Our Inner World

A Guide to Psychodynamics & Psychotherapy

SCOTT R. AHLES, M.D.

Associate Clinical Professor of Psychiatry
Fresno Medical Education Program
University of California–San Francisco
Fresno, California

THE JOHNS HOPKINS UNIVERSITY PRESS
Baltimore and London

© 2004 The Johns Hopkins University Press
All rights reserved. Published 2004
Printed in the United States of America on acid-free paper
2 4 6 8 9 7 5 3 1

The Johns Hopkins University Press
2715 North Charles Street
Baltimore, Maryland 21218-4363
www.press.jhu.edu

Library of Congress Cataloging-in-Publication Data
Ahles, Scott R., 1951–
Our inner world : a guide to psychodynamics and psychotherapy /
Scott R. Ahles
p. ;   cm
Includes bibliographical references and index.
ISBN 0-8018-7836-5 (pbk. : alk. paper)
1. Psychodynamic pshychotherapy.
[DNLM: 1. Psychoanalytic Therapy—methods—Case Report.
2. Psychological Theory—Case Report. WM 460.6 A286o 2004] I. Title.
RC489.P72A36 2004
RC489 14—dc21
2003012856

A catalog record for this book is available from the British Library.

For
my wife Leah
my son Jake
&
my daughter Cammie

Contents

III. *Psychotherapy*

Preface

The goal of this book is to teach some basic principles of psychodynamics and psychotherapy to trainees in psychiatry, psychology, social work, and counseling. Since Freud and Breur published *Studies on Hysteria* (1893–1895), in which they outlined their first theory of psychodynamics, a variety of psychodynamic theories have been developed: id theory, ego theory, interpersonal theory, object-relations theory, and self-psychology theory, to name a few. Trying to learn all of these theories can be a daunting task. Trainees frequently ask questions such as: "Which theory is the best?" or "How do I integrate all of these theories?"

Not only are there many different theories, there are many different psychotherapy techniques that are usually presented to trainees (e.g., psychodynamic psychotherapy, interpersonal psychotherapy, cognitive psychotherapy, short-term psychotherapy, etc.). After learning about these different forms of psychotherapy, trainees frequently ask questions such as, "OK, now what do I do? How do I treat patients?" Clearly, these are very good questions, and the hope is that this book will provide some answers for those attempting to navigate the often confusing world of psychodynamics and psychotherapy.

My intent here is not to discuss in detail all of the psychodynamic theories or all of the many forms of psychotherapy. Rather, this book presents selected concepts of various psychodynamic theories and then uses those concepts to develop a picture of a person's inner representational world. That inner representational world consists of a person's inner experience of himself or herself, of others, and of the world around that person. This book focuses particularly on the affective or emotional aspects of a person's inner world. After developing a picture of the inner representational world, we will trace the development of that inner representational world across the phases of childhood, adolescence, and adulthood. Finally, psychotherapy will be discussed, looking at techniques that can be used to help those whose inner world is causing them problems with their sense of self and/or their ability to form relationships with those around them.

Part I of this book reviews several psychodynamic theories, including id theory, ego theory, object-relations theory, attachment theory, and affect theory. It presents a variety of psychodynamic concepts and develops them into a pictorial model that we can use to understand that person's inner representational world. The goal is to use the understanding provided by this pictorial model to help in the treatment of the emotional instability of that person's inner world and to help that person relate better to the outer world. I do not assume that this model is correct in any absolute sense; it is simply a graphic shorthand that we can use as an aid in evaluation and treatment. It provides a checklist of psychodynamic issues, a representation of psychodynamic interactions that may be helpful in evaluating and treating patients.

Part II deals with development. It attempts to understand how different types of developmental interactions with significant others may lead to some of the psychodynamic problems discussed in part I. This is not to imply that all psychological problems have their roots in development. Certainly important constitutional/biological factors are involved as well. I will have more to say about these constitutional factors as I go along, but in this part, I concentrate on the contribution of developmental interactions in the genesis of psychological problems.

I begin by exploring early childhood interactions with parents and continue by reviewing development in the elementary school years and adolescent years. Next, I discuss the early, middle, and late periods of adult development. In each of these periods of development, I look inside the person to try to understand his or her inner world. I am particularly interested in (1) understanding the emotional balance of the inner world of the self and (2) understanding how a person (with his or her particular inner world) is relating to others in the world around him or her.

Part III, Psychotherapy, initially focuses on history, diagnosis, and treatment issues. After reviewing the various aspects of the patient's history that are important in the evaluation process, I discuss the use of the history obtained during evaluation to make a two-part assessment: (1) a symptomatic, descriptive *DSM* (*Diagnostic and Statistical Manual of Mental Disorders*) (American Psychiatric Association 2000) diagnosis and (2) a psychodynamic formulation that incorporates the concepts learned in parts I and II. In the last part of this chapter, I discuss a variety of psychotherapeutic interventions based on our understanding of the patient's inner world.

Subsequent chapters in this section consist of a series of clinical presentations. In each clinical presentation, I look at the person's symptomatic presentation and the treatments that might be used to help with these symptoms. Next I assess the underlying psychodynamic issues, develop a psychodynamic formulation, and discuss the psychotherapy that was used to treat that person. I am especially interested in looking at the emotional balance of the inner world of that person as well as that person's ability to form relationships with others.

The goal of this therapy described here is to work on those aspects of a person's inner representational world that are causing problems, either in how a person feels about him- or herself or in how a person relates to those in the world around him or her. The therapy described will be short term, as that is what is most available at present. By providing clinical case presentations to illustrate these techniques, this book should assist trainees in learning some basic principles of psychodynamic theory and psychotherapy technique to enable them to help people with psychological problems.

Many people gave me invaluable assistance in preparing this book. I thank the patients I have treated over the years who have shared the intimate details of their lives in the course of therapy and the pursuit of well-being. They have helped me immeasurably. I also thank the many trainees who have patiently listened to me express my ideas. Their thoughtful questions have helped me refine my thoughts. I also thank my editor, Wendy Harris, and the Johns Hopkins University Press for accepting my manuscript and guiding me through the editing and publishing process. Last, special thanks are due to Jane Ann LaMar, for her tireless and expert preparation of the manuscript, and to Yesenia Ramirez, for her excellent production of the diagrams that accompany the text.

⊚ I ⊚

A Model of Psychodynamics

Part I reviews some basic concepts of selected psychodynamic theories. Since most psychodynamic theories use the terms *id, ego,* and *superego,* chapter 1 provides definitions for these terms as they will be used throughout this text. Chapter 2 begins to develop a pictorial model of psychodynamics, arranging the id, ego, and superego along a horizontal axis. In chapter 3, Id Psychology and Ego Psychology, the dynamic interactions between the id, ego, and superego are discussed.

Chapter 4 reviews object-relations theory and self-psychology. The development of an internalized sense of self and an internalized sense of other via the separation-individuation process is described. This process is represented pictorially on a vertical axis orthogonal to the horizontal axis of id, ego, and superego. Chapters 5 and 6 use this vertical axis to explain some additional concepts. Chapter 5 describes how primitive defenses may be used when the separation-individuation process has not been completed. Chapter 6 describes how arrest along the separation-individuation pathway may lead to various forms of psychopathology.

Chapters 7 and 8 add some more concepts to the pictorial model. Chapter 7 focuses on attachment theory and discusses the concepts of internal working models or attachment patterns, concepts that are related to the internalized object relations introduced in chapter 4. Finally, chapter 8 reviews affect theory with an emphasis on how affects affect a person's inner emotional balance and his or her relationships with others.

The goal of part I is to help the reader understand the psychodynamic concepts that will be used throughout the rest of the book and to introduce the reader to a pictorial model that can be used to illustrate these psychodynamic concepts.

Definitions of Id, Ego & Superego

Part I will review selected aspects of certain psychodynamic theories. Since most of these theories use the terms *id, ego,* and *superego,* this chapter will discuss the definitions of id, ego, and superego and their related functions. Freud used these terms in discussing his structural theory of the mind (Freud 1923). While the id, ego, and superego are considered hypothetical constructs of the mind, they do correlate to some extent with brain anatomy and physiology. Let us pause just a moment to consider this.

In the structural model, the id subserves functions such as drives and emotions; in the brain the limbic system (amygdala, hippocampus, septal nucleus, hypothalamus, etc.) is the area of the brain from which drives and emotions originate. In the structural model, the ego is responsible for various functions such as perception (visual, auditory, and somatosensory), language, control of the motor apparatus, and cognition; in the brain these functions are subserved by the lobes of the neocortex (temporal, parietal, occipital, and frontal). The limbic system and the neocortex interact—for example, the neocortex gives us an objective perception of the world, and the limbic system adds affective and drive components to this objective perception to give us a combined cognitive-affective perception of the world. As we go along, we will discuss a similar sort of relationship between the id and the ego.

In a specialized cortical area in the frontal lobe of the brain, information from the limbic system (drives, emotions) and information from the neocortex (perception of the outside world) come together. This area of the brain decides whether to allow expression of a drive (an id function) based on not only a person's perception of the outside world (an ego function), but also the person's learned, internalized value system (a superego function). For a thorough discussion of these interactions within the brain, please see Mesulam (2000). In this volume I will be discussing these types of interactions as interactions between the id, ego, and superego. Before describing these interactions, I will first turn to definitions of these terms (see exhibit 1.1).

THE ID

The id is the agency of the mind that subserves the functions of drives and emotions.

Drives

The libidinal drive and the aggressive drive are the two drives discussed in traditional psychoanalytic theory. In general, libidinal drives bring people together and aggressive drives create distance between people. Here I discuss drives in a somewhat different manner—as other-directed drives and as self-directed drives. Other-directed drives (referred to here as attachment drives) are directed toward forming relationships with others. Self-directed drives (referred to here as assertive drives, or the drive to assert oneself) are directed toward preserving and developing the self.

Attachment Drives

The attachment drive is the drive to become attached to another person. Attachment drive will be discussed in more detail in chapter 8, but here I will briefly mention the various components of an adult attachment (pair bond) relationship. The attachment component itself is the component in which one person seeks a relationship with another for maintenance of his or her physical and emotional needs. There is a caregiver component in which one person meets the physical and emotional needs of the other. In a mutual adult relationship, each partner is in both the attachment role and the caregiver role. Another component is the affiliative component in which two people interact together around common interests, activities, and goals. There is a sexual component, which may lead to childbirth and then the formation of new attachment relationships.

Assertive Drives

Whereas attachment drives refer to developing a relationship with the other, assertive drives refer to the self. As used here, assertive drives refer to the drive to assert oneself on the environment for the maintenance and growth of the self. One might think of this as a self-preservative drive. Examples include basic physiological drives such as the drive to breathe or hunger/thirst drives, which bring in oxygen, fluids, and nutrients to preserve the body. We may also think of drives to develop and utilize ego functions such as the ability to walk, control the motor system, use the language system, or use the cognitive system—all of which may aid us in obtaining what we need to preserve the self.

Assertive drives may be expressed in a variety of contexts. For example, an assertive drive may be expressed in relative isolation (e.g., the person driven to use his language skills to read a book to acquire new knowledge, or the person driven to develop her musical talent by practicing piano). Assertive drives may be expressed in a competitive way in interactions with others in an academic or a work setting. Those who compete best get the best grades and the best jobs and may thus increase their chance of survival, of preserving the self. Assertive drives may be expressed in an aggressive manner, harming or killing the other to preserve the self.

Having discussed some basic concepts of attachment and assertive drives, let's discuss some interactions between attachment drives and assertive drives. Attachment drives may be used to promote the assertive drive of another—for example, a mother forming an attachment-caregiver relationship with a child to promote his or her self-preservation, or a mentor forming a relationship with a student to teach the student something to help him or her with self-development. Assertive drives may be expanded beyond self-preservation to preservation of the other (e.g., the person who uses his assertive drive to raise money to find a cure for an illness, or a person who uses her assertive drive to invent something or to develop a new technology that benefits others). Assertive drives and affiliative drives may be expressed together—for example, a group of people who get together and cooperatively use their assertive drive to accomplish a task or solve a problem.

Let's touch on the concept of variability of the intensity of drives. Drives may vary in intensity on either a constitutional basis or a psychological basis.

On a constitutional basis, drives may vary in intensity; a schizoid individual may be born with a very low level of attachment drive. A person born with a low level of assertive drive may have wonderful ego skills (his or her IQ, motor skills, musical skills) but no drive to develop them.

On a psychological basis, attachment drives may vary in intensity depending on one's experiences. On the one hand, if a person's experiences in interacting with others have always been painful or disappointing, then the intensity of that attachment drive may be decreased below its constitutional level because that drive is inhibited. If, on the other hand, interactions with others have generally gone well, then the person may approach new interactions with interest and enthusiasm. Similarly, assertive drives can vary in intensity due to psychological factors. If a child is criticized every time he tries to accomplish something (assert himself), he may become inhibited about asserting himself. If a child is rewarded and encouraged in her assertive efforts, however, she may continue to express that assertive drive without inhibition.

Finally, let's discuss the concept of conflict within the id over drive expression. A person may become conflicted over the balance of attachment versus assertive drive expression; that is, how much time does a person devote toward expression of attachment drive, and how much time does he or she devote to assertive self-development? For example, a person may become so absorbed in his work or studies (assertive self-expression) that his relationships suffer. Conversely, a person may become so involved in an attachment relationship (e.g., a parent caring for an infant) that she may feel as though she has no time for herself.

Having outlined a few concepts concerning drives, I next turn to a discussion of emotions and their relationship to drives.

Emotions

Various people (Tomkins 1962–1963; De Rivera 1977; Nathanson 1987; Ekman 1994) have developed theories involving affects and emotions. Still, there is no universally accepted theory of affects/emotions. I will discuss affect theory in a later chapter, but here my purpose will be to consider how emotions modify drives. Emotions may modify drives before, during, and after the expression of the drive. For example, an aggressive drive may be amplified by the degree of anger a person feels. A sexual drive may be amplified by the degree of love a person feels. An attachment drive may be amplified by the degree of affectionate emotion a person feels. These are examples of how a drive may be modified, by emotion, during its expression.

Once a drive is expressed by one person to another, the second person will receive it and experience a certain emotional reaction. In her response to the first person, she may send an emotion that the first person will perceive, thus stimulating an emotional reaction in him. This second emotion (the receiving emotion) may serve to modify subsequent expression of drives. So, for example, if a person extends an attachment drive to another with accompanying positive affect and receives a positive emotional response in return, then the person may continue to pursue an attachment with the other person.

If, however, the first person's expression of attachment drive–positive affect is met with rebuff, then he may discontinue pursuit of that attachment. If a person's experience throughout development is that attempts to form attachments are rejected, then he may inhibit attachment drives, or attachment drives may be expressed with less positive emotions and with cautious, anxious emotion. These are examples of how a drive may be modified after its expression—that is, how a drive may be modified by the emotional reaction a person receives in response to expression of a drive.

It may be that there exists constitutionally significant variation from one person to another in the valence of affect expressed in association with various drives and significant variation in the valence of affect experienced in reaction to events in one's world. One person may express his drive to interact with others very joyfully, and another may express it in a very shy manner. One person may react to a frustration from the environment with a little anger; another may react with much rage. Thus, one's constitution affective valence may have an effect on drives even before they are expressed.

This constitutional difference in the valence with which affects are expressed and experienced, along with the constitutional difference in the valence at which the drives are set, may be part of what we call temperament. Temperament, in this way, may be thought of as the variation of a person's reactivity to the world that can be attributed to his or her biological makeup.

Please note this discussion is not meant to imply that emotions occur only in association with id functioning. They certainly occur in association with other psychic functions such as superego functions. The above discussion concerns the relationship between drives and affects. I will have more to say about this as we go along and will also discuss other aspects of affective expression such as the affective expression of the superego.

Before moving on to discussion of ego functions, I want to make a few comments on memory. Memory obviously plays a very important part in this interaction between drives and emotions. A person remembers the emotional reactions she has received as a result of expression of drives and emotions. If the expression of drive and emotion is met with acceptance, she remembers that. If the expression of drive and emotion is met with rejection, then she remembers that. Obviously, these memories affect the subsequent expression of drive and emotion. Interestingly, the limbic system, which is intimately involved with drives and emotions, is also very much involved with memory, especially the initial encoding of memory.

THE EGO

The ego is the part of the psychic apparatus that interacts with the outside world and also interacts with drives and affects of the id. The ego is in the position of modulating between the demands of the id and (1) one's perception of the outside world and (2) the restraints of the outside world (which may be internalized into the superego). So, for example, if you are driving down the street and get cut off by another driver, you may experience anger and aggression toward the other driver (affects and impulses of the id). You may want to honk at or shake your fist at the other driver. The ego, before acting, may use its perceptual functions and perceive that the driver of the other car is large, muscular, and mean-looking. The ego, taking into account this perception of reality, may decide not to express the anger and aggression. Note, the superego may participate in this decision, telling you that it's not right to shake your fist at others even when they cut in front of you.

In the brain, these ego functions are carried out by the neocortex to a large extent. The neocortex has cells that are specialized for perceiving the outside world (visual, auditory, and somatosensory cells). The neocortex can provide us with a very objective view of the outside world. It can also provide us with a means of interacting with the outside world via cells specialized for motor function and language function. Prefrontal cells allow us to think, plan, and reason; make judgments; have insight; maintain and focus attention; concentrate; and follow a complex set of instructions. Prefrontal areas also receive information from limbic areas below the neocortex and can modulate between that limbic information (inner drive states and affects) and perceptions of the outside world, as in the example cited earlier.

In a general sense, ego functions can be divided into (1) those ego functions that deal mostly with the ego's relationship with the outside world and (2) those ego functions that have to do with the ego's relationship with the internal milieu, such as the relationship between the ego and the id. Though there is certainly some overlap, for purposes of discussion, ego functions will be divided into two categories: (1) the ego in relating to the outside world and (2) the ego in relating to the internal milieu.

The Ego in Relating to the Outside World

Perceptual. The ego can use various perceptual systems (visual, auditory, somatosensory) to perceive the environment.

Motor. Control of the motor apparatus is a major output channel via which a person can operate on the environment he has perceived.

Language. The use of language, both receptive and expressive functions, is another important means of interacting with the environment.

Cognitive functions. Abilities such as the capacity to attend, focus, concentrate, think, remember, plan, reason, have insights, and make judgments are all important cognitive functions. Cognitive functions provide us with means of interacting with the environment that are other than impulsive. Cognition allows for a way station between impulse and action. So, if a person sees something that she would like to have, rather than buying it impulsively, she can use her cognitive functions to think about whether she really can afford that item. Or she can use her cognitive functions to try out various solutions (if I buy this item, then I can't buy something else I want to buy) or to come up with new solutions (if I buy this item, then I can work some extra hours to be able to afford it).

Frustration tolerance. Here, frustration tolerance is used to refer to a person's ability to deal with frustrations from his environment. A person's ability to deal with frustrations from his environment is dependent to a large extent on the next ego function, coping and adaptation.

Coping and adaptation. Coping and adaptation refer to a person's ability to come up with adequate solutions to problems (frustrations) in her environment. So, if a person has ten tasks to do in an allotted period of time, and it is possible to get only five of them done, how does she cope so as not to become overwhelmed? Can she divide the tasks into those that are critical to complete now versus those that can be put off to another time? Can she get another person to help so that she can accomplish all the tasks? Obviously, an important part of coping and adaptation is one's ability to use the cognitive functions listed earlier.

Reality testing. Reality testing refers to the ability to test reality in one's mind before acting. Faced with a problem, a person can try out various solutions in his mind before acting. "If I do this, then that will happen." So, for example, faced with the problem of paying a credit card bill, a person can, before acting, test out various solutions along with their possible consequences:

Pay it all now.	I'll have less operating cash this month.
Pay part of it this month and part of it next month.	This spreads it out over time.
Get a loan to pay it off.	I can perhaps get a loan at a lower interest rate than my credit card.

Obviously, the development of language functioning is a great aid to reality testing. Reality testing is a great aid to the coping adaptations listed earlier. The failure of coping and adapting to excessive or traumatic stimuli in the environment is one of the factors in the development of stress disorders.

The Ego in Relating to the Internal Milieu

Impulse control. Impulse control refers to the ego's ability to control id impulses. So, even though a person may have sexual or aggressive impulses toward another person, it may be important to control those impulses in the given situation.

Delayed gratification. Delayed gratification refers to a person's ability to put off gratification of an impulse to a later time. If a person is hungry between meals, she can wait until mealtime. In part, this ability develops because her needs have been consistently gratified and she comes to trust that they will continue to be met in the future.

Ability to bind affect (anxiety tolerance). Ability to bind affect refers to the ability of the ego to prevent (repress) anxiety (and other unwanted affects) from entering the ego. Or, if anxiety does enter the ego, binding the anxiety refers to the ego's ability to contain the anxiety, to keep from being overwhelmed by anxiety. This likely relates to the ego's affective reserve. If the ego is mostly dominated by negative affects, the infusion of even a small amount of anxiety may lead to the ego feeling overwhelmed. If, on the other hand, the ego is dominated by positive affect, the infusion of some anxiety will not be so destabilizing.

Ability to modulate affect. The ability to modulate refers to the ability to experience a range of affects along a continuum. Some people tend to experience affects on the extremes of an affective continuum. Their affective experience is either extremely negative or extremely positive. Infants, for example, may vacillate between the extremes of joy and sadness; the same is often true of patients with borderline personality disorder. As development proceeds, the person develops the ability to experience a wide range of affects. So, for example, instead of just affects of extremely happy versus extremely sad, he can experience various gradations of happiness and sadness.

Mechanisms of defense. Mechanisms of defense refer to the means by which the ego deals with unacceptable id impulses or affects. Repression is thought to be the first-line defense. It prevents unacceptable id impulses and affects from entering the ego. If the repression breaks down, other mechanisms of defense may be recruited. This will be discussed more thoroughly later on.

Internalized object representations. Internalized object representations refer to a person's internalized view of others, which has developed via her experiences in interacting with others. This will be discussed more thoroughly later on.

Internalized self-representation. Internalized self-representation refers to a person's internalized view of himself. It includes his traits, characteristics, and attributes as well as how he feels affectively about those traits, characteristics, and attributes. This also will be discussed more thoroughly later on, along with its relevance to maintenance of self-esteem.

Internalized self-other patterns of relating. The internalized self-other patterns of relating refers to the patterns of interpersonal interactions a person has learned based on her experiences in interpersonal relationships.

Degree of separation-individuation. The degree of separation-individuation refers to the degree to which a person has separated self-internalizations from object representations and reached the point of establishing a cohesive sense of self that is not overly dependent on others for support. This will also be discussed more thoroughly later.

THE SUPEREGO

Superego is a term used to describe a specialized part of the ego that deals with our value system. In the neocortex, this function seems to reside in the prefrontal (orbitofrontal) cortex. Patients with injury or lesions to the prefrontal cortex become disinhibited—that is, they may act inappropriately hypersexual or hyperaggressive, as if they have lost the value system that would normally inhibit them from acting in these ways.

Two important superego functions are the punitive functions of the superego and the rewarding functions of the superego. In connection with the punitive function of the superego, a person might think of his or her conscience as a structure that contains a set of values, rules, standards of right and wrong. For purposes of this discussion, I define the conscience as the set of values that tell us what not to do or be. If a person transgresses that set of values, the punitive function of the superego induces guilt or shame.

In connection with the rewarding function of the superego, a structure that is often mentioned is the ego ideal. The ego ideal is our internal set of standards of what we should be. To the extent that we approximate our internal goals of what we want to be or do, the rewarding function of the superego induces pride or esteem.

These internal sets of values of what we should be (ego ideal) and what we shouldn't be (conscience) are learned throughout development. They are learned via internalizing the value systems of those around us, including parents, other relatives, significant others, peers, teachers, and so on. Obviously, the value system of the society, culture, or religious organization to which we belong plays a significant role in determining what these values will be.

For healthy functioning, rewarding and punitive superego functioning must be in balance. For example, if the punitive superego is poorly developed, a person may act in ways that are discordant with the value systems of those around him and, in a larger sense, with society. This may lead to conflicts in his interactions with peers and potentially ultimately with legal authorities. So, if a person does not share the belief that stealing is wrong, he might take something and not experience any guilt. Obviously, however, this may cause conflict with the person who owned the property stolen and may further cause problems with legal authorities.

If, however, the reinforcing function of the superego fails to develop, the person will have problems rewarding herself, being positive about herself. This inability to be self-rewarding may make it difficult to maintain self-esteem, leading to problems such as depression.

Optimal functioning depends on a healthy balance between the rewarding and punitive functions of the superego. Besides the balance between the rewarding and punitive aspects of the superego, there also needs to be an ability to modulate within each of these aspects of the superego.

With respect to the punitive superego, there needs to be an ability to modulate the amount of punishment and guilt that is induced in accordance with the degree of the transgression. Small transgressions induce a small amount of guilt; larger transgressions induce more guilt. In certain persons with primitive punitive superegos, this ability to modulate the inducement of guilt does not exist. They have only the ability to induce maximal amounts of guilt. This is a problem because even for minor transgressions, they induce maximal amounts of guilt. These barrages of large amounts of guilt make it hard to maintain an internal sense of well-being, a positive self-esteem.

With respect to the rewarding superego, there likewise needs to be an ability to modulate the amount of reward according to the achievement. Problems come in when a person's ego ideal is extremely perfectionistic—that is, when a person can reward himself only when he does something perfect. Since he never attains perfection, he never gets rewarded. Since reward from one's superego is important in maintaining self-esteem, persons with perfectionistic superegos may have difficulty maintaining self-esteem and may be prone to depression.

As a case in point, a patient came to therapy with chronic depression. She told the story of how as a child she would come home with straight A's on her report cards. Her parents' only response would be, "Why didn't you get A+'s?" Obviously she learned a very perfectionistic standard. She came to a session one day very distraught because she had received 75 percent on an exam in a college course she was taking. Clearly this was far from a perfect score, and thus one might understand her emotional reaction. It turned out, however, that her score was the highest in the class and twenty points above the next highest score. Thus, even though she had the best score (and she

Exhibit 1.1 Functions of the Id, Ego, and Superego

I. Id
    A. Drives
        1. Attachment
        2. Assertive
    B. Emotions
II. Ego
    A. In relating to the outside world
        1. Perceptual
        2. Motor
        3. Language
        4. Cognitive (thinking, attending, concentrating, remembering, planning, reasoning, making judgments, having insight)
        5. Frustration tolerance
        6. Coping and adaptation
        7. Reality testing
    B. In relating to the internal milieu
        1. Impulse control
        2. Delayed gratification
        3. Ability to bind affect (anxiety tolerance)
        4. Ability to modulate affect
        5. Mechanisms of defense
        6. Internalized object representations
        7. Internalized self-representations
        8. Internalized self-other patterns of relating
        9. Degree of separation-individuation
III. Superego
    A. Rewarding superego
        1. Ego ideal
        2. Pride and esteem
        3. Modulation of function
    B. Punitive superego
        1. Conscience
        2. Guilt and shame
        3. Modulation of function
    C. Balance of rewarding versus punitive superego

got an A+), it was not perfect and she was depressed. She had no ability to reward herself for having done the best.

SUMMARY

Exhibit 1.1 summarizes what has been discussed in this part with respect to id, ego, and superego functions.

The exhibit lists two important areas of id functioning: drives and emotions. Drives, emotions, and their relationships will be discussed further in subsequent chapters.

The next category includes the various ego functions that have been discussed. They are roughly divided into those that relate to the outside world and those important for internal functioning.

The last category is that of superego functions. The two broad superego functions are the rewarding function and the punitive function. In association with the rewarding superego is the ego ideal, our internalized view of what we should ideally be. In association with the punitive superego is the conscience, our internal set of rules of right and wrong. Also listed are various affects that the rewarding or punitive superego may stimulate in us. Under both the rewarding and punitive superego categories is listed the concept of modulation of function, referring to the ability to experience gradations of reward or punishment commensurate with the accomplishment or transgression. Finally noted is the concept of a balance of rewarding and punitive superego functioning, meaning that one needs to have both, not just one.

Using these definitions of id, ego, and superego, I will next discuss the interactions among these mental structures and develop a pictorial model to illustrate these interactions. If any of the previous concepts are not clear, it may be useful to review them after the presentation of the pictorial model in the next chapter.

2

A Pictorial Model of Id, Ego & Superego

H aving discussed the definitions of id, ego, and superego in chapter 1, I will first present a pictorial model of these three intrapsychic structures and then discuss some of the interactions among the inner world of the id, ego, and superego as well as the inner world's interaction with the outer world. The interactions between the id, ego, and superego can be put together as in figure 2.1. In the center of the diagram is the ego, and illustrated are the ego's interactions with the id, the outside world (for example, significant others), and the superego.

EGO AND OUTSIDE WORLD

In its interaction with the outside world, the ego may use its perceptual input channels (visual, auditory, somatosensory) to gather information on the outside world. It may use this information along with its abilities to think, reason, abstract, and make judgments to develop a plan of action that may be carried out along output channels (motor, language) to develop output behaviors. Faced, for example, with the task of preparing a dinner, someone might use the ego's perceptual apparatus to read about some recipes in a cookbook. Then the person could use the ego's planning ability to plan a menu. He or she might use motor and perceptual skills to go to the store and buy the necessary ingredients. Further motor and perceptual skills would be used in preparing the meal (output behavior). Other examples could include the ego using its abilities to plan a trip, organize group activity, or make a budget. In figure 2.1 these processes are diagrammed as the interaction between the ego and the outside world leading to output behavior.

ID AND EGO

The id is illustrated to the left of the ego along with the two functions mentioned previously: drives and emotions. Illustrated also are the two drives mentioned previously: attachment and assertive. The scale to the right of the drive box is meant to illustrate that the drives may be expressed with varying degrees of intensity. This variation in intensity of expression of the drives may be constitutional or may be as a result of one's experiences in interacting with the world.

Also illustrated are the emotions or affects. In this chapter, the terms *emotion* and *affect* will be used interchangeably, but a more thorough discussion of emotions and affects and their differences will be presented in chapter 8. These are roughly divided into the more positive emotions (love and affection are given as examples) and the more negative emotions (anxiety and anger are given as examples). The scales next to the emotion boxes are again meant to illustrate the variation with which emotions are expressed and experienced either on a constitutional basis or as a result of experience.

The juxtaposition of the drive box and the emotion boxes is meant to illustrate that drives may be expressed (either singly or in combination) along with varying degrees of various emotions. For example, an attachment drive could be expressed with varying degrees of positive affect or potentially with negative affect.

In the interaction between the ego and the id, the ego is in the position of modulating the id. The ego, for example, needs to decide whether or not to allow various drives to be expressed. It also may be in the position of deciding whether or not to allow memories of past emotional experiences to come to awareness. The general mechanism by which the ego modulates the id is called repression. The ego may repress the expression of current or past id drives and/or emotions, thus preventing their expression and/or awareness within the ego (see figure 2.1, repression).

In deciding whether or not to allow expression of id drives, the ego operates according to the reality principle. That is, the ego, before allowing expression of a drive, takes into consideration the reality of the outside world.

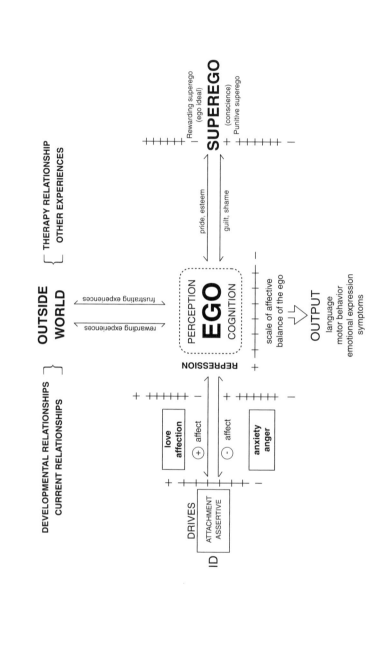

Figure 2.1. A Model of the Id, Ego, and Superego

The ego is depicted along with a couple of its ego functions, perception and cognition. The scale below the ego represents the affective balance of the ego.

The ego interacts with the outside world. Examples of interactions include developmental relationships, current relationships, the therapy relationship, or other experiences not involving interactions with others. In general, these interactions may be rewarding or frustrating.

The ego perceives the outside world, forming an objective cognitive perception of the outside world.

The ego sends its perception to the id, which may add elements to the perception, such as affective elements; the combined cognitive-affective perception then reenters the ego for further processing. The ego also sends its perception to the superego, which may, as a result of the perception, incorporate goals into the ego ideal or rules of right and wrong into the conscience.

Besides the outside world, the id and the superego may provide input to the ego. The id may strive to express various drives and/or affects; the ego may allow expression of these drives and affects, modify them, or attempt to repress them. The superego may send rewarding or punitive input to the ego, which may affect its affective balance.

Via its various interactions with the outside world, the id, and the superego, the ego may generate an output response. The output response may be a language response, a motor behavior response, or an emotional response. The output response may be adaptive or maladaptive, leading to symptoms.

The diagram uses various graduated scales $(+ -)$ to suggest variability of id, ego, and superego functions:

1. The scale next to the box labeled drives suggests that drives may be expressed with varying levels of intensity (on either a constitutional or a developmental basis)

2. The scales next to the terms $+$affect and $-$affect suggest that inputs into the id may elicit varying degrees of affective responses and that outputs from the id to the ego may be of varying degrees of affective intensity.

3. The scales next to the terms Rewarding Superego and Punitive Superego suggest variability in the degree of the rewarding input or the punitive input from the superego to the ego.

4. The scale below the term EGO is meant to represent the overall affective balance of the ego. This affective balance is a function of the baseline affective balance of the ego (from past inputs), along with the concurrent affective input from the id and superego.

So, for example, if a person is experiencing aggressive impulses toward someone, before acting out those aggressive impulses, he would assess reality. If the reality is that the person he is angry with is a very muscular person who is twice as big as himself, he may decide it is best to repress that aggressive drive. Note that the superego may enlist here on the side of the ego and further the repression, essentially telling the ego that hitting another is the wrong thing to do. Thus the superego enters the conflict evoking a set of values of right and wrong, while the ego deals with the conflict according to the constraints of reality.

In another example, if a person has sexual impulses toward a person she has just met, she likely does not express them because she probably is assessing reality correctly in believing that those overtures would be rejected. From a superego point of view, she might not express these sexual impulses because she believes that would be the wrong thing to do. In other words, she believes that she needs to follow the rules set by society before entering into a sexual relationship.

The above are normal examples of repression. Repression may occur in a more neurotic way, however. If someone is rejected every time he attempts to appropriately express a sexual drive, or if he is punished or criticized every time he attempts to express an assertive drive (competing in sports, for example), then he may chronically repress expression of those drives.

Attachment drives are subject to the same vicissitudes. Attachment drives begin in infancy; the infant has a propensity to become attached to significant others, especially mother. In terms of this model, one might say that the infant expresses an attachment drive associated with a certain affect—at times positive, at times negative. The mother responds in a reciprocal fashion, expressing attachment and affect. If the mother's expression of attachment is accompanied by positive affect (rewarding experiences in figure 2.1), this increases the probability of continued expression of attachment and positive affect and gradually leads to the building up of a memory trace of a positive interaction with another. It also leads to a state of well-being in the infant.

If the infant's attempts at attachment are met with the expression of ambivalence or with negative affect, or rejection (frustrating experiences in figure 2.1), then the probability of the expression of attachment associated with positive affect on the part of the infant may decrease, or attachment drives may become associated with a negative affect such as anxiety. Attachment may be expressed tentatively, cautiously, or not at all. The memory traces that develop are those of a negative interaction with another; and rather than the interaction inducing a state of well-being, it may induce a state of tension (see figure 2.1).

Of course, the child's response to the mother is not totally a function of the mother's emotional interaction with the child; temperament is also a factor. For example, if a child's attempts to form an attachment with her mother are met with ambivalence on the part of the mother, that child, with her temperament, may feel rejected and decrease her attempts to attach. Another child, with another temperament, may have a less negative emotional response and continue her attempts to attach or may even increase her attempts to attach.

As a person proceeds throughout development, he enters into a variety of attachment relationships. If those in general go well, then he develops positive memories of attachments, is uninhibited in expressing attachment drives, experiences a sense of well-being in relationships with others, and enters adulthood prepared to interact well with others and to form intimate relationships. If attachment relationships don't go well in development, if he is rejected, abused, and/or neglected, then his memories of relationships are negative affectively and he may repress attachment drives because they had been associated with tension. For that person, the inner sense of well-being that develops as a result of positive interactions with others may not develop; rather he is left with an inner sense of tension. He may enter adulthood with inhibitions concerning further attachments as he fears that they will not go well, as has been the case with interactions in his past. He is ill-prepared for intimacy.

ID AND SUPEREGO

The superego is illustrated in figure 2.1 along with its rewarding and punitive aspects as discussed earlier. The scales to the left of the words "Rewarding superego" and "Punitive superego" are meant to illustrate the ability to modulate rewarding and punitive superego responses—that is, the ability of the superego to respond with larger or smaller amounts of reward or punishment according to the situation (see previous discussion in chapter 1).

We have already discussed the superego's function of enlisting on the side of the ego in modulating the drives of the id. Again, for example, in the expression of an aggressive drive toward another person, the ego may repress the drive because in assessing reality, it believes that, because the other person is larger and more muscular, he or she will likely get hurt. The superego may enlist on the side of the ego to further repress the aggression because hitting someone goes against his or her internalized code of what is right and wrong. If someone were to actually hit the other person, the punitive superego might induce a feeling of guilt. If someone were to think of hitting another person, the superego might signal that it will induce guilt if the act is carried out. The ego's concern over experiencing guilt serves as a force to further repress the impulse.

Another major function of the superego in its relationship with the ego is the function of regulation of self-esteem (internal states of well-being versus internal states of tension). The ego (and id) may act on the environment in such a way so as to trigger the rewarding function of the superego. If, for example, one does a good job in work or school, the superego may induce feelings of esteem, and the person may experience increased self-esteem and an associated inner sense of well-being.

The ego ideal participates in this process by serving as a person's internalized image of what she would ideally like to be. In striving toward her ego ideal, the rewarding superego may reward the ego in proportion to the degree that the ego ideal is approximated. Small amounts of reward are given for distant approximations of the ego ideal, and larger amounts of reward are given for closer approximations of the ego ideal.

Shame may be induced for failures to live up to the ego ideal. For example, if a person is in school, it may be part of his ego ideal to do well in school. If he does not do well on an exam because he failed to study for the exam, the punitive superego may induce shame, leading to a sense of tension within the ego. Note that in this case, a failure to act (an act of omission) has led to the emotion of shame.

If a person deliberately commits a transgression against her internalized code of ethics and morals as defined by her conscience, then the punitive superego may induce a sense of guilt with resultant tension within the ego. Note that in this case, an intentional action (act of commission) has led to the emotion of guilt.

The balance of emotions induced by the rewarding and punitive superego is an important factor (among others to be discussed later) in the maintenance of self-esteem (i.e., balance of feelings of well-being versus tension within the ego system). Balance on the side of pride and esteem results in a sense of well-being within the ego. Balance on the side of shame and guilt results in a sense of tension within the ego.

AFFECTIVE BALANCE OF THE EGO

Below the word EGO in figure 2.1 is a scale that varies from a positive pole to a negative pole. Below the scale is the phrase "scale of affective balance of the ego." This scale is meant to represent the overall affective state of the ego at any given point in time. The affective state of the ego may vary from a state of positive affect (e.g., well-being or happiness on the positive end of the scale) to a state of negative affect (e.g., anxiety or sadness on the negative end of the scale).

As the ego interacts with the id, superego, and outside world, it receives many affective inputs. If we assume a certain level of affective balance of the ego at a given point in time, we can illustrate how that affective balance may move to either the right or the left on the scale of affective balance. For example, if the ego allows expression of an attachment drive in a current relationship, and if this leads to a rewarding interaction, then positive id affects may be stimulated and experienced by the ego, leading to a shift of a person's affective balance toward the positive pole. If, in this interaction, a person is rebuffed and criticized, then negative affects (e.g., anger, anxiety) may enter the ego from the id, and an affect such as guilt may enter the ego from the superego. The result is a shift of the person's affective balance toward the negative pole.

SUMMARY

In this chapter I expanded upon the concepts of id, ego, and superego that were introduced in chapter 1. The chapter has presented a pictorial model of the id, ego, and superego, and I have discussed interactions between the ego and the id, the ego and the superego, and the ego and the outside world. In the next chapter I will further develop these concepts by talking about id psychology and ego psychology.

3

Id Psychology & Ego Psychology

H aving defined the basic terms of the structural model—id, ego, and superego—and having presented a picture to illustrate the model, I will now go on to discuss some of the specific concepts of id psychology and ego psychology. In this chapter the focus will be on the interactions between the id and the ego/superego that lead to symptom formation. The theory of neurosis posits that neurotic conflicts arise out of a conflict between the id and the ego (and/or superego) (Fenichel 1945). Id drives are striving for expression; if those id drives are in conflict with ego and/or superego forces, conflict arises. For example, if a person's sexual impulses are unacceptable to the ego and/or superego, a conflict may exist between sexual impulses pressing for expression and ego and/or superego forces seeking to repress these sexual drives. Because expression of these impulses is forbidden by the ego/superego, expression of the impulse is associated with anxiety and perhaps guilt. To the extent that the ego and/or superego are successful in repressing the sexual impulses and associated emotion, no neurotic symptoms result, though the patient may suffer from the resulting sexual inhibition. If the ego/superego are not capable of totally repressing the id impulses and associated emotion, then either the impulses may be expressed (perhaps with accompanying anxiety or guilt) or neurotic symptoms may result. Neurotic symptoms result from a partial or alternate expression of the forbidden impulse or the associated anxiety. The partial/alternate expression serves to deintensify the conflict, allowing the ego/superego to bolster the repression.

An example of symptom formation would be the development of an anxiety symptom (panic, generalized anxiety). If the ego is not able to repress both the sexual drive and the associated anxiety, then a compromise may be reached in the interaction between the id and the ego. In this case, the anxiety associated with the conflict between the id and the ego is expressed in the form of symptoms, leaving less for the ego/superego to repress (just the sexual drive, not the associated anxiety) (see figure 3.1).

Alternatively, the impulse may be expressed in a disguised form such as a conversion symptom. The movements of a pseudoseizure, a conversion symptom, have been conceptualized as symbolizing the movements of sexual activity and to be an alternate/partial expression of the forbidden sexual impulse. Having partially discharged the id impulses striving for expression, the ego is now more able to repress the remaining impulse and associated affect. (For more discussion on the formation of conversion symptom, see the clinical presentation of Jane later in this chapter.)

Freud's early theory focused on id impulses (Freud and Breur 1895; Freud 1900). The goal of therapy was to make the patient aware of these impulses and the associated affect. Freud's case of Dora (Freud 1905) illustrates this type of therapy. In this case, Dora is brought to Freud by her father with physical symptoms that are thought to be of psychological origin. Dora complains to Freud that she is upset because her father is having an affair with a married woman, Frau K. While this is true, Freud speculates that on the basis of some of Dora's associations and dreams, Dora has amorous feelings toward Herr K., which she is repressing. Freud attempts to make Dora conscious of her unconscious drives and feelings toward Herr K., Frau K.'s husband.

In Freud's theory, making the person aware of his or her unconscious drives and emotions was the important first step in the therapy process. As long as these drives and emotions were unconscious, the patient was susceptible to symptom formation. If the unconscious drives and emotions could be brought into consciousness, then the person could work on these conflicts and hopefully resolve them.

As the structural model evolved, therapy also evolved. Besides striving to bring a person's past traumatic memories and unacceptable impulses to consciousness, therapy also sought to analyze ego processes. In particular, therapy became concerned with a person's ego mechanisms of defense, and hence the term *ego psychology*. Freud spoke of these processes in his writings—for example, in "Instincts and Their Vicissitudes" (1915). Anna Freud (1946) added significantly to this theory in her book *The Ego and the Mechanisms of Defense*.

Ego defense theory posits that the ego's primary mechanism of defense is repression. The ego attempts to deal with unacceptable id impulses and

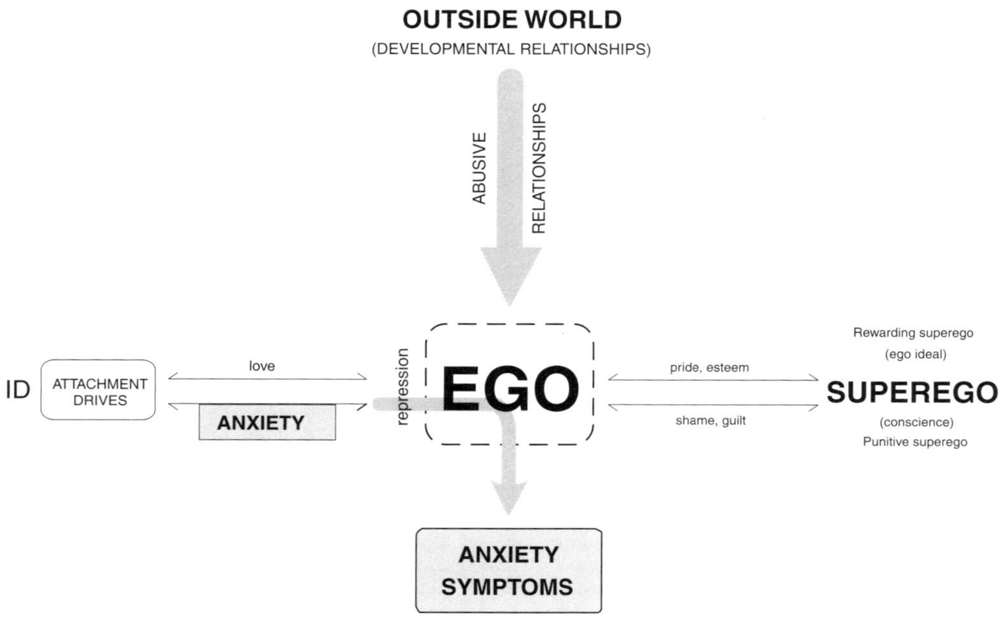

OUTSIDE WORLD
(DEVELOPMENTAL RELATIONSHIPS)

ABUSIVE RELATIONSHIPS

EGO

repression

love

ANXIETY

ID | ATTACHMENT DRIVES

ANXIETY SYMPTOMS

Rewarding superego
(ego ideal)

SUPEREGO

(conscience)
Punitive superego

pride, esteem

shame, guilt

Figure 3.1. The Development of Anxiety Symptoms

If a child expresses attachment drives in the context of a supportive, accepting family environment, these attachment drives may become associated with affects such as love and affection. If these attachment drives are expressed in the context of an abusive family environment (as in the diagram), attachment drives may become associated with affects such as anxiety.

As a result of the association between attachment drives and anxiety, the ego may repress the expression of attachment drives to prevent the associated anxiety from overwhelming the ego.

At some later time, the intensity of attachment drives may increase (e.g., a constitution increase in drives as a person moves from childhood to adolescence or an environmental increase when the person meets another to whom he or she is strongly attracted), or the ability of the ego to repress attachment drives may decrease (e.g., the person must deal with several new stresses, and there is less ego strength remaining for repression).

If the repression breaks down, one possible outcome would be the expression of anxiety (without the associated attachment drives), leading to the formation of anxiety symptoms such as panic attacks.

The expression of the anxiety without the associated attachment drives leaves those drives unexpressed. The ego now has less to repress and may be able to maintain the repression of the attachment drives.

emotions by repressing them. If the ego is successful, then those id impulses and emotions are not expressed and no neurotic symptom formation results. The only effect is that the energy used by the ego to repress the id impulses is not available to the ego for other ego activities (object relations, intellectual development, etc.). If too much ego energy is used in repression of the id, the ego may be stifled by its lack of energy, a syndrome that has been referred to as neurasthenia.

In a system in which the ego forces are able to balance the id forces via repression, the equilibrium may become destabilized in one of two ways: (1) id forces may increase (person enters a new relationship, leading to an increase in libidinal desires, which the ego had been trying to repress), or (2) ego forces decrease so the ego is less able to repress the id forces (new stresses come up, such as financial problems, which the ego must deal with, leaving less energy for repression).

Once the conflict is destabilized and the ego is no longer able to repress the id drives/emotions, one of two things may happen: (1) the drives/emotions may be expressed or (2) the ego may mount other mechanisms of defense to deal with the id drives/impulses. In the first case, the drive/emotion is expressed directly. In the second case, the drive/emotion is expressed in an alternate manner, which varies according to the mechanism of defense used. For example, if the mechanism of defense is displacement, the anxiety associated with the conflict is expressed but displaced to some outside object, leading to phobia formation. That is, the anxiety is taken out of the conflict and displaced to heights, elevators, bridges, or dogs, for example. The person has now developed a symptom, a phobia. He has a fear (anxiety) of heights, elevators, bridges, dogs, and so on. The anxiety associated with an unacceptable impulse has been displaced to an outside object. However, the anxiety that had been associated with the unacceptable impulse is no longer present. The ego has less to repress, and so the ego can now perhaps repress the unacceptable impulse, keeping it out of ego awareness and keeping it from expression. Thus, the defense (repression) has been reinstated, but at the expense of symptom formation (figure 3.2).

In another example, a person may recruit the mechanism of defense, isolation of affect, when repression fails. In this situation, the drive is expressed in thought, not action, without the associated affect, which is isolated back in the conflict between the id and the ego. The result is the formation of obsessive thoughts. The person experiences thoughts, often of a sexual or aggres-

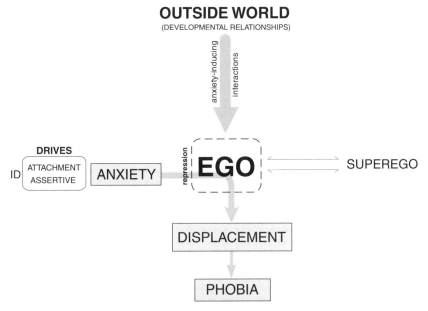

Figure 3.2. The Development of Phobic Symptoms

The experience of anxiety-inducing relationships may result in drive expression becoming associated with anxiety. Alternatively, from a biological perspective, excess anxiety may be associated with drive expression on a constitutional basis.

Because drive expression is associated with anxiety, the ego will attempt to repress the expression of drive and the associated anxiety to prevent the ego from becoming overwhelmed with anxiety. This results in a conflict between the id, which is striving to express drive, and the ego, which is trying to repress drive expression. If the repression breaks down, because of either increased drive intensity or decreased ego strength, anxiety may begin to enter the ego.

To prevent the ego from being overwhelmed by anxiety, the ego may recruit a secondary mechanism of defense, displacement. The anxiety from the id-ego conflict is displaced onto some outside object or situation (dogs, heights). The anxiety that was once associated with a drive within the interpsychic system is now displaced to an object or situation outside of the interpsychic system. Without the anxiety to repress, the ego may be able to remount its efforts to repress the drive that remains.

sive nature. These thoughts are often unacceptable to the patient, but they are expressed without the accompanying affect and without action. The expression of the thought, as a representation of the underlying unacceptable drive, decreases the intensity of the conflict, allowing the ego to restore the equilibrium by repressing what remains on the id side of the conflict, the affect. The conflict between the id and the ego has been brought back into balance, but at the expense of symptom formation (see figure 3.3).

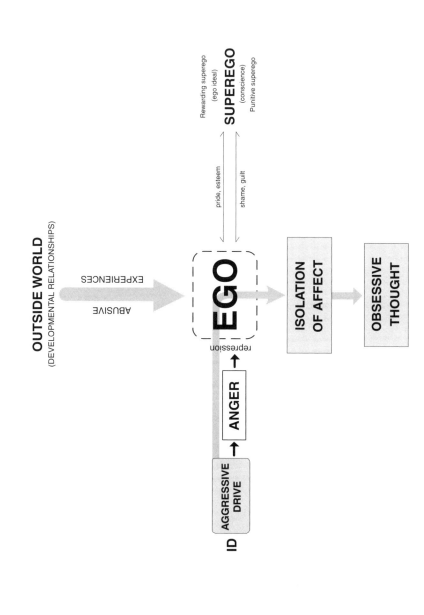

Figure 3.3. The Development of Obsessive Thoughts

In this example, abusive developmental relationships stimulate aggressive drives and angry affects at the level of the id. (Alternatively, those aggressive drives and angry affects may be present on a constitutional basis.) The ego (and probably also the superego) seeks to repress these aggressive drives/angry affects, resulting in a conflict between the id, which seeks to express, and the ego/superego, which seek to repress the aggressive drives/angry affects.

If the defense mechanism repression breaks down, a secondary mechanism of defense may be recruited—in this case, isolation of affect. What happens via this mechanism is that the aggressive device is expressed in thought, not in action, and is expressed devoid of the associated angry affect.

The term *isolation of affect* refers to the idea that the angry affect is isolated back in the conflict between the id and the ego after the aggressive drive is expressed in thought. The expression of the drive in thought decreases the intensity of the conflict, leaving less for the ego to deal with and enabling the ego to reestablish repression of the isolated affect. As a result, however, of expression of the aggressive drive in thought, the person develops an obsessive thought (e.g., the repetitive thought, "I am going to kill that person").

⑥ Jane is a twenty-year-old woman who was referred for therapy with symptoms of episodic visual loss. She had an extensive workup including ophthalmologic exam, chemistries, MRI, LP, EEG, evoked potentials, and visual field testing, all of which were normal. She saw several specialists and subspecialists, none of whom could find anything organically wrong with her. Jane gave the history that episodes of visual loss were episodic, lasting several minutes at a time and almost always occurring at work. She worked at a church as an organist/pianist where she played for Sunday services and for the choir practice. Further history revealed that the visual symptoms began after a certain young man joined the choir and Jane became attracted to him. The symptoms progressed to the point where she was no longer able to play the piano and had to leave her job. From the initial history, it was unclear why meeting this young man led to the loss of vision. Neither of them was attached to another, and no one at church objected—in fact, they encouraged her.

Her developmental history had been somewhat problematic. Her mother was a professional who spent much time away from home. Jane described her as angry, irascible, and critical when she was at home. She, however, was a gifted pianist and taught Jane to play piano.

Jane described her father as overly close, dependent on her, and judgmental. As she grew up, she was given the explicit message that he would feel betrayed if she were to date, marry, or leave home—that he needed her and depended upon her to maintain his stability. He would call her a slut if she wore makeup, lipstick, or a sweater he considered too tight. Other than being allowed to go to school, her activities outside the home were severely restricted to the point where she could not even go out to get the mail. One time when her father found out that she had shown some interest in a boy at school, he pushed her against the wall and put his hands around her throat to the point where she had trouble breathing. He demanded that she stop seeing this boy.

How might we understand this case in terms of id and ego psychology? The pertinent id drives/affects are her attachment/sexual drives and associated affectionate feelings toward the young man who joined the choir. These id drives/emotions are not allowed expression. What are the forces that serve to repress them? The ego, in considering its relationship to the outside world, in particular her father, would seek to repress the id drives/emotions. That is, the ego, in considering expression of the id drives/emotions, would take into consideration the almost certain angry, explosive reaction of her father. The anticipation of the father's reaction causes anxiety. Thus expression of sexual/attachment drives becomes associated with anxiety. Caught in the conflict between expressing the id drives/emotions and anxiety-inducing reaction of her father, the ego attempts to repress the id drives/emotions.

The superego may also participate in the conflict and add further repression of the id drives/emotions. That is, she has been taught that it is wrong to show interest in boys; this value has been internalized into her superego value system. If she transgresses against that value, guilt is induced, which is a feeling the ego does not want to have. To prevent guilt, the ego further bolsters the repression of the id drives/emotions. The threat of disapproval by her father and the fear of the inducement of guilt by her superego both lead to anxiety. Expression of the impulse becomes associated with anxiety. The anxiety serves as a stimulus (signal) for the ego to repress the impulse in order to avoid the potential disapproval and guilt.

Still, she goes to play piano for the choir practice every day and she sees the young man of her desires every day. The id forces grow to the point where the ego/superego forces can no longer contain them. The ego has two choices—to allow expression of the id drives/emotions and deny her father's and her superego prohibitions or to recruit additional mechanisms of defense. In this case, the mechanism of defense called conversion is recruited, and she develops the symptom of blindness. Her drive to see this young man is converted into an inability to see. With the id drive thus partially discharged through the development of a conversion symptom, the ego is now able to repress what is left of the id drive/emotion. Through the partial discharge of the id drive via the conversion symptom, the intensity of the conflict is decreased; this is called primary gain. The ego again gains control of the conflict (can repress the id forces) by allowing a distorted expression of the drive via symptom formation. Primary gain has to do with the gain achieved by the ego in its relationship to the id.

Note there is also secondary gain. The development of the blindness makes her unable to play the piano and stay in her job. Thus, secondarily, she is removed from the conflicted situation and no longer sees the young man she desires. Secondary gain refers to the gain the ego achieves in relationship to the environment. Other secondary gains in situations such as this might be the gain achieved by being taken care of by a caring physician, unemployment payments, and so on. The previous example seeks to illustrate the psychodynamic interactions between the id, the ego, and the superego and the ways in which neurotic symptoms may result. These interactions are illustrated in figure 3.4.

Jane entered into psychotherapy and became aware of the conflicts within her as described previously. She was able to express her feelings about the present

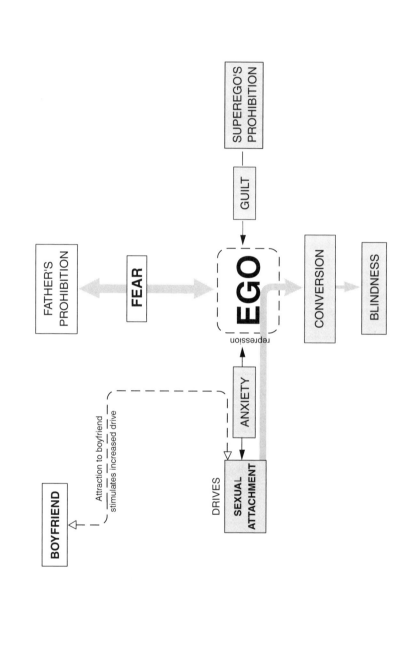

Figure 3.4. A Case of Conversion Blindness

Expression of id sexual and attachment drives is opposed by:

1. Father's prohibitions
2. Superego's prohibitions

Because of these prohibitions, expression of sexual/attachment drives would cause anxiety.

A conflict exists between the id, which is striving to express the sexual/attachment drives, and the ego, which (in deference to the father's and the superego's prohibitions) strives to repress those drives.

At baseline, the ego is able to repress the libidinal drives and avoid the experience of anxiety and guilt.

When Jane develops an attraction to the young man in the choir, sexual and attachment drives increase and the conflict falls out of balance; the ego is no longer able to repress the id.

The ego recruits a new mechanism of defense, conversion, resulting in symptom formation, blindness. The drive, the wish to see, is converted into an inability to see. This diffuses the conflict because, as a result of the blindness, Jane can no longer see or be with her boyfriend. Sexual and attachment drives decrease because the drives are expressed in a converted form. The ego now has less to repress. The ego is able to regain control of the conflict, but it is at the expense of symptom formation, blindness.

situation as well as her feelings about her past relationships with her parents; her symptom of blindness soon resolved.

Jane decided that she had come to the point in her life where she should move out of her parents' home and live on her own. Because she had lived such a restricted life, she was ill-prepared to live independently. This brings us to another aspect of ego psychology, coping and adaptation. Whereas the problems we described earlier have to do with how the ego deals with the id via various mechanisms of defense, the issue we are now addressing has to do with how the ego copes and adapts in its interactions with the outside world (i.e., what coping mechanisms does the ego have at its disposal). Jane had to learn basic coping mechanisms so that she could function independently in the world—find an apartment, interact in a job setting, budget money, and so on. This branch of ego psychology, dealing with how the ego copes with the outside world, was addressed by Heinz Hartman and his collaborators (Hartman 1964, 1986; Hartman, Kris & Lowenstein 1964, 1949; Hartman, Newman, Schur & Solnit 1966).

SUMMARY

In this chapter I have used the concepts of id, ego, and superego described in chapter 1 along with the pictorial model described in chapter 2 to illustrate how dynamic interactions between the id, ego, and superego may lead to symptom formation. We talked of how unacceptable drives and affects from the id may be repressed by the ego and superego and how if the repression breaks down, secondary symptoms of defense may be recruited, leading to symptom formation. These interactions occur along a horizontal axis on the diagram; in the next chapter I will move on to discuss object-relations theory and add a vertical axis.

4

Object-Relations Theory & Self-Psychology

I now move on to a discussion of objects (others) and of self as well as the relationship between others and self. The British Object Relations School (Fairbairn 1951; Winnicott 1960; Guntrip 1961; Klein 1975) and others focused on the internalized world of self and other. In America, Harry Stack Sullivan (1953) focused on the interpersonal relationship between self and others. The concept of self in the context of interpersonal relationship was a major focus of Heinz Kohut (1971, 1977) and his followers. My goal here is not to review the specifics of all these theories, but for an excellent critique of object-relations theory and self-psychology, please see the work of Frank Summers (1994). Here, my focus will be on the interaction between interpersonal relationships (and especially early developmental relationships) and internalized self-other object relationships, the inner representational world. In other words, we are going to look at the relationship between a child (the self) and his or her parents (the other) (an external relationship) and then try to understand the inner representations of self and other that the child develops. An assumption here is that the quality and quantity of the child's interpersonal relationships is one factor in determining what type of internalized self-other object relationships he or she develops.

In this chapter I will discuss early interpersonal relationships and internalized self-other object relationships in the context of Margaret Mahler's separation-individuation theory. The goal will be to try to understand how a person develops a healthy sense of self, a healthy sense of other, and healthy self-other patterns of relationships. At many steps along the way, problems may occur, leading to various pathological configurations. I will begin this chapter with a discussion of the separation-individuation process as de-

scribed by Margaret Mahler. I will then go on to discuss the separation-individuation process and the development of internalized self and other representations in the context of the pictorial id, ego, and superego mode
described earlier.

THE WORK OF MARGARET MAHLER

In the 1960s Margaret Mahler and her collaborators observed the day-to-day
interactions between mothers and children at the Masters Children's Center
in New York. The goal of the study was to learn how healthy children attain
their sense of individual identity; the results of the study are summarized in
The Psychological Birth of the Human Infant (Mahler, Pine & Bergman
1975). In this work, the authors outlined the following phases.

The Autistic Phase: Birth to Two Months

In the autistic phase, the infant sleeps much of the time. He awakes when
some tension such as hunger causes him to cry; he goes back to sleep once
his needs are met. The major goal of this period is to establish a state of
homeostatic equilibrium outside the intrauterine environment.

The Symbolic Phase: Two Months to Six Months

During the symbolic phase, the infant begins to react more to stimuli from
the outside world. The smile response develops; an infant will smile when
she perceives a face, facilitating bonding between self and other. At this
stage, however, the child has not yet developed the ability to perceive self
and other as different.

Separation-Individuation Phase

Differentiation (Six to Ten Months): The First Subphase

Mahler described the following aspects of the differentiation subphase:
   Hatching. The term *hatching* is used to describe a point in development
at which the child is able to maintain a more permanently alert sensorium
while awake; he has increased ability to perceive the outside world. Instead

of molding into the mother's arms when held, the infant may push away as if to get a better look at the mother. The infant may explore the mother's face, touching her nose, ears, mouth, glasses as if beginning to realize a differentiation. He may slip out of the mother's lap to play on the floor, but tends to stay close to the mother's feet.

The checking back pattern. At seven to eight months, the infant, when perceiving a face other than mother, will look at it and then "check back" by looking at mother's face. The infant seems to be comparing the two faces, seems to be starting to differentiate between mother and other.

Stranger reactions. If things have gone well in development, the infant begins to experience a sense of basic trust in others. As the infant becomes capable of differentiating other from mother, she will approach others with curiosity; if basic trust in others has not developed, encounters with others may be experienced with anxiety.

Delayed or premature differentiation. If development has gone well, the infant will develop not only a sense of basic trust toward others, but also a sense of well-being within the self. This allows the infant to begin differentiation (i.e., distancing himself from the mother) at the average time. If the mother is ambivalent about the child, abusive, or smothering, that independent sense of well-being may not develop, and the child's differentiation may be delayed or perhaps premature.

Practicing (Ten to Eighteen Months): The Second Subphase

Moving away. During the moving away subphase, the child becomes capable of locomotion (crawling, walking) and thus can determine her distance from or closeness to the mother. The child becomes interested in exploring the world around her and may for a short period of time seem oblivious to mother. By physically moving away, the child has taken a major step in the process of psychological separation and individuation.

Emotional refueling. The child returns periodically to the mother, seeming to need her physical proximity for emotional refueling before venturing out again. With time, the child develops an increasing ability to maintain emotional contact via eyesight without actual physical contact. The child has become more emotionally independent— less dependent on the mother to meet his emotional needs.

Rapprochement (Eighteen to Twenty-four Months): The Third Subphase

Seeming regression. During the seeming regression subphase, the child increasingly becomes capable of using language and symbolic play. Despite this ego growth and individuation, the child seems more concerned with the mother's presence; the obliviousness of the previous stage has diminished. At the same time that the child seems to be growing, developing, and separating, she seems to manifest an increasing need for the mother's love and support; that is, the child seems to regress to a more clingy, dependent state. The child has developed an increasing sense of her own separateness, and along with this comes anxiety; hence the desire for more closeness with the mother.

Shadowing and darting away. Mahler described a type of behavior in which the toddler would shadow the mother, following her wherever she went; suddenly the toddler would dart away and would seem to enjoy being chased and swooped up. Mahler explained the shadowing as a wish for reunion motivated by separation anxiety; the darting away represents the desire for separation motivated by a fear of re-engulfment.

Separation anxiety. Separation anxiety comes about as a result of the child now beginning to see himself as a person separate from his mother. The child is physically separate, yet has not yet developed the intrapsychic structure to psychologically maintain an inner sense of well-being separate from the mother. The child's demands for closeness represent an attempt to return to the symbiotic state of oneness with the mother so as to participate in the emotional well-being of the relationship.

If the mother is not able to respond to the child's anxiety in a phase-appropriate manner, if the mother is not available to the child, then separation anxiety may increase and demanding, clinging behavior may increase. The child may spend so much energy trying to maintain closeness with the mother that the development of other ego functions is retarded. A very ambivalent relationship may develop between the mother and child— one in which the child very much wants a close relationship with the emotionally soothing mother and at the same time experiences much anger at the frustrating mother. The child may then intrapsychically split his internal image of the mother into the good mother representation and the bad mother representation.

Alternatively, instead of being available, the mother may be overly engulfing, unable to let the child move away, unable to let the child move. In this situation, the separation-individuation process may become arrested.

Rapprochement crisis. Mahler used the phrase *rapprochement crisis* to describe the point in the child's development at which the child can no longer deny her own separateness. The child sees herself as physically separate from mother but has not yet attained a state of psychological separateness (i.e., has not yet internalized her own sense of psychological well-being so that she does not experience anxiety when separate). This is the stage of temper tantrums; if the child's needs for emotional closeness with the mother are not met, she becomes frustrated, anxious, and angry, and these emotions are manifested in the form of a temper tantrum.

Splitting mechanisms may increase, splitting the mother intrapsychically into the good mother and the bad mother representation. This splitting may become manifest in actual relationships between the child and others. For example, if the mother leaves the child with a baby-sitter, the baby-sitter (experienced as the bad mother representation) may be the recipient of the child's anger and temper tantrums; when the mother returns, the child may rush to the mother's embrace, experiencing her as the good mother representation. Alternatively, the baby-sitter may be experienced as the good mother representation, and the mother, as bad mother representation, may receive the child's anger when she returns.

By about twenty-one months, if development has proceeded in a phase-appropriate manner, the child continues to individuate and develops what is called object constancy. Object constancy is a term used to denote the development of an internal soothing representation of the mother. The child is now able to maintain this internal soothing image of mother when she is not present, the child is not dependent on the mother's presence for emotional soothing, the child can now separate from the mother without undue anxiety, and the rapprochement crisis diminishes.

If the rapprochement crisis is not resolved, object constancy does not develop and significant pathology may result. The child may grow up unable to tolerate separateness in relationships, and she may be very sensitive to any real or perceived rejection. Failure to negotiate this phase of development is thought to be a significant factor in the development of borderline personality disorder.

Consolidation of Object Constancy and Individuality

If development continues in a phase-appropriate manner beyond the twenty-fourth month, object constancy continues to become consolidated; that is, the child's cohesive emotionally soothing internal representation of mother becomes an increasingly solid and permanent intrapsychic structure. At the same time, the child's individuality, his internal sense of self, continues to develop. He develops a cohesive, emotionally positive sense of self. As the child continues to interact with mother and others, he identifies with them and internalizes characteristics of them into his own individual self-structure. With the consolidation of the child's intrapsychic structure, he is ready for the next step in development: to learn to relate to others as a separate individual.

DEVELOPMENT OF THE INTERNALIZED WORLD OF
SELF AND OTHER

In this section I will discuss the development of the inner world of self and other representations. The work of Otto Kernberg (1975, 1976, 1980) has been very helpful in providing a description of this process.

An internal self-representation refers to a person's conceptualization of him- or herself. It includes the characteristics, traits, and abilities that a person attributes to him- or herself, along with the affective valence associated with each of those characteristics. So, for example, if a person has good athletic ability, this characteristic may be associated with positive affect. If a person is poor at math, this characteristic may be associated with negative affect. The amalgam of a person's characteristics and their associated affects will be referred to here as one's sense of self.

In a healthy personality, the person is able to accept both her positive characteristics and her negative characteristics and integrate them into a cohesive whole. The hope is that there is a balance of positive over negative so that the person is feeling mostly good about herself and has a healthy self-esteem.

Problems result either when the positive and negative aspects of the self lack integration and/or when the negative aspects of the self outbalance the positive aspects of the self. Later I will describe the process of development leading to either a positive integrated sense of self or a negative and/or unintegrated sense of self.

An internalized object representation refers to one's internal conceptualization of another person. Again, this consists of a person's conceptualization of the characteristics or traits of the other person, along with an affective valence associated with these characteristics. For example, a person may view another person as kindly and feel positive about that. Alternatively, someone may view a person as mean and feel negative about that.

An internalized representation of another person is an approximation of what that person is like in reality. If someone knows another person very well, then his internalized representation of that person may fairly closely approximate reality. If he knows that person less well, his internalized object representation may be only a partially approximate reality. For example, if he knows a person only in the work environment, his internalized object representation of that person is based on his interaction at work and the characteristics that person displays at work. It will not include other characteristics/traits that the person does not exhibit at work, and thus his internalized object representation is only an approximation of the total reality of the other person.

Further, someone's internalized representation of another person may be distorted on the basis of her previous interactions with other persons. That is, she may project onto a current person traits and affects from past relationships. For example, if her experience with authority figures is that they have been derogatory and controlling, then she may project these characteristics onto a new authority figure (say, a new boss), and her internalized object representation of the new boss may include these characteristics along with various affects, even if the new boss is not like this at all. These distortions and their connection may play an important role in psychotherapy.

Internalized object representations might be thought of both in a narrow sense and in a broader sense. The narrow sense would include one's internalized representation of a single specific person. In a broader sense, one might think of the development of a general internalized object representation, which is an amalgam of all the specific internalized object representations.

For example, if someone grows up in a family, community, and environment in which most of the people are supportive, friendly, trustworthy, and honest, then this is what will predominate in the person's general internalized object representation. Further, this will influence future object representations, as he will expect that other people he meets will be supportive, friendly, trustworthy, and honest. Obviously, this may not be the case.

Contrariwise, if someone grows up in a family, community, and environment in which most of the people are critical, abusive, neglectful, and abandoning, then these characteristics will predominate in her general internalized object representation. And she will tend to expect that others she meets will interact in the same way. This may not be the case, and in therapy it will likely be important to help these people learn that other patterns of interaction are possible.

A person's experience with others during development will not likely be so polar as just described. That is, it is unlikely that everyone a person meets will be supportive or that everyone a person meets will be critical. Some people will be supportive and others will be critical. Certainly, even in interactions with a single person, the person may at times be supportive and at times be critical. The hope is that we are able to develop internalized object representations that can tolerate this ambivalence. That is, hopefully we can develop internalized object representations that fairly closely approximate the reality of that other person with all of his or her positive and negative characteristics. Hopefully, also, we can develop internalized object representations of others that are not encumbered by distortions that we project onto them from other relationships in the past.

Just as in the case of internalized self-representation, problems arise when (1) we are not able to integrate our positive and negative internalized object representations or (2) internalized object representations are seen as polarly negative. A third set of problems results from a failure to separate internalized self from internalized object representations. These problems will be discussed later, but first we need to outline the process of development of internalized self and object representations (see figure 4.1).

Let us start with the internalized world of the infant. Theories of development such as Mahler's theory described earlier suggest that the infant's self and object representations are combined and that they go through a process of separation throughout development. This is saying that at birth, the infant does not perceive a distinction between the self and other. To the extent that the child perceives the interaction with another, he perceives it as a self-object interaction. That is, the self and the other are perceived as part of the same whole. Certainly, if the fetus were able to perceive some aspect of its being and surround, the perception of the self and mother being part of one whole would be an accurate one. The hypothesis is that this perception of oneness in the interaction between self and other persists for some time after birth, until the perceptual apparatus matures more fully. Once the perceptual apparatus matures, the infant becomes capable of perceiving the physical separateness between the self and other. The age at which this capability develops is unclear, but work by Stern (1985) and others suggests that it occurs significantly earlier than Mahler originally proposed.

Let us assume that there is a period of time before which an infant perceives a separateness between self and other. The internal representations of these interactions are called self-object representations. A self-object representation is an internalized image of an interaction between a combined self-other (object). Associated with this internalized self-object representation (SO) is an affective valence. Gratifying self-object interactions will be associated with a positive affective valence (SO+). Frustrating self-object interactions will be associated with a negative affective valence (SO−). Clearly, the degree of gratification or frustration in the interaction may vary, so the degree of positive or negative affective valence associated with each interaction may also vary.

The internalized world of the infant's interaction with its mother will consist of a series of self-object representations with various affective valences (see figure 4.1):

$$SO_1 +1 \qquad SO_1 +2 \qquad SO_1 +3$$
$$SO_1 -1 \qquad SO_1 -2 \qquad SO_1 -3$$

As the child begins to interact with others—say, the father—more self-object representations are added (subscript 1 = mother; subscript 2 = father):

$$SO_2 -1 \qquad SO_1 -1 \qquad SO -2$$
$$SO_1 +1 \qquad SO_2 +1 \qquad SO_1 +3$$
$$SO_2 -3 \qquad SO_1 +2 \qquad SO_2 +3$$
$$SO_1 -2 \qquad SO_2 +2 \qquad SO_1 -3$$

Let us suppose an older sibling and a grandparent are also in this infant's immediate environment. We can then add sibling self-object representations (SO_3) and grandparent self-object representations (SO_4).

For purposes of this initial illustration, we will diagram development as it relates to the interaction between the child and the mother. Of course, real development is much more complex because many more people are likely to be present in the child's world. At this point we will simplify the interactions to just one, the mother.

In figure 4.1, the circle in the middle of the diagram contains a number of SO+'s and SO−'s. These refer to self-object representations that are gratifying (SO+) and self-object representations that are frustrating (SO−). (To

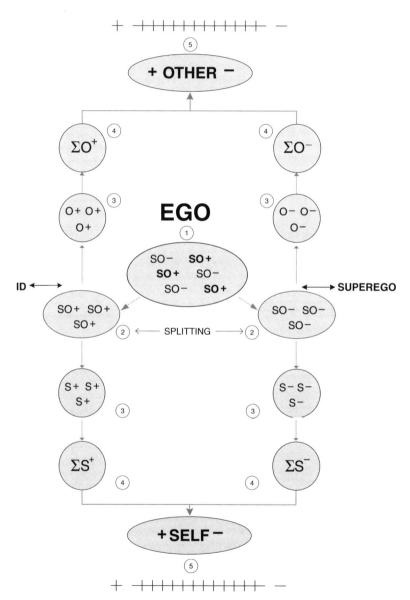

further simplify the diagram, only one valence [+1 or −1] will be assigned to each self-object representation, though in reality, multiple valences [+2, +3, −2, −3] could be assigned to illustrate that some interactions are more gratifying/frustrating and some are less gratifying/frustrating.) Each SO in this diagram refers to an interaction with the mother. Several SO's of positive valence and several SO's at negative valence imply that the infant does not, at this early stage, necessarily perceive each interaction with the mother as being an interaction with the same person.

As a way of decreasing inner states of tension, the infant separates self-object representations of positive valence from self-object representations of negative valence (see figure 4.1). This process is called splitting. The tense self-object representations (SO−'s) can be projected out, leaving the infant with internalized self-object representations of a self-other union that is only positive—a rather blissful state.

The next step on the diagram illustrates the separation of self-representations from object representations. This occurs as maturational development proceeds. Take, for example, the development of the motor system and the visual system. As the motor system matures, the child can crawl and then walk away from the mother and thus become physically separate from the mother. As the visual system matures, the child can look back at

Figure 4.1. Separation-Individuation

This diagram illustrates the separation-individuation process as well as the development of internalized self representations and internalized other representations. (The following numbers correspond to the numbers on the diagram.)

1. Earliest stage of development in which interactions between the self and other are experienced as a combined self-other (SO) representation.
a. Gratifying self-other interactions are illustrated as SO+.
b. Frustrating self-other interactions are illustrated as SO2.
2. Self-other representations of positive valence are split from self-other representations of negative valence.
3. Internalized self representations and internalized other representations are separated from each other.
4. Positive self representations are consolidated; negative self representations are consolidated. Positive other representations are consolidated; negative other representations are consolidated.
5. Positive self representations and negative self representations are integrated into a cohesive whole self representation; positive other representations and negative other representations are consolidated into a cohesive whole other representation.

the mother and visually perceive his or her physical separateness. Thus, the child is developing an ability to see himself or herself as physically separate from the mother. As memory systems mature, the child will be able to carry this perception, in memory, over gaps of time during which he or she is separate from the mother. This ability to maintain a mental image of the other when the other is not present is called object permanence. We still have a few more steps to go before we get to the object constancy, the ability to maintain an emotionally soothing image of the other when the other is not present.

At the level of development we are now describing, we see diagrammed a circle with several $O+$'s, a circle with several $O-$'s, a circle with several $S+$'s, and a circle with several $S-$'s. This implies that, even though self and other representations have been separated, the self and other are still experienced in a rather fragmented or unintegrated way. The self and other representations are unintegrated in two ways: (1) internal other representations of positive emotional valence are separated from internal other representations of negative emotional valence; internal self-representations of positive emotional valence are separated from internal self-representations of negative-emotional valence; and (2) within each circle the self or other representations have not coalesced into unified representations.

The next step on the diagram represents the coalescence of the self-representations of positive emotional valence into a unified positive self-representation $(S+)$; the coalescence of the self-representations of negative emotional valence into a unified negative self-representation $(\Sigma S-)$; the coalescence of the other representations of positive emotional valence into a unified positive other representation $(\Sigma O+)$; and the coalescence of the other representations of negative emotional valence into a unified negative other representation $(\Sigma O-)$.

At this point in development, then, the internal world of self and other representations consists of four representations $(\Sigma S+, \Sigma S-, \Sigma O+,$ and $\Sigma O-)$. That is, self and other representations have separated from each other and some degree of integration has occurred. Self-representations of positive emotional valence have become integrated; self-representations of negative emotional valence have become integrated; other representations of positive emotional valence have become integrated; and other representations of negative valence have been integrated. Integration, however, is not complete. The positive self-representation $(\Sigma S+)$ remains split from the negative self-representation ($\Sigma S-$), and the positive other representation ($\Sigma O+$) remains separate from the negative other representation ($\Sigma O-$).

At this point in development, then, the self may be experienced as either all good or all bad. The other may be experienced as either all good or all bad. It is this level of development that is often described as being characteristic of the borderline personality. It may also be characteristic of other disorders of the self besides borderline personality.

At the next level on the diagram, the final step of integration is illustrated. At this level, the positive self-representation and the negative self-representation have been integrated into a whole cohesive self-representation. The positive other representation and negative other representation have been integrated into a whole cohesive other representation. It is now possible to view the self and other ambivalently; that is, the self can be experienced as an integrated whole with both positive and negative characteristics; the other can be experienced as an integrated whole with both positive and negative characteristics. Obtaining this level of development is of significance, since being able to view the self and other ambivalently corresponds most closely with reality.

Thus, at this level of development, a person has developed the ability to view the significant others in her development as cohesive wholes with both positive and negative characteristics. This ability will also extend to new people she meets in the present and future; that is, she can view new people in this same ambivalent manner. Obviously, not everyone will have had the same experiences with significant others in development. Depending on what experiences a person has had in interactions with those significant others, she will have internalized object representation that colors how she expects future interpersonal interactions to go. If most of her developmental interpersonal interactions have been gratifying, then she will likely expect future interpersonal interactions to go well. If most of her developmental interactions have been frustrating, then she may approach future interpersonal interactions with caution. We might say that on the basis of past interactions, we develop a model of how interactions will go in the future. This model will be called an attachment model to refer to the way in which attachments are formed in interpersonal interactions. That is, via the separation individuation process, we form not only an internalized sense of self and an internalized sense of other, but also a sense of how self-other relations work (i.e., an internalized object relationship or attachment pattern). Since we usually develop with more than one significant other, we have probably learned more than one attachment model (perhaps a different model with the mother compared with the father). These different attachment models will be used in forming new relationships in the present and future. As an example, a person might use his or her father attachment model in relating to men and his or her mother attachment model in relating to women.

If a person has grown up with significant others who are critical and rejecting, then this is the attachment model he learns. He expects others to be critical and rejecting. As a result, he may be very cautious about entering into interpersonal relationships. Once in a relationship, he may not tend to extend much positive affect to the other, since this is not part of the attachment model he has learned. As a result, he may be rejected, which just confirms his original expectation.

It is possible, however, that through other interactions, as perhaps in therapy, he may learn that some people relate in ways different from their significant others. The hope is that he can internalize these new attachment models so that he can then go out and develop more fulfilling interpersonal relationships.

Two additional developmental aspects associated with the development of an internalized cohesive other representation are affective modulation and object constancy. Affective modulation refers to the ability to express affects across a wide spectrum of various possibilities. If a person is still experiencing others as split representations, then affective expression is very polar, either on the extreme of the positive pole or the extreme of the negative pole. Affects, however, exist across a wide spectrum. If one considers a dimension of affect varying from euphoria on one extreme to severe depression on the other, many degrees of happiness and sadness exist in between. The attainment of the ability to experience others cohesively and ambivalently correlates with the ability to experience emotions toward others (and analogously toward the self) that span the spectrum of possible affects and are in proportion to the nature of the interaction. This results in a person being a little sad at a small disappointment in an interaction with his or her significant other and very depressed by the loss of that significant other. (This ability to modulate affect is illustrated by the gradations above "Other" and below "Self" in figure 4.1.)

If a person has not developed this ability to modulate affects, then the affects she experiences toward others and toward the self will be very polar. A person has two affective responses—all positive or all negative. Thus, if someone has a date with a significant other and he is late, instead of feeling a small amount of irritation, she will feel rage.

The ability to experience others cohesively and ambivalently is thought to correlate with object constancy. Object constancy refers to the ability to maintain a soothing internalized image of a significant other. This is not the same as the ability to maintain an internal physical image of the significant other. Children can maintain a physical image of a significant other outside their presence long before they attain object constancy. Object constancy is a psychological function; it is the ability to maintain a soothing, stabilizing image of the other when the other is not present. Children may know that their mother exists physically when she is not present, but they may still be upset by her absence. Only her return can serve to calm them.

Children may for a period use a transitional object (doll, blanket) as a symbol of mother. It serves to soothe them when mother is not present. Eventually they give up the transitional object; that soothing function has been internalized. One might say that the child now has an internalized transitional object that serves to calm them in times of tension. This ability of inner soothing is one important mechanism for maintaining a sense of well-being within the child's inner world.

As development proceeds, if the majority of object relations are associated with a balance of gratification over frustration, the child will develop internalized object representations that are integrated and cohesive. The child will be able to see others as whole individuals with both positive and negative characteristics. The child will be able to use that mostly positive object representation to soothe himself when he is tense (the internalized transitional object). The child will grow up with the expectation that future object relationships can be rewarding.

Similarly, if development goes well, the child will develop a sense of self that is integrated and cohesive. He will be able to see himself as mostly positive, but will be able to acknowledge negative aspects within himself. As tension arises, he will be able, with his positive sense of self, to reinstate a sense of well-being.

This internal system of self and object representations will be referred to as the inner representational world. If the inner world has developed with healthy self and object representations, then the person has an inner sense of well-being and is poised to adapt to stressors from without that might threaten that sense of inner well-being (e.g., a problematic relationship).

If development has not gone well and if there have been problems in the development of healthy self and object representations, then the person may have difficulty maintaining a stable sense of inner well-being. Various defenses may be brought into play, and an assortment of disorders of the self may result.

SUMMARY

In this chapter I have described the inner world of self and object representations. The evolution of self and other representations across early development has been described using Margaret Mahler's theory of separation-individuation. This self-other inner representational world has been depicted along an axis vertical to the horizontal id, ego, superego axis presented in figure 2.1 in chapter 2. Next I will go on to use this illustration to describe the primitive mechanisms of defense (chapter 5) and the effects of developmental arrest at various levels along the spectrum of separation-individuation (chapter 6). The concepts of primitive mechanisms of defense and arrest of the separation-individuation process are both very helpful in understanding many forms of psychopathology.

5

The Primitive Defenses

In chapter 3 I introduced the concept of mechanisms of defense. There I discussed repression as a primary defense and the recruitment of secondary mechanisms of defense as a result of the breakdown of repression. The use of repression, however, is based on the presence of a certain amount of ego strength, which can mount the defense of repression to keep negative affects from flooding into the ego. If a person does not have sufficient ego strength to mount repression in the first place, negative affects will not be kept out of the ego but will enter and become associated with negative self and other representations. A predominance of negative self and other representations over positive ones may trigger the use of primitive defenses, the topic of this chapter.

This imbalance of negative affect within the ego may lead to chronic feelings of anxiety or other negative affects, which only gets worse when new stressors from the environment stimulate the influx of even more negative affect. If negative representations predominate over positive ones, then it may not be possible to complete the separation individuation process and get to the point of having separate, cohesive, mostly positive self and other representations. This predominance of negative over positive self and other representations can occur in one of two ways:

1. If, throughout development, frustrating object relationships predominate over gratifying ones, then the internalized self and object representations may be mostly negative. That is, negative interactions with significant others will stimulate negative affects and aggressive drives. Internalized self and other representations will become associated with these negative affects

and aggressive drives. For example, if a person grows up with significant others who are abusive, neglectful, and/or absent, and who always tell the person that he was unwanted, is no good, and will never amount to anything, then the person will grow up with negative feelings about others and the self (see figure 5.1). Of course it may be possible for someone to grow up in an abusive environment and somehow find a way to cope with the situation and develop a positive emotional balance.

2. A second way to arrive at this same configuration of a predominance of negative self and other representations over positive is on a more constitutional and less developmental basis. Naturally, if a person has an affective interaction with another, the result is a combination of the memory of the self and the other in the interaction along with the associated affect, either positive or negative. These affects can be thought of as entering the ego from the id's affective system. It may be possible that there exists within the affective system a problem on a constitutional basis that creates an imbalance in affective expression of positive versus negative affects.

If, in a given gratifying interaction, a person is unable to experience positive affect, then the self and object representations resulting from that interaction will not be associated with positive affect. If the person can only experience negative affect in association with frustrating interactions, then there will be an imbalance of negative introjects over positive introjects even if, in reality, there have been a balance of positive over negative interactions (see figure 5.2).

Regardless of the route, if negative self and other representations predominate over positive self and other representations, it becomes difficult to complete the separation individuation process and arrive at an internalized state in which self and other representations are integrated, cohesive, and mostly positive. Let us take the situation in which SO+ and SO− have separated into their respective self (S+ and S−) and other (O+ and O−) components, but have not yet consolidated into cohesive self (+ self−) and other (+ other−) representations (figure 5.3). If S+ and O+ are such that one has internalized very little in terms of positive self and other characteristics and feeling, and S− and O− are such that one has internalized much in terms of negative self and other characteristics and feelings, then completion of the separation-individuation process is difficult. It is difficult because if one were to try to combine S+ and S− (or O+ and O−) into a cohesive whole, that whole would be overwhelmed by the S− (or O−), leading to a chronically anxious and/or dysphoric state.

An alternative would be to stay at this unintegrated level and try to deal with the S− and O− defensively while preserving the S+ and O+. The types of defenses that are used in this situation are often called primitive defenses. They are distinguished from the neurotic defenses (e.g., repression, displacement, isolation, reaction formation, undoing, intellectualization, etc.) described earlier in the discussion of neurotic conflicts *between* the id, ego, and superego. The primitive defenses are used to deal with tension *within* the ego. Tension arises within the ego when there is an imbalance of negative self and other representations over positive self and other representations. Examples of these primitive defenses include projection (and projective identification) devaluation, primitive idealization, omnipotence, denial, and splitting.

Splitting is a key mechanism in dealing with tension within the ego. As described in chapter 4, splitting may be used early in development to split apart positive from negative representations; at this point it may serve the process of development. The persistence of splitting of S+ from S− (or O+ from O−) (see figure 5.3) prevents the development of a cohesive self and other internalization. However, in the situation in which negative representations (S− and O−) predominate over positive representations of self and other, splitting serves the defensive function of keeping S+ and S− (O+ and O−) apart so that S+ (O+) is not overwhelmed by S− (O−). It is the first step in the defensive struggle of the ego in attempting to keep itself from being overwhelmed by the tension of negative self and other representations.

With splitting in place, other mechanisms may be brought into play to decrease tension within the self system. Denial is a mechanism that can bolster splitting. It seeks to deny the importance of the existence of the negative self and other introjects, thus attempting to tip the balance in favor of the positive self and other introjects. If one can deny negative self and other introjects, it is as if they don't exist. Diagrammatically (figure 5.3), one might envision this as a process via which the negative self and other introjects are removed from the illustration. What would remain in the ego are the positive self and other representations allowing one's affective balance to shift from a negative state to a more positive state (see scale at the bottom of figure 5.3).

Other mechanisms that work on the negative self and other representations include projection and devaluation. In projection, the person projects

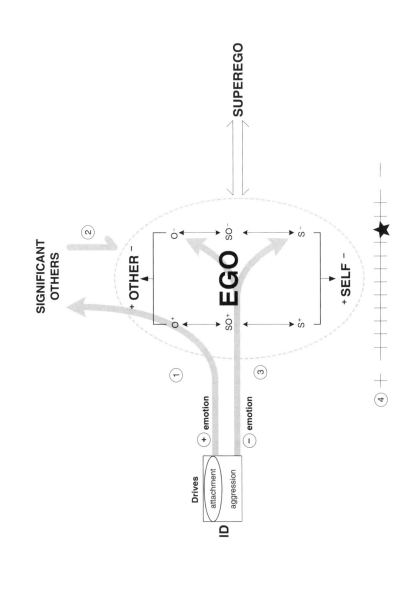

Figure 5.1. Developmental Basis of Excessive Negative Self and Other Representations

1. This diagram starts with the extension of attachment drive with (+) emotion toward the significant other (bold line 1).

2. The parent's reaction is very negative = frustrating, abusive, critical, neglectful (bold line 2).

3. When this negative reaction from the parent is received by the child, it leads to a negative emotional response (bold line 3). The ego is infused with negative emotions (e.g., anxiety, anger), and these emotions become associated with internalized object and self representations = other people will be mean, critical; I'm unworthy, bad, undeserving.

4. The star on the scale below the diagram symbolizes a negative affective balance within the ego related to the imbalance of negative self and other representations compared with positive self and other representations.

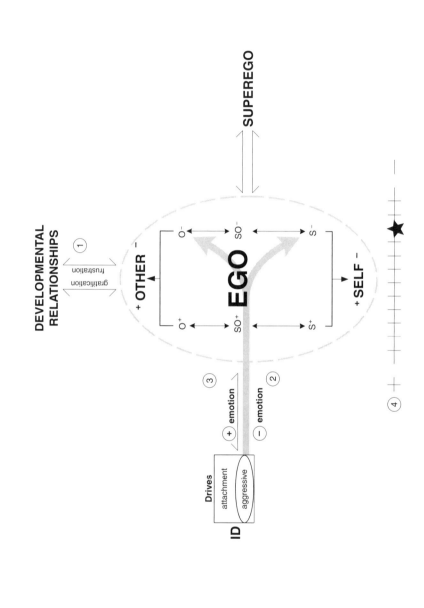

DEVELOPMENTAL
RELATIONSHIPS

① gratification / frustration

+ OTHER ⁻

O⁺   O⁻
SO⁺   SO⁻
S⁺   S⁻

EGO

+ SELF ⁻

SUPEREGO

ID
Drives
attachment
aggressive

③ + emotion
② − emotion

④ ★

Figure 5.2. Constitutional Basis for the Development of Excessive Negative Self and Other Representations

1. This situation assumes that we have the average expectable parents who are capable of interacting with the child using a healthy balance of gratification and frustration. Even a healthy parent-child relationship, however, will involve situations that are frustrating for the child (1).

2. In this child, any frustration stimulates, on a constitutional basis, an excessive aggressive response with associated negative emotion. This negative emotional response may then lead to excessive negative cathexis of self and other representation.

3. The previous dynamic may be combined with a constitutionally impoverished ability to experience positive emotions, leading to a paucity of positive self and other representations.

4. The consequence of this will be an excess of negative internalizations and a lack of positive internalizations, leading to an overall negative emotional balance in the ego.

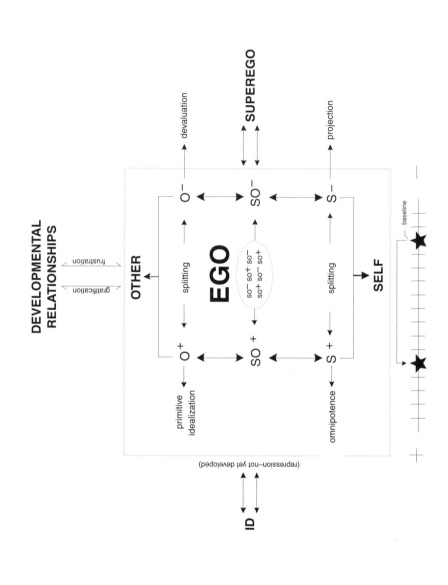

Figure 5.3. The Primitive Defenses

If the ego has not developed to the point of being able to use repression, the ego may become overwhelmed with negative affects. To deal with this baseline negative emotional balance, splitting may be maintained as a primary defense. This keeps positive self representations separated from negative self representations, and positive other representations separated from negative other representations, and allows for the use of other primitive defenses.

In this diagram, devaluation and projection are seen as moving negative self and other representations out of the ego. Primitive idealization and omnipotence increase the affective valence of the existing positive self and other representations. The overall effect is to decrease negative and increase positive emotional valence, shifting the affective balance from its negative baseline state to a more positive state.

or expels negative representations from the ego, often attributing them to someone else. Devaluation is often used with negative other representations. Someone devalues the other, thus decreasing the other's significance to herself. In essence, she says that the other is not important to her and attempts to devalue the other's significance to the ego. Diagrammatically (figure 5.3), projection and devaluation are illustrated by the arrows that extend outside the ego. This is meant to illustrate negative self and other introjects being extruded from the ego, allowing the person to shift her affective balance to a more positive state.

Other mechanisms may serve to bolster flailing positive self and other introjects. For example, in primitive idealization, the significance of positive other representations is increased. In omnipotence the affective valence of self representations is increased. In both primitive idealization and omnipotence, the attempt is to increase positive representations, tip the balance so that positive predominates over negative, and decrease tension within the ego. Diagrammatically (figure 5.3), projective identification and omnipotence are illustrated by the arrows that extend out from the positive object representation and positive self representation. Note that in this case, the arrows stay within the ego boundary. These are defensive maneuvers aimed at shifting the affective balance within the ego toward the positive.

In summary, splitting serves to separate S+ from S− (and O+ from O−). Projection and devaluation are illustrated as serving the purpose of decreasing tension within the ego (negative representations are moved outside the dotted line of the ego). Primitive idealization and omnipotence move positive representations to a more positive affective position within the ego, thus improving the affective balance of the ego.

The previous discussion assumes that the person has not been able to achieve a level of integration of cohesive self and other representations because of an excess of negative representations over positive representations. There may be another reason for the failure of the development of cohesive self and other representations; that is, cohesive self and other representations may fail to develop because the child has been given the message (overtly or covertly) that it is not all right to separate. The parent may need the child to stay closely attached because of the parent's insecurity. In these situations, the parent may not be overly critical, punitive, or neglectful. He may, in fact, be just the opposite. He may be very reinforcing, but he is reinforcing of things the child does because he, the parent, needs the child to do certain things to meet his (the parent's) own needs. For example, the parent may be very reinforcing of the child's performance in sports or on stage. The child is, however, given the message that she has to perform well because her performing well is very important to the parent. The parent is not able to reinforce the child because the child enjoys the activity, but rather reinforces the child's performance because he (the parent) needs the child to perform well in order to bolster his own faulty sense of self.

In this case, though the child may develop some positive self-characteristics, they may not be ones that she feels especially good about, not ones that she has invested with positive affect. Thus, though in this case there is not an excess of negative self representations, there also is a lack of development of positive self representations on which to build a cohesive sense of self. The child is not allowed to individuate, not allowed to be her own self, to develop characteristics based on her own interests that she can invest with positive affect. Rather, she is being told that she must stay closely attached to the parent and perform so as to meet the parent's needs. In this situation, object representations may be split, especially if the child experiences the relationship with the parent as very frustrating, leading to excessive negative object representations. Primitive defenses such as primitive idealization and devaluation may be used to deal with split object representations. Positive and negative self representations may also remain split (unintegrated). The splitting occurs not so much because of the excess of negative representations but rather as a result of the paucity of positive representations. The child may deal with the lack of positive representations via defenses such as omnipotence. This may especially be the case if the child has been told all of his life that she is special.

SUMMARY

In this chapter I have discussed the use of primitive mechanisms of defense, which are used when there is a failure in the completion of the separation-individuation process, a failure to develop cohesive positive self and other representations. As a result of the failure to develop cohesive positive self and other representations, these self and other representations remain split. At this level of ego development, there may not be sufficient ego strength to mount the mechanism of defense, repression, so from this split position, primitive mechanisms of defense are used. These primitive mechanisms of defense are used either to decrease negative affect by expelling it from the ego or to increase positive affect by enhancing positive self and other affects within the ego.

These concepts are useful in understanding various personality styles. For example, in borderline personality, we often see the use of projection (to expel negative) combined with primitive idealization. In this situation, the borderline forms a relationship with another whom he idealizes. That is, the affective valence of the internalized representation of the other is increased to idealized proportions, resulting in a shift of the affective balance within the ego of the borderline from negative to positive.

Another example would be the use of primitive defenses in the narcissistic personality. Here we frequently see the use of omnipotence to increase the affective valence of the self representation and the use of devaluation to decrease the affective valence of the other representation. The overall effect is to shift the narcissist's affective balance from a negative state to a more positive state.

In future chapters I will be coming back to many of the previous concepts and discussing them in the context of clinical cases.

6

The Psychotic, Borderline, Depressive &
Cohesive Levels of Separation-Individuation

Based on the model of separation-individuation discussed in chapter 4, we can describe various levels of separation-individuation that correspond to the different steps of the separation-individuation process and which are useful in understanding various forms of psychopathology. The levels we will discuss include the psychotic level, the borderline level, the depressive level, and the cohesive level. The psychotic level corresponds to the stage at which self and other representations have not yet separated (SO+ and SO−). The borderline level corresponds to the stage at which self and other representations have separated from each other but not yet integrated (O+ and O−; S+ and S−). The depressive level corresponds to the stage at which integration of self representations and other representations has occurred, but at which the affective valence associated with those +self representations (depicted in lowercase in fig. 6.1) and +other representations (lowercase) is not yet all that positive and may be quite negative. The cohesive level corresponds to an integrated level of +SELF− and +OTHER− (depicted in uppercase in fig. 6.1) development in which the balance of affect associated with those SELF and OTHER representations is positive. The psychotic, borderline, depressive, and cohesive levels are illustrated in figure 6.1 and will be discussed in more detail next.

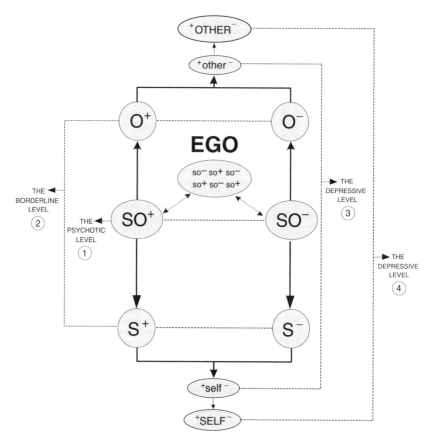

Figure 6.1. The Levels of Separation-Individuation

A failure to complete the separation-individuation process (i.e., to get to the cohesive level) may lead to an arrest at an earlier level. Four levels are illustrated:

1. The psychotic level: Self and other representations have not been differentiated (ego boundaries have not been established), though self-other representations of positive affective valence are split from self-other representations of negative affective valence. An even more primitive and disorganized variant of the psychotic level may be that which precedes the splitting.

2. The borderline level: Self and other representations have separated, but positive and negative self representations remain split, and positive and negative other representations remain split.

3. The depressive level (lowercase self and other): Positive and negative self representations have coalesced; positive and negative other representations have coalesced. Even though the self and other representations have become cohesive, there exists significant negative affect within these structures, so the person is chronically or frequently depressed, anxious, angry, and so on.

4. The cohesive level (uppercase self and other): There is a cohesive SELF representation, which is mostly positive affectively, and a cohesive OTHER representation, which is mostly positive affectively.

THE PSYCHOTIC LEVEL

At the psychotic level, self and other representations have not been differentiated. In other words, ego boundaries have not been established; that is, the self and the other representations have not differentiated one from another. The internal milieu consists of combined self-other representations of either a positive affective valence or a negative affective valence (SO+ or SO−).

This level of development may correlate with some of the psychotic symptoms that are seen in clinical situations. An object-relations model cannot explain all of the symptoms of psychosis, since many of the symptoms of psychosis are cognitive or perceptual. The object-relations model may explain symptoms of psychosis related to poor self-other differentiation. So, for example, a person may state that he (self) is God (other) as a manifestation of the SO+ introject. Or he may state that he (self) is the devil (other) as a manifestation of the SO− introject. In both of these examples, there is a failure in the separation of self and other representations. In another example, a patient hearing voices may be unable to distinguish whether the voices he hears are his own thoughts or are coming from other people. One patient, in the presence of other men, hears a voice saying, "I'm having sex with your girlfriend." He can't tell if one of the men is actually saying that (other) or if it's a thought within himself (self).

Persons may be at the psychotic position because of a failure to have progressed through the stages of separation-individuation (in which case constitutional factors may play a predominant role) or as a result of regression from a more advanced stage of separation-individuation such as the borderline level. In fact, many borderline patients describe, under stress, a fear of regressing to the psychotic level at which they would actually lose the self-other differentiation of the borderline level. Some borderline patients do, at least transiently, develop psychotic symptoms. This development of psychotic symptoms may correspond to the previously described regression from the borderline level to the psychotic level.

THE BORDERLINE LEVEL

At the borderline level, self representations have separated from other representations; that is, ego boundaries have been established. As a result, the per-

son distinguishes self from other. The problem is that the person at the borderline level has not taken the next step in the separation-individuation
process; she has not developed an integrated self-image and an integrated
other image. Rather, positive self-images remain split from negative self-images, and positive other images remain split from negative other images.

From a developmental perspective, this arrest at the borderline position
may occur for a variety of reasons (either singly or in combination):

1. An excess of negative representations over positive representations may
be one reason. If the balance of negative self and other representations is
greater than the balance of positive self and other representations, then the
tendency will be to stay at the borderline position. This is because integrating the mostly negative self (or other) representations with the few positive
self (or other) representations would lead to an integrated whole that is
mostly negative. Since that integration would lead to a chronic dysphoric or
anxious state, the tendency is to remain at a borderline level from which the
person may use various defenses such as projection or devaluation to decrease the imbalance of negative representations (or primitive idealization
and omnipotence to increase the valence of positive representations) and arrive at a more positively balanced emotional state.

Different mechanisms have been proposed via which a person may develop this excess of negative representations over positive representations.
From a developmental perspective, this imbalance of negative over positive
representations may result from relationships with significant others in
which a person is criticized, devalued, and/or abused. The person's internalized other representations would be of the critical, abusive other (O−), and
the person's internalized self representations would be of a worthless, devalued self (S−). This is opposed to the situation in which the person grows up
with significant others who are warm, supportive, and nurturing. The person then develops a positive other representation (O+) as well as a self representation of a person who is valued and worthwhile (S+).

It has also been hypothesized that one could develop an excess of negative
representations over positive representations on a constitutional basis
(Kernberg 1975, 1976). That is, a person may, on a constitutional basis, have
a tendency (temperament) to experience negative affects in excess of positive
affects. Thus, even if someone grows up in a family that is basically supportive, she has difficulty experiencing gratifying interactions as positive and

thus cathecting self (S1) and other (O+) representations with positive affect. At the same time, even minimally frustrating interactions with significant others may stimulate as excess of negative affect, which then gets cathected to self (S−) and other (O−) representations leading to an imbalance of negative representations over positive representations.

2. A second reason for an arrest at the borderline level may be the selective reinforcement of dependence over independence (Masterson 1976). In this situation the family may not necessarily be overly negative, abusive, or devaluing. In fact, they may be quite supportive and reinforcing of the child, but only if he remains dependent and does not try to individuate. Attempts at individuation are met with withdrawal of emotional support. Thus, because the development of individual characteristics is not reinforced, the person does not separate and individuate to the point of developing an integrated, mostly positive self.

3. A third dynamic may be that of the parent or parents who are neglectful or uninterested. In this situation, the parents are neither negative and abusive as in (1), nor are they reinforcing of dependence as in (2). Rather, they are uninterested or don't seem to have the time for the child. As a result, empathic mirroring interactions do not occur between the parents and the child. The lack of this type of interaction leads to the failure to stimulate the positive affect that is necessary for the cathexis of healthy self and other representations.

THE DEPRESSIVE LEVEL

In chapter 4, I discussed an integrated level of separation-individuation. Here, that integrated level is divided into two subcategories, the depressive level and the cohesive level. The depressive level will be designated by the terms *self* and *other* in lowercase letters; the cohesive level will be designated by the terms *SELF* and *OTHER* in uppercase letters.

At the depressive level, positive and negative self representations have been integrated, and positive and negative other representations have been integrated. However, the integrated self and integrated other representations are not predominantly cathected with positive affect. From the perspective of the developing child, one may see this as a normal stage—a stage where the child has just begun to develop an integrated identity, but at which that identity is still quite fragile. If development were to proceed normally, that identity, that sense of self, would gradually grow as the child developed more and more characteristics that were invested with positive affect, and eventually the child would arrive at the normal cohesive level. Instead, in some persons, development gets arrested at this level at which integration has occurred but at which the negative affective investment outbalances the positive affective investment in the self and other.

The reasons for this arrest may be similar to the reasons for the arrest at the borderline level. The difference may be more quantitative than qualitative. So, in the example where the pathology results from the parents being critical and abusive, if the criticism is extreme, development is arrested at the borderline level. If the criticism and abuse are less extreme, development is arrested at the depressive level. In other words, in the borderline level the balance of negative investment over positive investment is greater than it is in the depressive level. As a result, at the depressive level integration occurs even though it leads to a chronically depressive state. In this situation, the advantages of integration (at the depressive level) likely outweigh the disadvantages of being at the split, unintegrated level in the borderline.

The term depressive is used to identify this level of separation-individuation, and indeed some persons at this level may manifest the symptom depression, while others may present with different symptom pictures. So, the depressive level may be the stage at which most dysthymic people reside on a chronic basis. Some narcissistic people (those who usually appear more integrated than borderline) may also be at the depressive level. They have, however, been able to deal with it by shoring up narcissistic defenses (omnipotence, for example). Dependent people may be at the depressive level. They deal with it by finding someone to cling to in order to help balance their negative emotional state. Many persons with anxiety disorders are operating from this level.

THE COHESIVE LEVEL

At the cohesive level of development, positive and negative self representations are integrated, and positive and negative other representations are integrated. As opposed to the depressive level, now the majority of the affective cathexis in the integrated self representation and the integrated other representation is positive. That is, now the person has developed an internalized view of himself that is mostly positive and an internalized view of other that is mostly positive. The person is able to acknowledge negative characteristics within the self and realize that others may have negative characteristics. But for the most part, he sees himself positively and realizes the possibility of others who can be mostly positive themselves and who can interact in a mostly positive manner.

Achieving this level of development is important for maintaining an inner sense of well-being. The person who achieves this level of development will have mostly positive self and other representations, which help him maintain and sustain positive emotional balance.

I would like to make one more point before concluding this chapter: it is best to think of separation-individuation as existing along a continuum from a very early undifferentiated level to a mature cohesive level. I have merely described four reference points along the continuum. While a given person may be at one of these reference points, another person may be in between them (e.g., between the borderline level and the depressive level; between the depressive level and the cohesive level, etc.).

SUMMARY

In this chapter I have further discussed separation-individuation, adding various levels at which the separation-individuation process can become arrested. The levels discussed were the psychotic level, the borderline level, the depressive level, and the cohesive level. I shall come back and talk about these levels further when I begin discussing psychotherapy, because, in treatment, it is very helpful to try to determine the patient's level of separation-individuation.

7

Attachment Theory

hapter 1 introduced the concepts of attachment drives and relationships; now we turn our attention in more detail to attachment
theory, a theory that grew out of the observations and research of
John Bowlby. Bowlby (1907–1990) received his psychoanalytic training
in Britain in the middle part of the twentieth century. He was supervised
by Melanie Klein and associated with Anna Freud and Donald Winnicott
and so was well versed in traditional Freudian psychoanalytic theory as
well as object-relations theory. Bowlby came to believe that these theories
underestimated the effect that environmental factors, such as the quality
of the relationship between a parent and a child, had on childhood development and psychopathology. His views put him at odds with the
psychoanalytic establishment of his times. Peter Fonagy's (1999) review
in the *Handbook of Attachment* provides an excellent description of the
points of divergence as well as the points of convergence between attachment theory and psychoanalytic theory. The following are just a couple of
differences:

1. Attachment theory looks at the child in the context of the child's relationship with the mother; psychoanalytic theory looks at the child in the context of the child's drives, fantasies, and unconscious mental processes.

2. Research in the field of attachment tends to be prospective, starting
with the child and studying that child in a variety of environmental situations; psychoanalytic theory tends to start with the adult and attempts to re-
construct the childhood experience from the adult's memory.

Bowlby and many others, notably Mary Ainsworth, studied attachment and the related issues of separation and loss in investigations that began in the 1940s and have continued up to the present. Bowlby presented his theory and findings in a trilogy entitled *Attachment and Loss* (Bowlby 1969, 1973, 1980). In this chapter I will review selected aspects of attachment theory including (1) some of the separation studies that significantly influenced Bowlby's thinking, (2) the specifics of the mother-infant attachment relationship, (3) Mary Ainsworth's concept of internal working models, (4) the evolution of attachment relationships across development, (5) the contribution of attachment theory to our understanding of the inner representational world, (6) attachment theory and adult psychopathology, and (7) attachment theory and psychotherapy.

SEPARATION STUDIES

Bowlby became interested in understanding the attachment relationship between a child and a mother because of some of the problems that had been observed in children who had been separated from their parents. One of the first people to study the effects of separation of a child from its mother was Rene Spitz, who began his studies in the 1930s and who published his observations in a book entitled *The First Year of Life* (Spitz 1965). In one study he observed 123 infants who were growing up in an institutional setting with their mothers. The children developed normally for the first several months, but at some point between six and eight months, they were separated from their mothers for periods of three months or more. The infants developed weepy behavior and became withdrawn from their surroundings. When approached by adults, they ignored the adults; if the adults persisted in attempting to interact with the children, they cried or screamed. After three months the weepy phase subsided, and now the children would sit or lie with wide-open, expressionless eyes and immobile faces staring, seemingly in a daze, refusing contact with adults. Spitz likened the facial expression of these infants to that of a depressed adult. He called this syndrome anaclitic depression to distinguish it from adult depression.

In another study, Spitz observed ninety-one infants in a foundling home from which children were going to be placed for adoption. Women came to this institution, gave birth, cared for the children for three months, and then left. Thereafter, the children were cared for by nurses, each of whom was responsible for eight to twelve infants. All of the infants' physical needs were met, but obviously one nurse could not provide the same degree of emotional care to eight to twelve infants as a mother in a one-to-one relationship. Spitz observed that these children went through the previously described period of anaclitic depression. After three months, these infants became passive and did not develop the ability to turn over. At two years they had a developmental quotient that was 45 percent of normal, and by the end of two years, one-third had died. Those that survived to four years could not sit, stand, walk, or talk. Spitz concluded that the absence of a mother led to emotional starvation and resulted in an arrest of psychological and physical development.

In the years after World War II, Bowlby began his studies on the effects of separation. He hired a research assistant, James Robertson, who had worked with Anna Freud during the war and had observed children who had been separated from their mothers as a result of the war. After the war, Robertson and Bowlby observed children who had been separated from their families as a result of the child's hospitalization. In London in the 1940s and 1950s, parents were allowed to visit their children in the hospital only one hour per week; this provided a naturalistic setting for the study of separation. Between 1948 and 1952, Bowlby and Robertson (1952) observed children ages eighteen months to four years who had been separated from their families for periods of one week or more due to hospitalization. As a result of their observations, three stages of separation were identified: protest, despair, and detachment.

In the first stage, protest, the child cried and screamed, manifested anxiety, and attempted to find the mother to effect a reunion. During the stage of despair, the child became withdrawn, was less active, disengaged from people and the environment, and appeared depressed, in mourning over the loss of the mother. The final phase, detachment, was most obvious when the child was reunited with the mother. The child did not show any joy at the mother's return, seemed to have lost interest in her, refused to acknowledge her or accept her comfort. If the separations were not too long, the children reattached to their mothers; however, in the case of prolonged separation, the detachment persisted.

Besides the human infant studies, Bowlby was also interested in animal studies of separation, such as those by Harry Harlow in the 1950s and 1960s.

In Harlow's (1971) surrogate mother studies, rhesus monkeys were separated from their biological mothers and raised by two surrogate mothers, one a wire mesh mother with a feeding tube and another wire mesh mother covered with terrycloth. The baby monkey would spend time feeding on the wire mesh monkey with the feeding tube, but most of the rest of the time was spent clinging to the terrycloth surrogate mother. The terrycloth surrogate seemed to stimulate attachment behavior, because if the baby monkey was frightened, it would scurry to the terrycloth surrogate mother, not the wire one. When these monkeys grew up, they were incapable of providing adequate mothering for their offspring.

In other experiments, Harlow (1969, 1973) studied separation; infant monkeys were initially raised by their mothers and then separated. They seemed to manifest Bowlby's stages of (1) protest—they attempted to regain contact with their mother; (2) despair—they sat in the same posture and did not engage in play; and (3) detachment—when reunited, they rejected their mothers.

ATTACHMENT

These and other studies convinced Bowlby of the significance of separation and loss. Bowlby hypothesized that an important parent-child bond had been broken. To understand this, Bowlby became interested in the field of ethology. He was aware of Konrad Lorenz's (1957) imprinting studies, which showed that infant geese form a strong bond to their mothers; this bond was called a behavior system. Bowlby (1973) used this concept to define the attachment behavioral system in human infants. This attachment system assures that the child will remain in the proximity of the parent and, from an evolutionary perspective, maintaining proximity assures protection and increases the probability of survival. This system is particularly important in a species like the human, which goes through a prolonged period of immaturity and dependency before becoming self-sufficient.

The attachment system is related to the fear system; that is, if the child is threatened or in pain, he will experience fear, which triggers the attachment system, leading the child to seek the proximity of mother for protection and safety. Bowlby and Ainsworth, however, stressed that physical proximity was not enough to assure the security of the child; the mother must be available and responsive to the child. As the child gets older, that availability can be assured by means other than physical proximity. The child can talk with the parent and understand that the parent is going to be away (separated), but that the parent will return and thus will continue to be available and responsive. The child's expanding cognitive facilities greatly facilitate this understanding because the child can eventually realize that the mother continues to exist even when not present. If the parent demonstrates continued availability and responsiveness, then the child develops confidence in the parent's availability and responsiveness, resulting in a secure attachment. If the parent can maintain attunement to the child's physical and emotional needs, the child develops a secure base; if not, the child may become insecure. Mary Ainsworth studied the concepts of secure and insecure attachments, and it is to her work that I now turn.

MARY AINSWORTH—INTERNAL WORKING MODELS

Mary Ainsworth's research provided much empirical evidence for Bowlby's attachment theory. She studied attachment relationships between children and their mothers—both in the laboratory and in the home—and provided evidence for Bowlby's hypothesis that differences in the attachment styles of children were related to differences in the availability and responsiveness of their caregivers.

In the laboratory, Ainsworth developed a paradigm known as the strange situation for assessing the quality of the infant-caregiver attachment relationship. Briefly, in the strange situation, a mother and one-year-old child enter a room in which a stranger is present; the child is allowed to explore in the room, and at some point the mother leaves for a short period and then returns. So, in this paradigm, there is both a separation and a reunion. The goal is to activate the child's attachment behavioral system and learn something about the child's expectations about the availability and responsiveness of the mother.

Using this method, Ainsworth et al. (1978) defined attachment relationships as either secure or insecure. Among the insecure attachment relationships, two subtypes were differentiated: avoidant and resistant (also called anxious/ambivalent).

In the strange situation, the secure child can use the mother as a secure base from which to explore the room. Upon separation the child becomes distressed and stops exploration. The stranger may be able to comfort the child. Upon reunion, the child will seek proximity with the mother, be comforted quickly, and return to exploration/play.

The avoidant child will play with toys available in the room but will not usually engage the mother in playing together. When the mother leaves, the child is not distressed; she may actually be more responsive to the stranger than the mother. When the mother returns, the child may ignore or actually move away from the mother.

The resistant (anxious/ambivalent) child has a hard time using the mother as a secure base for exploring and playing—that is, he has a hard time leaving the mother to initiate play; he is generally very wary of the stranger. Upon separation he is very distressed, and upon reunion he is difficult to calm.

Since Ainsworth's original studies, a third insecure attachment style has been described: the disorganized/disoriented style (Main & Soloman 1990). In the strange situation, these children were not classifiable into one of the previously described patterns. They tended to show contradictory behaviors. For example, they might cry for the mother at separation and then move away from her during reunion—that is, show elements of both the resistant and the avoidant pattern.

Ainsworth (1978) had made home observations of the interactions between these mother-child dyads in the year leading up to the strange situation study. Mothers of secure children were available and responsive to their children's needs. Mothers of children later classified as anxiously attached (resistant) were less responsive to their children's needs, interfered more with their children's behavior, and were less accessible to their children's bids for attention compared with the mothers of securely attached children. Mothers of children later classified as avoidant seemed to have an aversion to physical contact with their children and expressed little emotion during interactions with their children.

These various secure and insecure attachment patterns are known as internal working models. This means that, as a result of numerous interactions between a child and a mother over time, the child develops an internal model of what to expect from the mother in terms of availability and responsivity. We can think of this internal working model as consisting of an internal image of self interacting with other according to a certain interactional style and associated with various affects. In the secure pattern, the mother is available and responsive. In situations in which the mother is less available and responsive, the child may try to find a strategy that increases the mother's availability and responsivity, such as being clingy as is seen in the resistant (anxious/ambivalent) pattern.

In the previous discussion, it is clear that the type of internal working model (attachment pattern) a child develops is dependent on the mother's availability and responsivity. Others (Goldsmith & Alansky 1987) have suggested that the child's temperament is a factor, and that what is important is the interaction between the child's temperament and the mother's availability/responsivity. From this perspective, we might consider the child with a very irritable temperament and a mother with an average ability to be available and responsive. That mother might become overwhelmed with that child's irritability and, as a result, become less available and responsive, resulting in an insecure attachment. If that irritable child is paired with a mother with an above average ability to be available and responsive, then a secure attachment may result. If the irritable child is paired with the average mother, but the average mother has some help (e.g., a husband or grandparent in the home, who can help out when the mother becomes overwhelmed), then things may work out. If that irritable child is paired with a parent who has less than average ability to be available and responsive, then we might speculate that there would be a bad outcome.

Much of the early research of attachment focused on the relationship between a mother and a child in the early years of a child's life. More recently the issue of attachment over time has been the subject of investigation, and it is to that topic that I now turn.

THE EVOLUTION OF ATTACHMENT

This section will discuss the attachment behavioral system as well as other interpersonal relationship systems over time to help us understand the components of an adult-adult relationship. Earlier I described the child's attachment relationship with the mother as one in which the child seeks the proximity of the mother for protection and to have his or her physical and emotional needs met. A key component of this relationship is the availability and responsivity of the mother. In a relationship between a mother and a child in which the mother is available and responsive, the child develops an inner working model of that relationship, which includes the expectation that the relationship will continue on that same available, responsive basis.

With that secure base, the child is increasingly able to move out into the world away from the mother and explore his or her universe and return to the mother when he or she needs her security.

In attachment theory, the other behavior system that is activated in the mother-child relationship is the caregiver behavior system (Bowlby 1988; George & Soloman 1999). Just as the attachment behavior system is activated in the child, so the caregiver behavioral system is activated in the mother. Thus in this attachment-caregiver system, the goal of the child is to be protected and taken care of; the goal of the caregiver is to protect and give care. A key feature of the caregiver behavioral system is sensitivity; this refers to the caregiver's ability to sensitively perceive and evaluate the child's cues appropriately. Another feature of the caregiver behavior system is that it is goal corrected, which means that the type of caregiving behavior will vary according to the age of the child and according to the amount of caregiving the child needs in a particular situation.

The caregiving behavioral system seems to evolve gradually over time. We may see some of the early vestiges of caregiving in children's play with dolls or in a child's care of a pet. In some families, a child may have caregiving responsibilities for a younger sibling. As children develop affiliative relationships and especially as they get into adolescence, we may see significant amounts of caregiving in peer relationships such as a boyfriend-girlfriend relationship. The caregiver system likely becomes most activated when one makes the transition to parenthood.

The next system to talk about is the affiliative system (Ainsworth 1989). If the attachment-caregiver relationship has gone well (i.e., the child has formed a secure attachment), then she has a secure base from which to explore her environment. The exploratory system becomes activated, and child is able to move away from the mother and investigate the world around her. Eventually, in her exploration she will come in contact with other children, in the neighborhood, the day care, the preschool. As a result of these encounters, the child may form affiliative relationships, relationships with other children involving jointly exploring the environment, playing games, and engaging in activities. Some of these affiliative relationships may develop into close friendships.

As a person moves into adolescence, affiliative relationships may take on caregiving and attachment qualities. Though attachments to parents continue to be important throughout adolescence, there may be a gradual shift in attachment relating from a parent to a peer, and this may ultimately culminate in a significant other/mate relationship.

In adulthood one may have a variety of affiliative relationships that may vary according to the amount of emotional involvement there is in the relationship. There may be affiliative elements in the relationship with one's mate in which there is much emotional investment. Varying degrees of emotional investment may be present in affiliative relationships with friends, relatives, coworkers, social acquaintances, and so on.

The next system to discuss is the sexual mating behavioral system (Feeney 1999), which becomes activated during adolescence. Certainly one of the tasks of adolescence is to begin to explore aspects of sexual relating. The sexual mating behavioral system may be activated in a variety of contents. It may be activated in the context of an attachment-caregiving relationship in the formation of significant other/partner relationship. It may be activated outside of an attachment-caregiver relationship in a less committed relationship. As a person moves through adolescence into adulthood, sexuality can become an important part of an emerging pair bond relationship, our next topic.

The pair bond (Reedy, Birren & Schaie 1981; Hazan & Zeifman 1999) relationship refers to a relationship between a pair of people who form a committed bond. The pair bond relationship contains elements of all of the previous forms of relating. The pair bond relationship is an attachment relationship, but now the attachment relationship is mutual. In the mother-child attachment relationship, the mother met the attachment needs of the child. In the pair bond relationship, each partner meets the attachment needs of the other. Because each partner is meeting the attachment needs of the other, each partner is also a caregiver, so the caregiver behavioral system is activated. The sexual mating system is likely part of the pair bond relationship. One feature of sexual intercourse is that it leads to the release of oxytocin, which facilitates bonding. The affiliative system is also part of the pair bond relationship; the members of the dyad share common goals, interests, and activities, which they engage in together. Another aspect of this may be increased intimacy of sharing (i.e., sharing with one's partner one's innermost thoughts and feelings). Finally, children are often a product of a pair bond relationship. Having children stimulates new caregiving and attachment bonds, and the whole cycle starts over again.

We have discussed the various interpersonal behavioral systems including the following:

1. Attachment
2. Caregiving
3. Affiliative
4. Sexual mating
5. Pair bond

These systems evolve over development and, if things have gone well, culminate in the pair bond relationship, which contains elements of all those above it in the list.

THE INNER REPRESENTATIONAL WORLD

Earlier I talked about the concept of internal working models in attachment relationships. We might think of an internal working model as having cognitive, affective, and relational properties. In other words, it contains an internal representation of self and of other as well as a representation of an interaction between self and other that has a certain affective coloring to it.

Mary Ainsworth described categories of internal working models: secure, avoidant, and anxious/ambivalent (resistant). These are very useful concepts, and in this section I want to elaborate on the concept of internal working models or attachment patterns and suggest that in clinical work, it may be useful to understand a person's internal working model a little more specifically. That is, for a given category of internal working model, say avoidant, there may be many specific patterns, one that is unique to one person, another to another person, and so on. In a therapy situation, understanding the specifics of that person's internal working model may be very useful in helping that person. The specifics of a person's internal working model is what I call that person's inner representational world. Let's look at an example.

⑥ Claire, a woman in her twenties, comes in asking for help with relationships with men. She states that she's very reluctant to get into relationships with men for fear that she will get hurt; when Claire has been in relationships, they have been short-lived because she becomes anxious and breaks off the relationship.

From the previous description we might hypothesize that she is using an avoidant internal working model.

Let us now go on and try to understand a little bit more about her inner representational world. Claire grew up in a family in which her parents were divorced when she was three and her mother remarried when she was five. The family then consisted of herself, her mother, and her stepfather; she would see her father on alternate weekends, on holidays, and during the summer.

Claire described her mother as a kind, giving, loving, artistically talented woman who always had time for her. She used her artistic ability to engage Claire in many projects and activities that Claire has fond memories of. She feels close to her mother and says she can talk to her about anything.

She described her stepfather as a critical, judgmental man with a temper. He was not able to be complimentary to Claire. Claire was an excellent student in grade school and high school, but her stepfather always found something to criticize about her performance. With any minor transgression to his many rules, he would fly into a rage and yell and scream. Claire dealt with her stepfather by trying to stay out of his way, by avoiding him.

Claire's father was an alcoholic. Her major memory of visiting her father was of going to the bar. Since she was underage, she would wait in the car while her father and his buddies and/or current girlfriend would go inside and get drunk. When they came out, they would drive recklessly down the road and often either get stopped by the police or get into a car accident (fortunately no one was ever hurt). When her father was not drunk, Claire described him as a fun-loving guy but characterized him as rather immature, "like a big kid." As she got older, Claire tried to find more and more excuses to not go visit her father, to avoid him.

Now let's make some comments about Claire's inner representational world; the following are three relationship patterns:

1. *Mother pattern.* A kind, giving other interacting with a valued, worthwhile self with the associated emotions of love and affection.
2. *Stepfather pattern.* A critical, judgmental other interacting with a worthless, criticized self with the associated emotions of anger and guilt.
3. *Father pattern.* An uncaring, intoxicated other interacting with an insignificant, undeserving self with associated emotions of fear and anxiety.

Understanding these patterns is helpful in psychotherapy. We can see that Claire developed a secure attachment pattern with her mother and rather avoidant patterns with her stepfather and biological father. If she used either the stepfather pattern or the biological father pattern in a current relationship with a man, the negative affects associated with those patterns were triggered, making Claire uncomfortable and resulting in her tendency to leave the relationship. Understanding the specifics of these two avoidant patterns helps the therapist in two ways: (1) the therapist can help Claire work through the emotions she has over these two avoidant patterns so that she can resolve them and so, hopefully, they will not come up in current relationships with men, leading her to leave those relationships; and (2) the therapist can serve as a model to help her internalize a new relationship pattern, which she can hopefully then use to form a happy, healthy relationship with a man.

ATTACHMENT THEORY AND ADULT PSYCHOPATHOLOGY

Many studies have looked at the relationship between adult psychopathology and childhood attachment events such as trauma, separation, and loss. Dozier, Stovall, and Albus (1999) provide an excellent review of these studies. The list that follows summarizes a few of the findings from their review:

1. Children who lose a parent by death are at risk for later depression.
2. Children who lose a parent by separation experience less severe, but angrier, forms of depression.
3. Persons with depression describe their parents as unsupportive and rejecting.
4. Infants with resistant (anxious) attachment are more likely than infants with secure or avoidant attachments to be diagnosed with an anxiety disorder in adolescence.
5. Persons with panic disorder had frequently experienced early loss of a caregiver or inadequate caregiving.
6. Persons with generalized anxiety disorder report rejection by their parents and more role reversals with their parents.
7. Infants with disorganized attachment tend to be reported in later years by their teachers as having dissociative symptoms in grade school and high school.

8. Children with disorganized attachments who are repeatedly abused may be more susceptible to the development of dissociative symptoms.

9. Persons with anorexia tend to have mothers that are overcontrolling and perfectionistic as well as unsupportive of their children's autonomy; their fathers tend to be emotionally unavailable and rejecting.

10. Persons with borderline personality disorder report experiencing early abuse, prolonged separations from caregivers, and emotional neglect when caregivers are present.

Thus, many studies suggest an association between problematic childhood attachment relationships and the development of adult psychopathology. Bowlby stressed that while insecure attachment relationship in childhood was a risk factor for the development of psychopathology, insecure attachment did not determine psychopathology. Attachment is an evolving process, and while a child may be insecurely attached at one point in time, he or she may be able to cope and adapt and become securely attached at a later point in time.

In addition, the child who is securely attached is not necessarily immune from psychopathology. He may experience trauma or losses later on that predispose him to the development of problems. An important issue is whether or not attachment theory has anything to offer in terms of treatment to those people who do develop psychopathology. It is to that question that I turn next.

ATTACHMENT AND PSYCHOTHERAPY

Psychotherapy will be discussed in more detail in part III, but here I will discuss a few concepts derived from attachment theory. Bowlby presented many of his ideas on treatment in a book entitled *A Secure Base* (1988). From an attachment perspective, a person may develop problems such as anxiety, depression, or difficulty relating to others because she was never able to develop secure attachments. The failure to develop secure attachments is seen as related to caregivers not being available and responsive. As a result, the person develops internal working models that are associated with anger, anxiety, sadness, or other negative affects. The therapist serves as the available, responsive secure base for the patient, providing her with a relationship that she can use to express and resolve some of these emotions and a relationship that she may be able to use to develop a new internal working model that is associated with more positive affects.

Patients often come to therapy when there is some stress in their life that leads to affective dysregulation; like the child who feels threatened, the patient seeks out an attachment relationship. The empathy and support of this relationship allows patients to reexperience the unhappy and unfortunate experiences of their lives, enabling them to see those experiences in a new light. Hopefully, they can change their views of themselves as unlovable and unworthy, and their views of others as uncaring and punitive, into representations of themselves and others that are much more positive.

In her book *Attachment and Adult Psychotherapy* (2000), Pat Sable discusses "narratives of attachment." She describes asking patients to travel mentally through time in order to create a narrative of their life and in particular of their attachment experiences. The therapist provides the secure base from which patients can explore their traumas, losses, separations, and unsuccessful attachment experiences. They can look at how these experiences have shaped their representations of self and other; hopefully they can reconsider and restructure these representations in a way that allows them to be free of symptoms. In the context of an affectively attuned relationship, the therapist allows the patient to express emotions that previous attachment figures did not allow the person to express. This gives the person the chance to deal with these emotions associated with old working models and the opportunity to develop new working models that can be associated with more positive emotions.

SUMMARY

This chapter reviewed some basic ideas of attachment theory. I started with the history of how Bowlby began to think about attachment and how he defined the attachment relationship. I reviewed studies of maternal separation as well as Mary Ainsworth's studies on internal working models. In addition to the attachment caregiver system, information on affiliative, sexual, and pair bond behavior systems was presented. After a discussion of the inner representational world, I went over some concepts of pathology and treatment as they relate to attachment theory. Next, I will move on to a discussion of affect theory. The end of that chapter will return to attachment, and I will talk about the relationship between affect theory and attachment theory.

8

Affect Theory

DEFINITIONS

This chapter will attempt to further delineate a theory of affects as they relate to the previously described psychodynamic model. My first goal will be to try to define some of the words used to describe feeling states. Words such as *emotion, affect,* and *mood* are commonly used to describe feeling states. Sometimes these words are used interchangeably; sometimes these words are used to describe different aspects of feeling states, though not always in a consistent manner.

The following are some definitions of the words *emotion, affect,* and *mood.* Once these words are defined, I will use them in a manner consistent with these definitions.

Emotion

Emotion is a term used to refer to the psychic as well as the physiological components of a feeling state. The psychic component is the subjective feeling itself (e.g., happiness, sadness, anger). The physiological components are the autonomic (e.g., blushing, sweating, increased heart rate, etc.), endocrine (e.g., increased cortisol), and motor (e.g., facial expression) components of the emotion. Emotional responses appear to be coordinated by the limbic system in response to a stimulus that may be either external (e.g., a visual perception) or internal (e.g., hunger, a memory).

Consider the following example. Suppose a person sees a frightening stimulus. The information received from this stimulus is processed at the level of the visual cortex, giving rise to the objective visual recognition of the stimulus. The stimulus is also received at the limbic system where further processing is carried on. One aspect of this further processing is the emotional processing that occurs at structures such as the amygdala. The amygdala may assign feeling (e.g., fear, anxiety) to the perception. This is the psychic component of the emotion, which then may be combined with the objective visual perception.

The amygdala connects to (1) autonomic nervous system nuclei to initiate an ANS response (e.g., increased heart rate, increased respiratory rate), (2) the hypothalamus leading to an endocrine response (e.g., increased cortisol), and (3) the basal ganglion leading to a motor response (e.g., frightening facial expression, assumption of a bodily posture for fight or flight) (Mesulam 2000). Emotions are thought to be relatively brief responses to a stimulus. This part of the definition differentiates emotions from mood, which are thought of as relatively enduring over time.

Affect

The term *affect* is used here to refer to the psychic component of an emotion; it is the subjective feeling part of the emotion (as opposed to the physiologic components of the emotion). Of central importance to our discussion is the concept that an affect may be cathected to a thought, idea, and so on via memory. In terms of our psychodynamic model, we are particularly interested in the affective cathexis of self and other representations. In a general sense, the affective cathexis of either self or other representations will be either pleasurable or unpleasurable.

Consider an example of a pleasurable affective cathexis. Suppose a child is engaged in playing a game with his parent. They are both having fun; it is a pleasurable experience. The self representation consists of a memory that includes a cognitive component (e.g., the memory of the self engaged in a game) and an affective component such as joy, which is cathected to the cognitive component. The other representation similarly consists of a cognitive component (i.e., the parent engaged in the game) and an affective component of a happy, giving parent.

Now consider an example of an unpleasurable affective cathexis. This time suppose we imagine a parent shouting at a child in a verbally abusive manner. Now the self representation consists of a child being yelled at (the cognitive component) along with an affective component, anxiety, fear, cathected to the cognitive component. The other representation consists of a cognitive component (the yelling parent), to which is cathected an affective component, anger.

Mood

The term *mood* is used here to refer to a more stable, enduring, long-lasting (but changeable) feeling state. In terms of our psychodynamic model, a mood is the result of the sum of the affective cathexes of the self and other representations. So, if one's internal milieu consists of an abundance of pleasurable (+) representations and a paucity of unpleasurable (−) representations, then one's mood may be happy, peaceful, content. If, on the other hand, there is a greater balance of unpleasurable representations compared with pleasurable representations, then one's mood may be angry, anxious, or depressed.

Note that these moods may change depending on the ongoing influx of affects that get cathected to self or other representation. Consider the person with a happy mood. If she has an unpleasurable interaction with another, this may lead to the influx of much negative affect, which may change her mood to sadness until she is able to discharge (decathect) that negative affect. Now consider the person whose mood is unhappy. A pleasurable interaction with another may lead to a positive affective influx, which allows his mood to change to a happy one.

BASIC EMOTIONS

It has been proposed (Darwin 1872; Tomkins 1962, 1963; Ekman & Davidson 1994) that humans and other primates possess basic emotions. The term *basic* refers to the conceptualization that these emotions are inherent, biologically based, hardwired from birth. This is not to deny the fact that sociocultural learning plays a part in the development of a person's emotional responses. I will return to the issue of learning at the end of this section, but first I will further explain the concept of basic emotions.

The concept of basic emotions dates back to Darwin, who in 1872 published a book entitled *The Expression of Emotions in Man and Animals* (Darwin 1872). Darwin studied emotional facial expressions in man and in other primates; he noted similarities in the facial expressions of man and these primates. He believed that humans and primates inherited basic emotional reaction patterns that served as a form of communication (e.g., a happy facial expression communicates receptivity to a person we encounter; an angry facial expression communicates the possibility of attack to the other).

Darwin's work lay dormant for many years until Silvan Tomkins (1962, 1963) began studying emotions and facial expressions. He listed a series of emotions and associated facial expressions that he believed are inherited and under the control of subcortical centers in the brain. The following is a listing of Tomkins's basic emotions and their associated facial expressions:

1. *Surprise-startle.* Eyebrows up, eyes blink
2. *Interest-excitement.* Eyebrows down, tracking behavior, attitude of looking and listening
3. *Enjoyment-joy.* Smile, lips widened and out, slow and deep breathing
4. *Distress-anguish.* Crying, arched eyebrow, corners of the mouth turned down, tears and rhythmic sobbing
5. *Contempt-disgust.* Sneer, upper lip lifted
6. *Anger-rage.* Frown, jaw clenched, face red
7. *Fear-terror.* Eyes frozen open; pale, cold, sweaty; facial trembling with hair erect
8. *Shame-humiliation.* Eyes cast down, head down

According to Tomkins, these patterns are all inherited. The first five can be observed from birth. The last three appear later and seem to require learning for them to be manifested.

More recently, others, such as Paul Ekman (1992a, 1992b) at the University of California, San Francisco, have done additional work on basic emotions. Ekman has studied facial emotional expressions in a number of literate and preliterate cultures. When people of many different cultures are shown a picture of a person with a specific facial expression, they all identify the same emotion. For example, when shown a picture of a smiling face, people from different cultures identify the emotion happiness.

This has been found to be true for the emotions surprise, enjoyment, happiness, anger, fear, disgust, and sadness. It may also be true for contempt, interest (excitement), shame, and guilt, though more study is needed. Some of these emotions (interest, joy, sadness, disgust, distress) can be identified in the infant at birth. Others, such as surprise and anger, can be expressed by the infant at three to four months; fear can be expressed by six months.

Ekman talks about emotions as important signals between people that give us clues about the interaction between ourselves and another. For example, if I am walking down the hall and see someone walking toward me with a smile on her face, I get one emotional message; if that same person is walking toward me with a frown on her face and her fists clenched, I get a different emotional message. Thus, emotions are an important component of interpersonal interactions.

Ekman (1992c) goes on to list several characteristics of basic emotions:

1. *Distinctive universal signals* (facial expressions).
2. *Presence in other primates.*
3. *Distinctive physiology* (such as a specific ANS reaction for each emotion).
4. *Distinctive universal antecedents.* This implies that there are certain stimuli that will elicit each of these basic emotions (i.e., that we are preprogrammed evolutionarily to react to certain stimuli with specific emotional responses). This is not to deny the importance of learning in emotional responsiveness because certainly learning contributes to the establishment of a connection between a stimulus and an emotion.
5. *Coherence of response system* (i.e., coherence between a given emotion, its facial expression, an ANS pattern, and CNS activity).
6. *Quick onset.* Emotions can begin within milliseconds of an emotionally provoking stimulus.
7. *Brief duration.* Usually in seconds rather than minutes or hours. This distinguishes emotions from moods.
8. *Automatic appraisal mechanism.*
9. *Unbidden occurrence.* Emotional responses occur automatically to a given stimulus; they happen to us, they are not chosen by us.

Ekman (Ekman and Friesen 1975) also suggests that each basic emotion may actually represent a whole family of emotions. Within the family of a given basic emotion may be other emotions that express varying degrees of the basic emotion. For example, within the basic emotion family of fear we might find apprehension, alarm, worry, trepidation, shock, terror, horror, and dread. Other examples follow.

Surprise family. Astonished, amazed, astounded
Disgust family. Aversion, contempt, repugnance
Anger family. Displeasure, fury, wrath, rage
Happiness family. Contentment, pleasure, enjoyment, joy
Sadness family. Unhappiness, somberness, misery, sorrow, grief

Finally, I need to mention a little more about the distinction between an emotion and a mood. I have already said that in general, an emotion is more short-lived and a mood more long-lasting. Another aspect of a mood may be that it is made up of various combinations of emotions, the affects of which have been combined with cognitions to form affective-cognitive structures. Thus, depression may be a mood that is a result of various affective-cognitive structures derived from basic emotions such as sadness, anger, disgust, and shame.

AFFECTS AND OBJECT RELATIONS

It is interesting to look at affects from an object-relations perspective. The work of Joseph De Rivera (1977) has been helpful in this regard. He suggests that an emotion directed from one person (let's say a parent) toward another person (let's say a child) results in a second emotion in the child. He gives numerous examples of such emotional interactions. Let us examine a few as they may occur in a relationship between a parent and a child. If a parent expresses the emotion "love" toward the child, the child experiences the emotion "security." If love is the dominant emotion that the parent expresses toward his or her child, then the child may grow up with a strong sense of security and well-being.

De Rivera suggests that the emotion "anger" in one person elicits the emotion "depression" in another. So, if a parent's predominant manner of relating to his or her child is with the emotion anger, the child may become depressed.

Table 8.1 lists some of the emotions De Rivera describes in his book. In the left-hand column are a list of emotions called "it emotions"; these are emotions that have an other as their object (i.e., they serve to move an other). In the right-hand column are a list of "me emotions"; they are the emotions that occur as a result of an "it emotion." We might say that the "it emotion" from one person leads to an emotional movement in the second person, resulting in the "me emotion."

Table 8.1 Emotions

IT Emotion		ME Emotion
Love	→	Security
Desire	→	Confidence
Anger	→	Depression
Fear	→	Anxiety
Esteem	→	Humility
Admiration	→	Pride
Contempt	→	Shame
Horror	→	Guilt
Acceptance	→	Serenity
Wonder	→	Joy
Rejection	→	Sorrow
Dread	→	Panic

As stated before, love in a parent leads to security in a child; anger in a parent leads to depression in a child. Also, desire leads to confidence, fear leads to anxiety, and so on.

A few comments about this schema are in order. First, it is not entirely clear that the connections between "it emotions" and "me emotions" are universal. That is, does love always lead to security, and does anger always lead to depression? It would seem that to some extent, the "me emotion" that is elicited by the "it emotion" is in part dependent on the person generating the "me emotion." For example, while anger may lead to depression in one person, might it not lead to anxiety in another. This is a question that needs further exploration.

Second, might we not think of there being a reciprocal relationship between the "it emotions" and the "me emotions"? That is, could we conceive of there being a two-way arrow between the "it emotions" and the "me emotions"? For example, if love leads to security, does security lead to love? If anger leads to depression, does depression lead to anger? If fear leads to anxiety, does anxiety lead to fear? This, too, is a question that needs further exploration.

At this point, I would like to further develop the concept of emotions in object relationships by talking about the concept of emotions in the context of the previously proposed psychodynamic model. Emotions will be discussed in terms of developmental relationships—the relationships between parents and children. We will explore the effect of the emotions of the parent on (1) the internal development of the child and (2) the emotional relationship between the child and the parent.

Let us start out with an emotion that is sent from a parent to a child (see figure 8.1); we will call it a sending emotion. This sending emotion, along with whatever language ("I love you") or behavior (a hug) that accompanies it, is first received and processed at the level of the ego (cortex). The processed information is then sent to the id (limbic system), where an emotional reaction is elicited. We will call this the elicited emotion. As noted previously, this elicited emotion may have several components: affective, autonomic, endocrine, and motoric (e.g., facial expression). The affective component may reenter the ego, where a couple of things may happen: (1) the affective component may become cathected to various internal representations and fixed into memory, and (2) the affect may lead to the development of a new sending emotion, which is sent back to the parent.

For some examples, see figure 8.2. Suppose we imagine a parent in a loving interaction with his or her child. The sending emotion from the parent to the child is love. What is the elicited emotion in the child? If we follow De Rivera's schema, the affective component of the elicited emotion would be security (well-being). This sense of security or feeling of well-being might then be cathected with the child's internalized self representation. Might there be other affective components to this elicited emotion? Perhaps the affect of love would be elicited; this then might be cathected to the child's internalized other representation. Thus, as a result of the love sent from the parent to the child, we have affected the inner world of the child such that the internal self is cathected with security and well-being, and the internal other

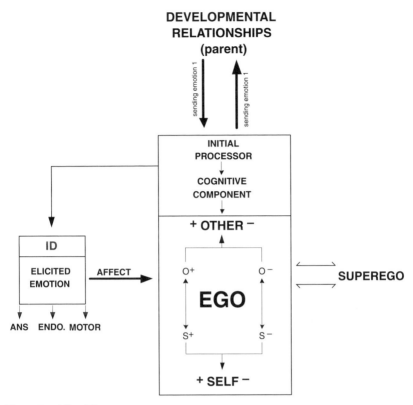

Figure 8.1. Affect Theory

A sending emotion (1) from a parent to a child is initially processed at the ego and then further processed at the id, leading to an elicited emotion, which may have affective, autonomic, endocrine, and motor components.

Affective components may reenter the ego and become combined with the cognitive components; the combined affective-cognitive components may be cathected with self and other representations and contribute to the development of attachment patterns.

A second sending emotion (2) may then be sent back to the parent from the child.

is cathected with love. If, over time, there is a predominantly loving interaction between the parent and the child, these well-being self cathexes and loving other cathexes will continue to grow and may lead to a predominantly positive mood in the child.

The previous description applies to the internal reaction of the child. We might also consider an external reaction of the child—that is, a tendency to send an emotion back to the parent. In this case, the sending emotion might be love, which might lead to another loving emotion being sent back to the child, and so on. In this manner, a loving bond develops between the parent and the child, which includes the child's positive self and other cathexes as well as an internalized attachment pattern of a loving relationship between one person and another.

Another example is shown in figure 8.3. Suppose the sending emotion from the parent to the child is anger. The elicited emotion in the child would be, according to De Rivera, depression. A depressive affect might then become cathected with the child's internalized self representation. Another component of the elicited emotion might be anger, which could then become cathected with the child's internalized other representation. The internal world of the child as a result of this interaction would then consist of a depressive self representation and angry other representation. If the predominant style of interacting between the parent and the child is an angry one, then depressive self cathexes and angry other cathexes would increase, and the overall mood of the child may be angry and depressed.

Besides the internal reaction of the child, we can again consider an external reaction. The elicited emotion in the child may trigger a sending emotion, which is sent back to the parent (alternatively, it may be repressed). If the sending emotion is anger, then a reciprocal angry interaction between the parent and child may be precipitated. As a result, the child may internalize an angry self-other attachment pattern.

As a result of the numerous emotional interactions between a parent and a child, the child internalizes a variety of affectively cathected self and other representation, some positive and some negative. The scale on the bottom of the page (see figures 8.2 and 8.3) is meant to symbolize the sum of affective cathexes within the ego. The sum of affective cathexes is what we defined earlier as mood. In part III, Psychotherapy, I will be using these concepts to discuss how we might help a person with a negative mood to change his or her affective cathexes and improve his or her mood.

AFFECT THEORY AND ATTACHMENT THEORY

We have already discussed one association between affect theory and attachment theory; this is that internal working models or attachment patterns are associated with affects. For example, a pattern between a nurturing other and secure self with the associated affects of love and affection, or a pattern be-

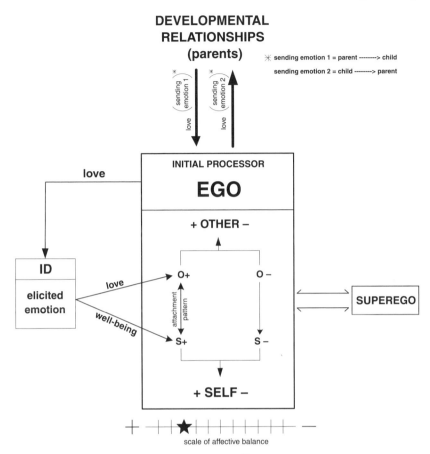

Figure 8.2. Affect Theory: Exchange of Positive Affect

A sending emotion 1 (love) is sent from the parent to the child. That sending emotion 1 and the interaction that accompanies it are perceived at the ego as well as the id. At the level of the id, the sending emotion stimulates elicited emotions, which have affective components. In this example, the elicited emotions are love and well-being, which can become cathected to the child's self and other representations.

This type of interaction can affect the overall mood state of the child (see scale of affective balance) and contribute to the development of a positive attachment pattern.

The child may send a sending emotion 2 (love) back to the parents, and a reciprocal interaction may ensue.

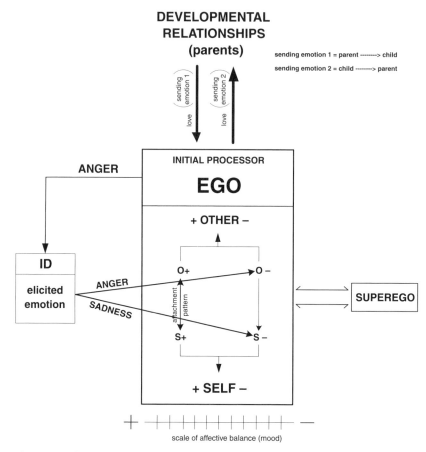

Figure 8.3. Affect Theory: Exchange of Negative Emotion

A sending emotion 1 (anger) is sent from the parent to the child. That sending emotion 1 and the interaction that accompanies it are perceived at the ego as well as the id. At the level of the id, the sending emotion stimulates elicited emotions, which have affective components. In this example, the elicited emotions are anger and sadness, which can become cathected to the child's self and other representations.

This type of interaction can affect the overall mood state (see scale of affective balance) and contribute to the development of a negative attachment pattern.

The child may send a sending emotion 2 (anger) back to the parents, and a reciprocal interaction may ensue.

tween a critical other and an insecure self with affects of anxiety and anger. Researchers have begun to look at other aspects of the interface between affects and attachment; one such area is that of affect regulation in the context of attachment relationships (as reviewed by Cassidy 1994).

An infant in an attachment relationship with a caregiver turns to that caregiver for affect regulation (i.e., when the infant is anxious or distressed, she turns to the caregiver, who calms the infant, regulates her affective disturbance). In a securely attached child, the child gradually becomes more capable of regulating her affect on her own and needs the mother less for affective regulation. Still, even the securely attached child may become overwhelmed by affect and turn to her mother for aid in affective regulation, just as a secure adult may turn to her attachment partner during times of affective dysregulation. Securely attached individuals thus can regulate affective dysregulation either by internal processes or by turning to an attachment figure, allowing them to return to a baseline calm state.

This may not be true for insecurely attached individuals. Avoidantly attached individuals have learned to inhibit affective expression and, as a result, are not able to express affect as a means of affective regulation. Affect is inhibited, but then may be expressed episodically and explosively. The anxiously (resistant) attached individual has learned that he has to enhance the expression of affect in order to get a response from his caregiver; this affective enhancement may have deleterious consequences in subsequent relationships. The securely attached individual, for example, may find the anxiously attached individual's affective enhancement unpleasant or dysregulating. The avoidantly attached individual who inhibits affect may require others to stimulate his inhibited affect so it can be expressed and as a result may seek out the anxiously attached individual. To the extent that the avoidantly attached individual is angry and the anxiously attached person is anxious, we may see the exchange of these negative affects back and forth, leading to a rather tumultuous relationship.

Another way for the insecurely attached individual to regulate affect would be via the use of drugs or alcohol. Drugs and/or alcohol can be used to regulate affect by decreasing negative affect or increasing positive affect or both. The suggestion has been made that the affectively enhanced anxiously attached individual drinks alcohol to quell negative affect and the affectively inhibited avoidantly attached individual drinks to allow disinhibition of positive affects (Cassidy 1994).

SUMMARY

We have reviewed the concepts of basic emotions, affects, and moods. Affects are the subjective feeling components of emotions; our moods are an amalgamation of affects. Central to our discussion is the concept that in attachment relationships, affects are stimulated and cathected to internalized self and other representations. The accumulation of these self and other cathexes over time is what determines mood. In psychotherapy we can attempt to help people with mood disorders (anxiety, depression) by changing their self-other affective cathexes from negative to positive.

⊚ II ⊚

Development

Part II looks at development and focuses on two important developmental issues: (1) How does a person develop a healthy sense of self? and (2) How does a person develop healthy relationships? We will be looking at the development of sense of self and relationship ability across the life span.

Chapter 9 proposes an outline for the development of sense of self and relationship ability from childhood through late adulthood. The focus here is on healthy development. Chapter 10 describes problems with the development of a healthy sense of self, and chapter 11 presents problems in the development of the ability to form healthy relationships. Both chapters are illustrated with clinical cases. Chapter 12 consists of a clinical presentation and discussion of a person who illustrates both problems with sense of self and interpersonal relatedness.

9

The Developmental Lines of Sense of Self &

Interpersonal Relationships

Persons presenting for psychotherapy often describe problems that, in one way or another, concern either (1) how they feel about themselves or (2) how things are going in interpersonal relationships. Frequently they describe both problems.

A person seeking treatment because he doesn't feel good about himself may say that he has low self-esteem or lacks self-confidence or feels worthless. Alternatively, he may describe himself as tense, anxious, or depressed; that is to say, he has difficulty feeling good about himself, difficulty maintaining a positive inner emotional balance. This category of problems will be defined as a problem of sense of self.

A person with relationship problems may say that she is unhappy with her current relationships or that she has experienced a string of failed relationships or that she can't seem to form a relationship. Usually those persons who initially present with relationship problems also have underlying sense of self problems. Occasionally, a person comes in with a quite healthy sense of self who has just relationship problems. Persons who present with sense of self problems almost always have relationship problems.

An underlying hypothesis here is that sense of self problems are more basic or primary compared with relationship problems. In other words, a person must first develop a healthy sense of self before he or she can have healthy relationships. Thus, persons with problems with their sense of self will also have problems with interpersonal relationships. Persons with a healthy sense of self will usually have healthy relationships. At times, persons with a healthy sense of self have problems with relationships, especially intimate relationships.

The evolution of a mostly positive cohesive sense of self and the growth of the ability to form meaningful, intimate relationships are two important developmental tasks. These two tasks, sense of self and relationship ability, develop gradually during childhood, adolescence, and into adulthood. It is proposed that the development of sense of self and the ability to form interpersonal relationships (1) are inextricably intertwined across the various phases of development and (2) are dependent, at least in part, on the quality and quantity of the object relations that the person experiences during these phases of development. In addition to developmental or environmental factors, constitutional (temperamental) factors are also important; this discussion, however, will focus on developmental factors. An attempt will be made here to illustrate the process by which sense of self and relationship ability grow throughout the developmental periods of life. A broad outline of the chapter is included in exhibit 9.1.

SENSE OF SELF AND RELATIONSHIP LEVELS

First, however, let us look at some of the building blocks of a sense of self and a relationship.

Sense of Self

1. *Inner well-being associated with object and self-constancy.* This means an inner representation of self and an inner representation of other that are cathected with positive affect.
2. *Internalized characteristics associated with pleasurable affects (from the id).* This means a characteristic that a person associates with pleasure and enjoyment. An example would be a person's enjoyment of his or her ability to ride a bike.
3. *Internalized characteristics associated with pride (from the superego).* This means a characteristic that a person associates with pride. An example would be a person feeling proud of his or her ability to play the

---

**Exhibit 9.1 The Developmental Lines of Sense of Self
and Interpersonal Relationships**

I. Sense of self and relationship issues
  A. Sense of self
    1. Self and object constancy
    2. Characteristics associated with pleasure
    3. Characteristics associated with pride
  B. Relationship type
    1. Attachment relationships
    2. Caregiver relationships
    3. Affiliation relationships
    4. Sexual/mating relationships
    5. Pair bond relationships
II. Sense of self and relationship ability across development
  A. Separation-individuation phase
    1. Self
    2. Relationships
  B. Preschool years
    1. Self
    2. Relationships
  C. Grade school years
    1. Self
    2. Relationships
  D. Adolescence
    1. Self
    2. Relationships
  E. Early adulthood
    1. Self
    2. Relationships
  F. Middle adulthood
    1. Self
    2. Relationships
  G. Late adulthood
    1. Self
    2. Relationships

piano. Obviously a person may experience pleasure and pride in the same ability, and a person may engage in some activities that stimulate pleasure but not pride.

These components will be expanded upon later.

Relationship Types

For a more detailed discussion of relationship types, see chapter 7.

1. *Attachment relationship.* Bowlby originally defined attachment relationship as a relationship between an infant and a mother in which an infant forms an attachment with his or her mother and seeks out the mother's proximity for purposes of physical and emotional security.

2. *Caregiver relationship.* This is the other side of the attachment relationship (i.e., the mother meeting the physical and emotional needs of the child).

3. *Affiliative relationship.* If attachment relationships have gone well, the child develops more of a sense of inner security and doesn't have to maintain such close proximity to mother. The child may venture out and explore his or her environment. In doing so (e.g., preschool), the child may meet other children with whom he or she can explore the environment via play, games, activities, and so on. These affiliative relationships seem to be organized more around participating together in an activity (exploratory behavioral system) than around meeting attachment needs for security. Throughout life a person may form a variety of affiliative relationships that may vary in their degree of emotional investment. For example, we may have an affiliative relationship with a friend in which there is significant emotional investment or an affiliative relationship with a coworker in which there is less emotional investment.

4. *Sexual/mating relationships.* As a person goes through puberty and adolescence, he or she experiences an increased interest in sexual relationships. Adolescence and young adulthood become a time of learning how to form a sexual relationship.

5. *Pair bond relationship.* Adolescence and young adulthood also become a time of lessening of the attachment bond between a person and his or her parents. An individual may find a mate and establish a pair bond relationship. In a pair bond relationship, the attachment needs of an individual are

transferred to his or her mate. This form of pair bond attachment relationship is different from the parent-child attachment in that in the pair bond attachment relationship, each person is meeting the attachment needs of the other. The pair bond relationship also contains elements of the caregiving relationship in that each member of the pair serves as a caregiver in meeting the attachment needs of his or her mate. The pair bond relationship also contains elements of the sexual mating relationship. The sexual relationship may strengthen the bond and pave the way for mating and the raising of children and then the addition of another caregiver element to the relationship. There will also likely be affiliative aspects of the pair bond relationship in that most pair bond relationships are based on some common interests and activities. Perhaps an additional element of the affiliative component of a pair bond relationship is the mutual sharing of more intimate thoughts and feelings.

SENSE OF SELF AND RELATIONSHIP ABILITY ACROSS DEVELOPMENT

Let us now move on to make a few comments on the evolution of sense of self and relationship ability throughout the various periods of development.

Separation-Individuation Phase—Birth to Age Three

Self

Margaret Mahler described a process of development that she called the separation-individuation process, which occurs between birth and approximately age three (for more detail, see chapter 4). During this period of time, the infant goes from a quite undifferentiated state at birth to one in which he, through the continuing development of the nervous system and especially the perceptual apparatus, comes to perceive himself as separate from those around him (object permanence). In addition, if there is adequate caregiving during this time, the child will develop object constancy and self-constancy. Via the interaction between the child and mother (and others), the child is internalizing a representation of the mother (other) and of the self. If this interacting is emotionally positive, the representations of the mother and the self are associated with positive emotion. To say this a slightly different way, if there is an emotionally positive interaction between the mother and the child, the child internalizes from this interaction an emotionally positive feeling about the mother and about himself. Statements and actions that convey a sense of love and affection lead to inner positive feelings about the self and other. If a child is told that he is loved and is treated in a loving manner by his mother, then the child develops an inner image of a loving mother and a self that is loved.

On the other hand, emotionally negative interactions lead to negative representations of the self and other. If a person is always told in an angry manner that she is no good or worthless, she internalizes an emotionally negative other representation and an emotionally negative self representation. She does not feel good about either self or other. In development we all experience some positive and some negative interactions. Hopefully, the balance of positive interactions is greater than that of negative interactions so that the balance of emotionally positive self and other representations is greater than that of emotionally negative self and other representations.

The attainment of a mostly positive other representation and a mostly positive self representation affords a person significant sense of inner well-being and correlates with what we call object (self) constancy. That is, a person with these positive representations has a means of maintaining a positive internal emotional balance. He is no longer totally dependent on external resources, such as the mother, to calm and soothe him when he is anxious; he has some ability to do this for himself. The growth of this object-self constancy is a fundamental core self-development. It facilitates the separation-individuation process and further self-growth by allowing a person to maintain an inner sense of well-being even in the absence of a soothing maternal figure.

If early interactions are mostly negative, leading to the internalization of mostly negative self and other representations, then a person is ill-prepared for further growth in terms of separation-individuation. This is because the person's inner emotional states will not be that of well-being but of tension and anxiety. She will not have developed an ability to maintain a state of emotional well-being and thus will be dependent on external resources for maintaining some sense of well-being. In this case, energies may be directed away from further self-development and away from the development of healthy mutual relationships and toward maintaining dependent contacts with others that help preserve an inner emotional sense of well-being. Persons who have never developed a core positive sense of self may be chronically anxious and/or depressed and may seek out treatment for these problems.

Table 9.1 Sense of Self and Relationship Ability across Development

Stage	Self	Other
Separation-individuation phase	Internalization of the mother and object constancy	Parent-child attachment relationship
Preschool year	Identification with the father and others in the environment	Relationships with mother and father—learning to relate to parents
Grade school year	Growth of the self through learning in school—teachers, coaches, religious leaders	Relationships with authority figures outside the home, continued peer affiliative relationships—especially with same-sex friends
Adolescence	Continued growth of the self via learning and identification	Learning to relate to members of the opposite sex, exploration of sexual relationships
Early adulthood	Self growth via pursuing an education and beginning a career	Pair bond relationship—beginning an intimate relationship, relating as a parent, relating with colleagues
Middle adulthood	Continued growth of the self leading to the assumption of a mentor role in one's career and with one's children	Continued growth of intimacy of a pair bond relationship, changing relationships with children, parents, grandparents
Late adulthood	Continued mentor role or new life activity	Continued pair bond relationship, becoming a grandparent

Relationships

As we can see, this early period of life is very important for self-develop-ment. It can potentially begin the process of the development of a core self that is infiltrated with a sense of well-being, which can continue to grow throughout subsequent phases of development. This early phase of life is also important in relationship development. During this phase, the person experiences a certain quality of relationship(s). As a result, he begins to learn something about how relationships work. If relationships have been mostly gratifying, he tends to experience relationships as pleasurable and will probably have a tendency to seek out more relationships. If relation-ships have been mostly frustrating, he tends to experience relationships as painful and may then approach relationships rather hesitantly or perhaps begin to avoid them.

Looking at this from the perspective of one's internal world is useful. I have already discussed how interactions with significant others (mother, for instance) throughout development lead to the internalization of both self and other representations. Another aspect of this internalization process is the internalization of a relationship or attachment pattern between self and other. That is, in addition to the internalization of self and other representa-tions, a person internalizes a pattern of how self and other relate, how one person relates to another. So, if relationships have been mostly gratifying, the person learns this pattern of relating, and a gratifying self-other relation-ship pattern gets internalized. If relationships have been mostly frustrating, the person learns this pattern of relating, and a frustrating relationship pat-tern gets internalized.

The internalization of relationship patterns begins early in life and contin-ues across subsequent developmental stages. This earliest phase of develop-ment begins the process of development of relationship or attachment pat-terns (see figure 9.1).

Preschool Years—Ages Two or Three to Five

Self

In this stage, the developmental processes mentioned earlier continue and new processes ensue. During the early years of development, the child forms a very close relationship with the mother. The continuation of this relationship is obviously critically important throughout subsequent stages of development. However, if self-development is going to evolve, the process of separation and individuation must proceed. How can the child maintain a relationship with the mother and at the same time separate from a totally dependent relationship with her? One way to solve this dilemma is by forming relationships with others, such as the father. By moving closer to the father, the child can become less dependent on the mother while still maintaining a relationship with her. This facilitates self-development in two ways: (1) it allows the child to move away from the dependent relationship with the mother, and (2) it provides the child with a new identification figure—the father—with whom, along with the mother, the child may form identifications that further self-development. The presence of others in this environment—grandparents, aunts, uncles, older siblings—may also be very important in this process.

For the young boy, the relationship with the father is likely important in the consolidation of male gender identity, as the relationship with the mother provides an important model for relating to females. At the same time, for the young girl, the relationship with the father provides an important model for male relationships, as the continuing relationship with the mother is important for consolidation of female gender identity.

As opposed to the infant, the preschool child has now developed to the point where she can operate in her environment in a much more significant way. The child gradually evolves from a point where her interaction with the environment is very passive to a point where her interaction is much more active. Play is a major way in which the child actively interacts with the environment. This allows for a new level of interaction between the child and the parents. In the earliest years, the parents were doing things for the child (feeding, clothing, changing, holding, rocking, etc.). Through play, the interaction between the child and parents changes to one in which the parent does things with the child.

The capability of the child to interact more actively with the environment while interacting with a parent allows for continued self-development. The child, for example, may begin to color in a coloring book or build with building blocks. Hopefully, the parent is able to mirror the child's enjoyment in the activity he is pursuing. That is, hopefully the parent can participate in the

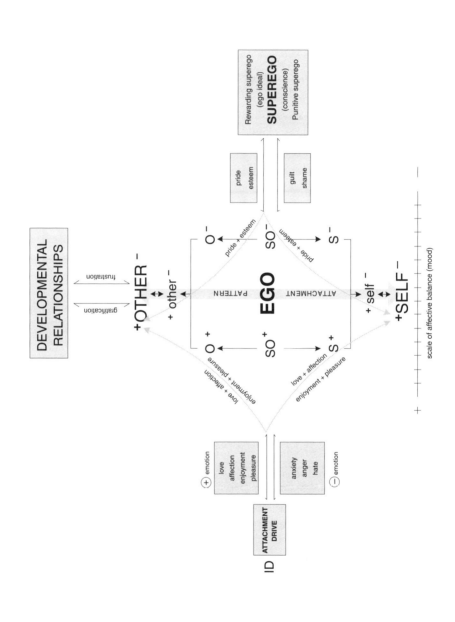

Figure 9.1. Development of a Healthy Sense of Self and Other and Healthy Attachment Patterns

In healthy, loving, nurturing relationships between a parent and child, emotions such as love and affection are stimulated and become cathected with the child's internalized self representation and his internalized other representation. That is, in the context of a loving, nurturing relationship, the child learns to feel good about himself and his significant other.

If the parent is able to share in the child's joy as he explores the world and begins to master tasks, the child develops a sense of pleasure in those acquired skills and a further sense of love toward the parent with whom he was interacting (as above), as well as a sense of enjoyment and pleasure in the interacting with the other. The parent may serve as a model from which the child internalizes further skills that can be cathected with affects such as enjoyment and pleasure.

If parents are able to be rewarding toward the child as he accomplishes tasks and acquires skills, the child internalizes a rewarding/reinforcing superego. This reinforcing superego can serve as the source of emotions such as pride and esteem, which can be further cathected with internalized self and other representations.

If development proceeds as just described, then the child progresses through the separation-individuation process and develops a cohesive, mostly positive sense of self and a cohesive, mostly positive internalized other representation. These two internal structures (SELF and OTHER) help the person maintain an inner sense of emotional well-being. In addition, in the context of healthy, nurturing developmental relationships, a child learns an attachment pattern that can be used in forming relationships throughout life.

child's enjoyment of his activity (coloring, block building.) If this is the case, then the child, via play, not only acquires a new skill (the ability to color, to build with blocks) but comes to associate that skill with a positive affect, enjoyment, pleasure. This not only facilitates the further development of the skill but also facilitates important self-development. The child has now internalized into his sense of self a skill that is associated with positive feelings such as enjoyment and pleasure (see figure 9.1).

Let us contrast the previously described situation with one in which there is a different kind of interaction between the parent and child. Suppose as the child plays, the parent ignores the child or tells her that her coloring is no good or not good enough, or the parent must show the child that he or she can do it better. This type of interaction may interfere with the development of skills that could be important building blocks of self-structure or lead to those skills being associated with negative affects. In either case, self-development is stymied.

Another aspect of self-development is the growth of self-structure of the child via the identification with and internalization of skills and characteristics of the parents. This process may coincide with the play interactions between the parent and child. For example, the parent may model the skill of throwing a ball or drawing a face. The child, using the parent as a model, practices the skill, hopefully in the context of an emotionally pleasurable interaction with the child. In doing so, the child internalizes that skill as a characteristic of him- or herself that is associated with positive affect. In a similar manner, the parent serves as a model from which the child may internalize personality characteristics: the ability to control impulses, to share, to be generous, and so on.

Finally, with respect to self-development at this stage, we might mention interactions outside the family. Many children go to a preschool and interact with other adults as well as children their own age. These interactions provide additional possibilities for identifications from which self-structure may be built.

Relationships

During the preschool phase of development, we see the continued growth of relationship or attachment patterns. As the child begins to interact with more and different people, he experiences and learns more about relationship patterns.

For the boy, the relationship with the mother continues to be an important model of a pattern for relationships with females; the relationship with the father becomes an important model of a pattern for relationships with men. For the girl, the relationship with the father becomes an important model of a pattern for relationships with men, just as the relationship with the mother continues to be an important model of a pattern for relating to women. If there are siblings present in the home or extended family members involved with the family, then the interactional patterns learned in the interactions with them are also important.

Increasingly during this period, the child moves from a dyadic form of relating to a triadic form of relating. In the previous period, the child may have enjoyed a close dyadic relationship with the mother. As the child grows older, interactions become increasingly triadic and competitive. A not uncommon example would be in the situation in which another infant is born when the child is two or three. Now the first child loses her exclusive relationship with the mother and must compete with the infant child for the mother's attention. The birth of a second child likely accelerates the first child's separation from her dependence on the mother as this child moves on to find new and perhaps more available attachment figures such as the father. If the child moves toward the father, however, she may learn that she has to compete with older siblings and mom for dad's attention. The same may be true as the child moves toward an extended family member such as a grandparent. The child learns that the relationship with each of the others is not exclusive—that the other must be shared with another. At the same time, the establishment of relationships beyond the relationship with the mother helps repair the loss of the exclusive relationship with the mother. If all of these relationships go well, self-structure will continue to grow; there will be an increase in the growth of positive self-structure, and the child will become less dependent on a relationship with another for stabilizing herself emotionally. In addition, the child will continue the development of internalized attachment patterns.

Outside the home, the child may begin to interact more with peers in the neighborhood and/or the preschool. These relationships, too, are by nature triadic. They do, however, provide important models from which to develop relationship patterns for interactions with peers.

The Grade School Years (Latency)

Much of what has been said heretofore continues to apply. There are, however, significant new aspects of both self-development and relationship development. During the grade school years, the child continues to expand his horizons beyond the family. More interactions with teachers, peers, and other adults (i.e., coaches, religious leaders, scout leaders, etc.) now take place. All of these interactions provide new opportunities for the growth of a sense of self and relationship ability.

Self

Self-structure can continue to grow via interactions with family members in all the ways described earlier. First, the child can continue to identify with and internalize characteristics via his or her interactions with family members. Second, the child can continue to learn skills from family members. To the extent that these characteristics and skills are associated with pleasurable affects, they contribute to the building up of an emotionally positive self-structure.

The expanding interactions that occur during the grade school years allow for the possibility of building self-structure further via the acquisition of more skills and characteristics. Besides parents, the child now interacts in meaningful ways with teachers, who may thus serve as significant identification figures for the internalization of characteristics. In a similar manner, interactions with other adults and peers may be important in the acquisition of personality characteristics.

School provides the opportunity for the acquisition of new skills. The child goes to school (secular and perhaps religious) and learns the skills of the society and culture to which she belongs. Hopefully, the acquisition of these skills and characteristics can occur in such a way that they become associated with pleasurable affects, which help build an emotionally positive self-structure.

In addition to pleasurable emotions, which we might think of as id emotions (see figure 9.1), we can now introduce the concept of emotions such as pride and esteem, which we might think of as superego emotions. Can our self-skills and characteristics, in addition to becoming associated with emotions such as enjoyment and pleasure, now also become associated with emotions such as pride and esteem? Can we take pride in the skills we have acquired; can we esteem our self characteristics? If so, we can further strengthen self-structure because in addition to the positive emotions such as pleasure and enjoyment, we can now also associate the positive emotions of pride and esteem with our self-skills and characteristics. This helps to further solidify an emotionally positive self-structure.

By adding these comments on the superego at this time, I do not mean to imply that the superego was not important earlier in development. It is, however, a structure that is very important in the latency years and in all subsequent periods of development.

Another aspect of superego functioning to consider is the ego ideal. The ego ideal is our concept of what we would ideally like to become. It is formed through our idealization of parents, other adults in our environment, and perhaps also sports or performance stars, political figures, and so on. Thus, through identification with others we not only develop characteristics in the here and now, but also develop goals for what we want to be like in the future. These goals are ideals we can strive toward in the future.

One final aspect of self-development to mention during the grade school years has to do with sexual identity. This is a period of time when boys play with boys and girls play with girls. This phenomenon, along with continued identification with the same-sex parents (and other same-sex adults), furthers the consolidation of sexual (gender) identity.

Relationships

The relationships with the parents continue to provide important models for the establishment of relationship patterns. Now, however, expanding interactions with others outside the home expose the child to new relationship patterns, which can hopefully reinforce healthy patterns that have been developing through family interactions. Relationships with teachers, recreational leaders (coaches, camp counselors), and religious leaders may not only reinforce relationship patterns learned in the home; they may also provide patterns for relating to authority figures outside the home. Increasingly important during this period are peer relationships. As noted previously, this is a time when boys play with boys and girls play with girls. Usually, during this period, a child will pick a same-sex best friend, a "chum," as Sullivan (1953) called it. These peer relationships are important for establishing patterns for relating to peers in general and friends more specifically.

Another thing to mention about relationships during this period is that we see increasing amounts of mutuality in relationships. Earlier, relationships were for the most part on a nurturing level—that is, a relationship in which a child receives emotional supplies from the other person in the relationship. Increasingly, relationships begin to move to a companionship level in which the child not only receives emotional supplies from the other but also gives them back. This growing degree of mutuality in interpersonal relationships is facilitated by the growth of the self. In earlier periods, self-growth was facilitated by positive relationships with others. At some point, if self-growth has continued in a maturationally appropriate manner, the child has the strength to begin to give in relationships. This obviously greatly facilitates the development of best friend relationships.

One point to make is that as the child increasingly moves away from the home in the preschool and grade school years, there may be a difference in the quality of interaction experienced in the home versus outside the home. For example, a child may come from a very warm, nurturing home environment. If, however, the child is a member of a minority group, or if he has a physical deformity, he may experience interactions outside the home that are far less warm and nurturing. This may have a profound effect on the development of sense of self and relationship ability.

Adolescence

The next period to discuss is that of adolescence. The onset of adolescence marks the ending of childhood and the beginning of the transition from childhood to adulthood. As such, adolescence is important for the continuing consolidation of the sense of self and the ability to interact in relationships.

Self

Adolescence can be a period of tremendous self-growth. A person, within the span of a few years, goes from being a child to becoming a young adult. To a large extent, the processes of self-development are those already discussed. The adolescent can form identifications with others (both in their immediate environment as well as in their extended environment) and internalize characteristics via those identifications. Increasingly the person can choose which characteristics he or she wishes to develop. In this manner, internalization can become more of an active process and less of a passive process.

In a way we might think of adolescence as another major separation-individuation process. The adolescent must develop (individuate) enough self-structure in order to be able to appropriately separate from his or her family of origin. It is perhaps the anxiety associated with the necessity of this self-development that, in fact, propels the development of the self during the developmental years. Hopefully, the family can interact with the adolescent in a phase-appropriate manner so that the adolescent will be able to develop the self-structure necessary for separation and at the same time maintain harmonious interactions with his or her family of origin so that those relationships can continue into adulthood.

If the family is not reinforcing of self-development, the adolescent may not develop a self-structure sufficient to allow her to function as an independent adult. That person may go through adulthood seeking out dependent relationships to support a flailing self-structure. If the family is not supportive of separation, the person may have a hard time leaving the family. Or she may leave by creating a large distance between herself and her family in order to continue her self-development. As a consequence, she may lose the salutary effects of continued interactions with her family of origin.

One part of self-development that must continue the consolidation process is that of sexual identity. This is especially important in light of the fact that a major relationship ability to master during adolescence is that of relating to the opposite sex—an issue we will return to shortly.

Relationships

A major relationship task during the latency period was to form a peer relationship with a member of the same sex, a best friend, a chum. During adolescence a major relationship task is to develop a relationship with a member of the opposite sex, a boyfriend for girls or a girlfriend for boys. If past self-development has gone well so that the person has a mostly positive sense of self, and if past relationships have gone well so that the person has learned good models for relating to members of the opposite sex, then one's first boyfriend-girlfriend relationship may proceed without undue anxiety.

A certain amount of normal anxiety will be involved in these relationships. If the person has not developed a good sense of self; that is, if his sense of self is fraught with anxiety already, then the addition of an anxiety-provoking relationship may be an inhibiting force in the development of that relationship. If the relationship patterns he has learned (especially those involving relating to members of the opposite sex) are associated with anxiety, then, again, the addition of this anxiety in a new relationship may be inhibiting.

But even if the person has developed a good sense of self and has developed good relationship patterns, a certain amount of anxiety will still be present in these new relationships. This is because even if the person has experienced healthy attachment and affiliative relationships, he or she must now enter a relationship and eventually learn to relate in a sexual mode.

This beginning ability to form relationships with members of the opposite sex is clearly an important developmental task that can continue to evolve throughout other periods of development. In addition, one's continued relationships with parents, same-sex peers, and mentors are also important for solidifying healthy relationship patterns.

Early Adulthood (Twenty to Forty)

Self

The early adult years can be years of tremendous self-growth. These are years during which a person often pursues an education and begins a career. Relationships with mentors in school and at work can be important sources of identification from which to form internalizations into the person's self-structure. Hopefully, via these interactions and via the person's experiences in school and work, she begins to consolidate an identity centering around her life work. Developing the skills of a career can be very important in that self-consolidation process. If she can enjoy what she does, and if she can take pride in what she does, her sense of self can continue to grow in a milieu of positive emotions.

This period may be associated with other new aspects of self-development. The person may begin to take on new self-identity as a spouse and a parent. In addition, parts of the person's self-identity may be tied to the religious, civic, and recreational activity he gets involved in. To the extent that these new roles are activities associated with gratification and a sense of pride, they help to build a self-structure that is emotionally positive.

Relationships

Early adulthood is frequently the time during which one forms one's first major, committed heterosexual relationship. This relationship may culminate in marriage. This pair bond relationship may combine elements of earlier levels of relating including the attachment relationship, caregiving relationship, affiliative relationship, and sexual/mating relationship.

Other relationships that may continue and deepen during this period include relationships with parents, mentors, peers, and colleagues. If one has established healthy relationship patterns earlier in development, then these interactions with mentors and peers in school, work, and recreational activities may be very rewarding and sustaining types of relationships.

A new type of relationship that may begin during the earlier adult years is the relationship a person has with his own children. Relationships with children have the potential for being some of the most rewarding and satisfying relationships of one's life. However, to the degree that one has unresolved issues from one's own childhood, having children may stimulate a reemergence and perhaps a reworking of these issues.

Middle Adult Years (Forty to Sixty)

Self

In the middle adult years, we can see continued growth of the self via consolidation of one's role identity at work, in the family, and in one's religious, civic, and recreational activities. An important new aspect of self-development during this time may be the assumption of a mentor role in one of these areas. In a person's work for example, she may be one of the more senior persons. If self-development has continued during the adult years, then she may be accomplished and respected. As a result, she may be sought out as a mentor by those more junior. Other aspects of the mentor role may include being a mentor in the family to her own children or being a mentor in a religious, civic, or recreational activity. Achievement of the mentor role, along with the interactions with others that it brings, can have a very sustaining effect on the self.

Relationships

The middle adult years can be years of growth in terms of relationships. If self-development has proceeded successfully over the years, then the increased strength of the self may form the base from which a person can be more open, giving, and sharing with his or her partner. If a person's partner can do the same, there are opportunities for increasing intimacy in the relationship. The middle adult years may be years in which a person's children grow into adulthood. This provides the opportunity for a new kind of relationship with them, one that is less of a parent-child relationship and more of an adult-adult relationship. Relationships with peers and colleagues at work may also be gratifying, as may the relationships with those for whom one serves as a mentor.

The middle adult years may also be a time of loss in terms of relationships. A person may have to deal with the loss of his or her own parents (grandparents). Working through these losses and facing his or her own mortality may have a significant organizing effect on the person's own self-development. Another potential loss may be the loss of a person's spouse through divorce. This may provide the opportunity for reworking relationship patterns so he or she can form a new, more gratifying relationship (as opposed to forming another relationship based on the relationship pattern that failed previously).

Another loss may be the loss of children who grow up and leave home. This may be an especially painful loss for a person who has devoted many years to the raising of those children. The loss of children may be balanced by the arrival of grandchildren or by the opportunity to pursue interests that the person has put off during the child-raising years.

The Late Adult Years (Sixty to Eighty)

Self

During the late adult years, or for at least part of them, a person may continue in a mentor role. Alternatively, if a person retires from what had been his major life activity, the self may be organized into new activities, perhaps activities that he has postponed until the retirement years. A certain degree of satisfaction may be obtained from looking back with pleasure and pride on his accomplishments.

Relationships

Retirement, with the concomitant increase in time available, brings up the possibility of increasing intimacy in a relationship. These later life years also bring up the possibility of the termination of a relationship as a person's partner passes on. Other relationships that may continue to be important are those with children and friends.

A type of relationship that may be new to this period is the relationship with a grandchild or grandchildren. Relationships with grandchildren may be extremely gratifying types of relationships. They allow a person in the later years of life to reexperience the youth of children unencumbered by the responsibilities of parenthood.

SUMMARY

Table 9.1 provides a summary of the development of sense of self and interpersonal relationships across the various phases of the life cycle. In this chapter we have discussed the healthy development of a sense of self and of an ability to form interpersonal relationships. Next we move on to talk about problems in the development of sense of self (chapter 10) and relationship ability (chapter 11).

10

Pathology of the Self

Now that we have examined an outline of the development of sense of self and interpersonal relationships, let us turn to a discussion of how this development may go awry, leading to pathology. This chapter will focus on developmental problems that lead to pathology of the sense of self. The goal will be to present a series of different types of developmental interactions that can occur between a child and his or her significant others, leading to pathological self-development. A number of broad categories of developmental interactions will be presented, followed by case examples. The list of developmental interactions is not meant to be exhaustive. Everyone's development is unique, and so any one individual's developmental history may not coincide with a category presented here or may include elements of more than one type of development described here.

The focus of this chapter will be on pathology of the self. Most of the case examples will be of people who came in with complaints such as, "I am depressed," "I don't feel good about myself," "I have low self-esteem." All of these people also had problems with interpersonal relationships, but in this chapter, in order to attempt to understand self pathology better, the focus will be on their difficulties with sense of self. In the next chapter, the focus will shift to interpersonal relationships, and the chapter following that will discuss a case that illustrates problems with sense of self and interpersonal relationships together.

Before discussing different types of developmental interactions that can lead to self pathology, I want to briefly return to the issue of constitutional factors that the previous chapter alluded to briefly. Our focus heretofore has been on developmental interactions between children and parents. It is important to emphasize that constitutional variables of both the child and the parent are significant. Development occurs in the context of constitutional givens. Two important constitutional givens are the temperament of the child and of the parent. Let us contrast the child with a relaxed, easy to please type of temperament with a child who has an irritable, hard to please type of temperament. The irritable, hard to please child may do well with parents who are very nourishing and giving and able to tolerate a lot of frustration. However, if the parents have low frustration tolerance and are not so nourishing and giving, then they may become frustrated in their attempts to satisfy this irritable, hard to please child. This frustration may lead to anger, which increases the possibility of negative and potentially abusive interactions between the parent and the child.

The relaxed, easy to please child may do well with a wide variety of parents who have different types of temperaments. However, even this child may have difficulty if paired with parents of a very irritable temperament. Still, even in this situation, some children will somehow learn to cope with a less than optimal home environment.

My focus here is to look at the effects of developmental interactions on the growth of sense of self and the ability to form interpersonal relationships. My intent is not to deny or minimize constitutional factors. Indeed, in some cases, these constitutional factors may be the most important ones. However, in order to examine developmental factors more closely, I will be speaking about them predominantly, but will ask the reader to keep in mind the fact that development always occurs in the context of the constitutional makeup of the parent and of the child.

Let us now return to the issue of development and look at a series of types of developmental interactions that may lead to problems with the sense of self (see exhibit 10.1).

DEVELOPMENTAL INTERACTIONS THAT LEAD TO AN EXCESS OF NEGATIVE SELF AND OTHER REPRESENTATIONS

Under this heading would be interactions between parents and children in which the parent is physically or sexually abusive. In addition, included here

---

Exhibit 10.1 Pathology of the Self

I. Developmental interactions that lead to an excess of negative self
   and other representations
   A. Alice
   B. Betty
   C. Carley
II. Developmental interactions that fail to lead to the development of
   positive representations
   A. Diane
   B. Ed
   C. Frank
III. Developmental interactions that lead to a failure in separation
   A. Greta
   B. Martha
   C. Chris
IV. Developmental interactions of over-involvement
   A. Heather
V. Developmental issues related to loss
   A. Ingrid
   B. Janice
   C. Kevin

---

would be parents who are emotionally abusive in that they do not meet the
emotional needs of their child, or parents who are verbally abusive by being
very critical and guilt-inducing (see Figure 10.1).

⑥ Alice is a thirty-year-old woman who came in stating that she's always strug-
gling to maintain her self-esteem. She described difficulty maintaining a positive
emotional state and said that she is frequently sad, frustrated, irritable, anxious,
or angry. She feels pessimistic about the future, has little she enjoys, and doesn't
see life as very worthwhile. She described these things as characteristic of the way
she has felt most of her life. Besides mood symptoms, over the years she has also
been bulimic and has abused alcohol and amphetamines. She has never been
married but has been in a series of relationships that have not worked out. Alice
does have a master's degree and supports herself teaching at a junior college.

She described her developmental interactions as unhappy. Her parents were
divorced when she was born, and her mother moved to another part of the coun-

try, leaving her with her father. She feels that her father was loving, but he was also alcoholic and spent his time outside of work in the bar and was thus never available to her.

She was initially raised by a series of baby-sitters. She remembers the last one from her early grade school years, who would beat her with a belt and lock her in the closet for hours at a time. When her dad found out, the baby-sitter was fired, and his mother moved in to care for her. Alice's grandmother was not physically abusive but was always critical and negative toward Alice. She remembers her grandmother hated Alice's mother and always told her that she didn't think that Alice was her father's child. Her grandmother continually blamed her for the failed marriage and for Alice's father's alcoholism.

At age twelve she was raped by a neighbor and thereafter sent to live with her mother. She describes her mother as someone who didn't want her in the first place and who was not happy to have Alice come to live with her. She remembers her mother frequently telling her that she hated her. The home environment with the mother was quite chaotic throughout her teenage years as her mother entered into a series of relationships with different men and moved frequently. None of these men were abusive to her, but neither did any of them pay her any attention. She had a stormy high school career but did graduate and move out to college and has lived on her own ever since.

This case is meant to illustrate the history of a person whose development is characterized by a series of negative interpersonal interactions. It is hypothesized that these negative interactions would lead to significant negative representations of self and other. There were a paucity of positive interactions on which to base any positive self or other representations. As a result, negative representations predominate, and Alice developed the self pathology described in which she complained of chronic difficulty maintaining self-esteem as well as chronic feelings of sadness, frustration, irritability, anxiety, anger, and feelings that life was not pleasurable and not very worthwhile.

As a final note, I may add that in addition to her problems with sense of self, she also had, as one would expect, significant problems with interpersonal relationships.

⑥ Betty is a twenty-three-year-old woman who also gave a history of chronic low mood and chronic low self-esteem. She dated the symptoms back to age ten, at which point her grandfather had died. Her relationship with her grandfather had been the one happy relationship of her childhood.

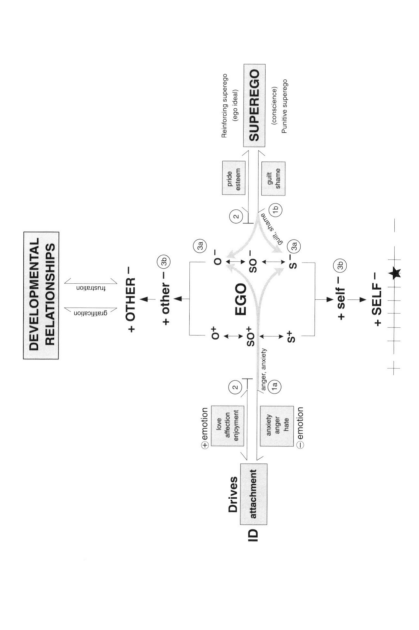

Figure 1C.1. Pathology of the Self: Excessive Negative Interactions, Lack of Positive Interactions

1. Pathology of the self may result from excessively negative interactions between a child and the important developmental figures.

   a. Those interactions may be abusive, stimulating much anger/anxiety, and so on, which gets cathected with self and other representations.

   b. Those interactions may be very critical, stimulating much guilt and shame, which get cathected with self and other representations.

2. Pathology of the self may also result from neglectful relationships, which may not necessarily be overtly abusive. In this case, there is a failure of the stimulation of (+) emotions such as love, affection, pride, and esteem, which could become cathected with self and other representations

3. Either (1) and/or (2) may lead to a failure of completion of the separation individuation process, resulting in an arrest at either the borderline (3a) level or the depressive (3b) level.

   Note: The referenced numbers correspond with the numbers on the diagram.

Her development includes a history of being adopted when she was seven months old. She was told that her biological mother was unable to care for her; she never knew her biological father. Her adoptive parents adopted her because they were unable to have children, but subsequent to adopting her they had two biological children, three and seven years younger than Betty. She reported that she did not get along with either sister; the parents gave the sisters preferential treatment over her. Betty recalled always being singled out as the bad one and as a consequence was yelled at and spanked and could never do anything right. The sisters, on the other hand, could never do anything wrong.

She described her mother as very critical and demanding; she wanted Betty to be the ideal daughter. Betty remembered frequently being told she was not good enough. She described her father as very strict; she never felt any support from him.

In summary, she experienced her parents as verbally and emotionally abusive and as quite demonstrative with corporal punishment. There was no sexual abuse. The one positive relationship was with her grandfather who lived nearby and whom she visited frequently, but who died when she was ten.

The case is presented as another example of a person who has chronic low self-esteem and difficulty maintaining an inner positive emotional balance. She experienced her childhood interactions as ones in which she was abandoned by her biological parents and treated negatively by her adoptive parents. Thus, the predominate interpersonal interactions in her development led to negative self and other representations. The one positive relationship with the grandfather did seem to be a source of some positive self and other representations, but not enough to overcome the excess of negative representations. Thus Betty was left with chronic low self-esteem and depressed mood.

Ⓖ Carley, age twenty-six, gave a similar history of chronic low mood and inability to feel good about herself. Her parents, like those of Alice, were divorced shortly after she was born, and until age nine, she lived with her mother and had little contact with her father. She remembered that her mother was always negative toward her; they frequently fought. She believed that her mother preferred her brother, whom she frequently praised.

When Carley was nine, her mother remarried and moved to another part of the country with her new husband. She felt that her stepfather did not like her and did not want to take her with them. In fact, she was left behind and lived with her maternal grandmother from age nine to fourteen. She experienced a warm, nurturing relationship with her grandmother and looks back on those years as the best of her life. Unfortunately, her grandmother died when she was fourteen, and she was sent to live with her father. By this time, he had remarried and started a new family. He welcomed Carley reluctantly; the relationship between her, her father, and her stepmother rapidly deteriorated. Her father was verbally abusive, often making demeaning comments such as calling her a slut or a whore. He also became physically abusive, and on more than one occasion, she ended up in an emergency room after he beat her up.

Again, we have a story of a person whose developmental relationships (except for the relationship with the grandmother) were characterized by negative interactions and abandonment. Again, there is little here on which to base the development of emotionally positive representations of self and other.

DEVELOPMENTAL INTERACTIONS THAT FAIL TO LEAD TO THE DEVELOPMENT OF POSITIVE REPRESENTATIONS

The failure to develop positive representations is certainly present in the previously described category in which abusive relationships have led to an excess of negative representations. There are those, however, who do not come from overtly abusive relationships who still have problems developing and maintaining a positive sense of self. The problem here is not one of abuse and the development of negative representations, but rather more the presence of neglect and the failure to develop positive representations. In other words, parental figures are either physically or emotionally unavailable to form the kinds of rewarding, emotionally positive interactions with the child that lead to the development of positive self and other representations.

Diane is a twenty-three-year-old woman who had recently graduated from college with a teaching degree. Though she had done well in college and had been on the honor roll, she reported that she had not enjoyed college much and was not especially proud of what she had accomplished. She had received a rather competitive teaching job, that would start in the fall semester. She, however, was not looking forward to it much and described a sense of hollowness about herself and emptiness about her future. She felt that she was not a very happy person and that she was realizing that she never had been.

Diane denied any history of any form of abuse during her developmental years. She came from an intact family in which there was no history of separations, losses, abandonments, frequent moves, or any acute stressors that she could identify. Her major memories of her family centered around the lack of interactions that occurred.

Her father ran a business, and she described him as a workaholic who was hardly ever home. When he was home, he showed little emotion—either positive or negative. Her mother also worked; when she was home she was preoccupied with cleaning the house and putting things in order. Diane described her as a very perfectionistic woman who would not go out to get the mail without her hair done and her lipstick on.

The family did not go on vacations or engage in activities together. She recalls as a small child often being dropped off at the day care center. As she progressed through grade school and into high school, she increasingly became involved in sports and other activities such as debate. Her parents never came to watch her in any of her activities.

She always did very well in school because she felt that was expected. She never received praise for doing well but believed she would be criticized if she didn't. When Diane graduated from high school, she talked her parents into coming to the graduation banquet. They were shocked when she received an award for her accomplishments. Afterward, her parents commented, "Here you are all grown up and we don't even know you."

The point of this case vignette is to illustrate a situation in which a person comes from a family that appears outwardly stable and in which there is no abuse. Yet Diane does not feel very happy with herself or her life. The main problem here appears to be that there was no one present to engage in activities with her, no one available to share a sense of enjoyment and pleasure with her. There was no one present to praise or reward her for her accomplishments. Thus, now she has difficulty feeling a sense of pleasure or pride in her accomplishments and activities.

Thus, in this case, while there is no excess of negative self and other representations, there is a paucity of positive self and other representations upon which to develop a positive sense of self.

ⓖ Ed is a young man in his mid-twenties who came in stating he was having difficulty with his mood. He described that he was rarely happy and that his predominate moods were depression, anger, or irritability. According to him, he has had difficulty maintaining a positive mood for as long as he could remember. He described his self-esteem as low, and he said that he often feels rejected. He tends to be self-critical. Life was described by him as "dark" and "not all that worthwhile."

Ed grew up in a family in which his parents were divorced when he was one year old. They, however, maintained an amicable relationship with each other and lived on the same block. Thus, as a child he had frequent interactions with both of them and would often see each of them every day. Some days he would stay with his mother and some days with his father.

He describes his parents as "old hippies" whose main message to him was, "Do your own thing." He felt they never gave him any guidance or support. So, when he would develop an interest in an activity, such as a sport, and look to his parents for guidance and support, he would be told to "do your own thing." His sense was that while they didn't discourage him, neither did they support him in terms of encouraging him or participating in the activity with him. As a result, he felt that he never developed a sense of direction and that in his mid-twenties, he is still trying to find some sense of direction.

Again, in this case, there was nothing particularly abusive in the relationship between Ed and his parents. He seemed to describe an inability on the part of his parents to participate in activities with him in an active, enthusiastic, joyful manner. Thus, there was no opportunity for his interests and activities, via his interactions with his parents, to become associated with positive, pleasurable, pride types of emotions. Rather, the message to him was, "Do your own thing," which meant, "Do it by yourself and leave me alone to do my own thing."

⑥ Frank is a thirty-year-old man who also presented with chronic low self-esteem, sadness, and loneliness. He said, "I always feel glum."

He described his family as one that did very little together. He felt that his father never spent any quality time with him. In fact, he remembers his father saying on more than one occasion, "I wish I was not a father." He felt much closer emotionally to his mother, but interactions with her were limited, as she worked long hours. In addition, because the family lived in a fairly remote area, there was little opportunity to interact with others outside the home.

Again, this is a case in which there were no abusive interactions leading to negative self and other representations. At the same time, absent in this family were the type of positive interactions leading to the kind of positive self and other representations upon which one could build a positive self-esteem and inner sense of well-being.

DEVELOPMENTAL INTERACTIONS THAT LEAD TO A FAILURE IN SEPARATION

In the previous two categories I have talked of situations in which there is either an excess of negative representations or a paucity of positive representations (or both). Certainly, these types of development may lead to problems in separation-individuation (see figure 10.2).

In the case of some borderline personality disorders, for example, if there exists an excess of negative self representations over positive self representations, then it may be difficult to take the step of integration of both positive and negative representations into a combined self representation that contains, at the same time, both positive and negative elements. This is because the excess of negative elements in an integrated self representation would lead to a very tense/dysphoric state. The solution to this is to remain at an unintegrated state where positive and negative self representations remain split. The separation-individuation process thus becomes arrested at this level.

The type of developmental interaction to be described here is one in which there is a failure in separation due to developmental interactions in which dependency is rewarded and support is withdrawn for moves toward independence. (Certainly this mechanism may occur in conjunction with a development that induces an excess of negative representations.) What occurs in these situations is that the family encourages dependency on the family and discourages moves toward psychological separation and individuation.

Obviously, families and cultures vary significantly in the degree to which they encourage staying close to the family versus encouraging separation from the family. What we are discussing here is not the family's or the culture's tendency to encourage staying physically close to or separating physically from the family. What we are talking about is the person's ability to develop an inner sense of psychological separateness (i.e., an ability to generate at least some of their emotional well-being from within). The person who has achieved psychological separateness does not necessarily need to maintain physical separateness from his or her family; in fact, he or she may be very physically close to them.

What we will discuss here is the extreme of encouraging dependence on the family of origin to the degree that sufficient separation-individuation does not occur. As a result, a person does not develop a positive internal emotional milieu, does not have his or her own internal sense of well-being. This pathological situation may be the result of an interaction with a significant other who is extremely dependent himself and thus cannot allow separation of the child because he needs the child to meet his own dependency needs.

To illustrate this type of developmental interaction that leads to problems in separation, a brief case vignette will be presented, followed by two more in-depth case presentations.

⑥ Greta is a twenty-eight-year-old woman who came in with a complaint of depression after she broke up with her boyfriend of six years. Her boyfriend was an alcoholic and had numerous affairs with other women. The relationship ended when he gave her a sexually transmitted disease.

Greta stated she was aware of his drinking and affairs since early on in the relationship but stayed in the relationship because she feared being alone. Now that the relationship is over, she described that her anxiety over being alone was as great as her sadness over the loss of the relationship.

Greta described growing up with a mother who was very controlling, and she feels that at age twenty-eight, she is still trying to develop some emotional distance from her mother. She recalled that she and her mother constantly fought throughout her childhood and adolescence. The major conflict was over whether Greta would be able to play with girlfriends, be involved in extracurricular activities, or go out on dates. Her mother always wanted her to stay home and spend time with her rather than go out and do things with other people. Greta reported that throughout grade school and into high school, her mother would frequently come to the school and take her out of school with the excuse that Greta had a doctor's appointment. In reality, her mother just wanted someone to be with, and they would spend the time shopping or going to lunch.

Interestingly, Greta was the third child in this family. She was adopted into the family at a time when the two older children were about to leave home, and at a point in Greta's mother's life when she could no longer have children. Greta remembered often being told that her mother adopted her so that she could have a companion. Greta's adoptive father was involved in the family very little.

The point of this vignette is to describe a situation in which the mother has an overly dependent relationship on her daughter. The mother discouraged separation by her daughter and encouraged Greta to stay close to meet her mother's de-

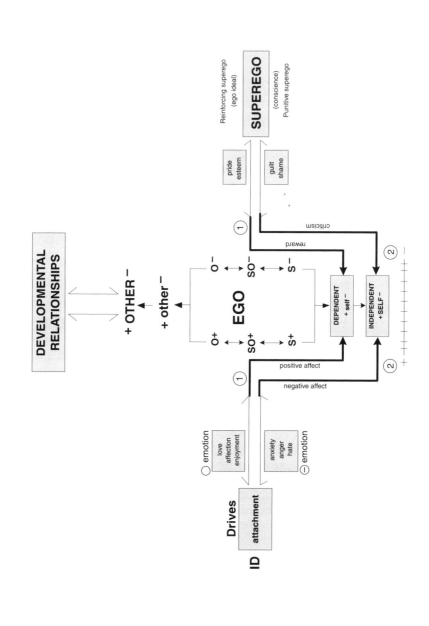

Figure 10.2. Pathology of the Self: Reward for Dependence

The separation-individuation process may become arrested at a dependent level because of the following:

1. Remaining at a dependent level is associated with pleasure (positive affect) and reward.
2. Moving to an independent level is associated with anxiety and criticism.

Note: The referenced numbers correspond with the numbers on the diagram.

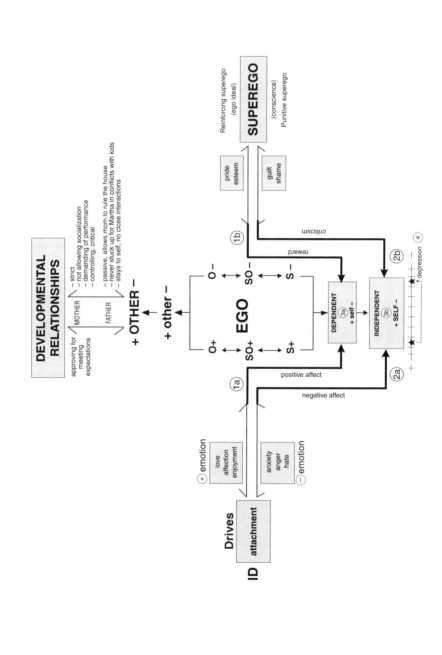

Figure 10.3. Pathology of the Self: Reward for Dependence: Martha

1. Martha's parents could be positive (1a) and rewarding (1b) with respect to her scholastic and athletic achievements and for her compliance with her mother's demand that she stay close to the family.

2. Martha's parents would be negative (2a) and critical (2b) for attempts to separate, such as going over to other children's homes, dating, leaving home for college.

3. Maintaining a positive affect balance was contingent on staying close to home (dependent self [3a]). Moving to a more independent level of separation-individuation was associated with anxiety and criticism (independent self [3b]).

4. Martha's attempt to go to college was an attempt to move from a dependent self to an independent self. The effect was the withdrawal of positive affect (love, affection) and reward and the addition of negative affect (anxiety, anger) and criticism, which shifted her affective balance from a relatively positive balance to a negative balance, resulting in depression.

Note: The referenced numbers correspond with the numbers on the diagram.

pendency needs. The effect was that Greta never separated sufficiently to develop an emotionally positive independent sense of self and thus was herself quite dependent.

She described that during high school, she tried to separate from her mother by forming relationships with boyfriends. To the extent that her mother allowed these relationships, the mother tried to micromanage the relationships by telling her what to do in the relationships, including how to act sexually.

Greta did leave her mother shortly after high school by marrying a man from a nearby military base without her family's knowledge. Unfortunately, this was not a good relationship, and she was soon divorced and returned home. She next made an attempt at independence by moving away to college. She, however, became anxious and depressed and returned home after one semester. Eventually she met the man described earlier, with whom she had the six-year relationship and with whom she did move away from home.

Although she separated physically from her family, she had really not progressed in her development to the point of being emotionally separate. Her development had not prepared her to be emotionally independent. She, to a large extent, was dependent on her boyfriend. When that relationship broke up, she was not able to maintain an inner state of emotional equilibrium and became anxious and depressed.

Now I will discuss two cases in more depth to illustrate this problem of failure of separation.

⑥ Martha is a twenty-one-year-old woman who came to treatment stating she'd been depressed for three months since she had left home to attend college some two hundred miles away from where her parents lived. Prior to coming to her present college, she had lived at home and attended a local junior college. Symptoms of depression included sadness, crying spells, decreased concentration, decreased motivation, decreased enjoyment, decreased self-esteem, decreased appetite, and initial and intermittent insomnia. There was no suicidal ideation (see figure 10.3).

She described the major stressor as being away from home. Martha had not established a circle of friends in her new environment. Though there was a part of her that wanted to leave home, there was another part that felt insecure being on her own. Her parents, and in particular her mother, were unsupportive and critical of her move away from home. Her mother told her she would fail in school because she, her mother, was not there to tell her when to get up, when to go to school, to make decisions for her, and otherwise take care of her. Her mother frequently tells her that if she fails, she must return home; Martha described that her mother calls her almost daily to see if she's flunked out yet.

Though Martha said that her self-esteem has always been rather low, she had never felt depressed like she did now. She had no history of alcohol or drug abuse, and there was no family psychiatric history. Her medical history was positive for allergies, ulcers, and asthma. The asthma and allergies are episodic ongoing problems for which she takes medication occasionally. The ulcer occurred at age sixteen and has not recurred. She did have knee surgery during her senior year in high school for an injury sustained while playing sports.

Developmentally, Martha described growing up in a family that consisted of herself, her parents, an older brother, and an older sister. The brother and sister were many years older and had left home when Martha was quite young so that she grew up as an only child for most of her childhood.

Martha described her mother as very controlling and very demanding of performance. If Martha does something that her mother disapproves of, her mother gets angry, becomes critical, and won't let Martha forget it. On the other hand, her mother is approving with Martha's compliance with the mother's expectations.

The father is described as more passive, letting mother rule the house. He supported the mother in conflicts with the children and would never stick up for any of the children. She did not experience her father as critical but says they did not have a very close interaction, as he tends to stay to himself.

She experienced her parents as very strict. They would not allow her to go play with neighborhood children, have other children over to her house, or go to birthday parties. She remembered spending a lot of time at home in her room reading.

As a child, she was involved in many activities that her mother picked for her: Brownies, Girl Scouts, tennis, soccer, swimming, dance, and piano. She recalled her mother driving her around to all these activities in a compulsive manner, always demanding that she perform at a high level. Her mother would give her approval for the expected performance. Though she was allowed to interact with other children during these activities, any interactions outside the structured activities were curtailed.

During grade school and high school, Martha always got good grades. In high school she continued to be very active in structured activities, especially sports (soccer, tennis, and swimming) at which she performed at a high level. Her parents were approving of her scholastic and athletic accomplishments. Her parents, however, continued to limit her social activities, telling her she could not date until she was twenty-two and putting restrictions on the use of the phone and on watching TV.

She did well enough in sports to be recruited by several universities. However, the knee injury during her senior year put an end to her desires to compete on a collegiate level as several of her friends were planning to do. Instead, after high school, she attended a local junior college and continued to live at home. Her parents, and particularly her mother, encouraged her to move on to a local four-year university after she completed junior college. Though she feared moving away, part of Martha felt she should separate from her family and attend a university some distance from home. She convinced her parents to allow her to move away by expressing interest in a program at a distant university that was not offered locally. Her parents were very reluctant to allow her to leave home. She feared that they might sabotage her plans by withdrawing economic support. To circumvent that possibility, she had worked during junior college and had saved up a significant amount of money so that she could support herself if need be.

Though at first she was proud of herself for leaving home, she soon found herself becoming depressed. She struggled with the options of trying to stick it out at the university versus returning home to her parents.

Martha's case will be discussed in terms of separation-individuation. If we look at her sense of self, we can hypothesize that she has not developed an independent, mostly positive sense of self that is separate from that of her parents. Why is this?

In part it may relate to the fact that the abilities that she developed (both scholastically and athletically) and which she internalized into her sense of self were largely abilities based on activities that her parents picked for her. So, we might consider that her athletic ability was something that her parents felt good about but not necessarily something that she felt good about. Athletics might be something she did to please her parents but not necessarily things she was invested in. As a result, her athletic self-attributes could be characteristics of her self that were not invested with significant positive affect and thus not all that helpful for her in maintaining a positive sense of self.

Although this may have been somewhat of an issue for Martha, it doesn't appear to be a major issue. That is, even though Martha's parents picked which activities Martha should participate in, and Martha was not allowed to pick her own interests, it seems as if the things her parents picked for her were things that she could invest in emotionally—things that could lead to positively cathected self-attributes, which could serve as a core of a positive sense of self.

In understanding Martha's failure to develop a positive independent sense of self, we should look at her parents' reluctance to reinforce separation. Her parents encouraged activities that they picked for her and discouraged many activities that would separate her from the family. We have mentioned how her family discouraged going over to the neighborhood children's homes, having neighborhood children over to her house, going to birthday parties, dating, speaking with friends on the phone, and ultimately moving away to college.

In summary, her parents are rewarding if she is compliant and remains attached to the family and are critical if she is noncompliant or tries to separate from the family. This seems very much in line with the type of dynamics that Masterson (1976) talks of in his discussions of problems related to separation-individuation.

Masterson describes a rewarding object relations unit (RORU) and a withdrawing object relations unit (WORU). In the normal situation of the RORU, the parents are rewarding for the development of positive attributes in their children, including being rewarding for appropriate steps at separation. They are critical (WORU) and withdraw support for the development of undesirable characteristics.

In the case of Martha, we see a situation in which the parents are rewarding for the development of scholastic and athletic abilities but are critical of steps toward separation from the family. In other words, the development of positive scholastic and athletic abilities activates the RORU, but attempts at separation from the family activate the WORU. Thus, although Martha could feel good about some of her positive characteristics, she could not feel good about separation. So, when Martha moved away from home and went to college, the family withdrew support (WORU) and became critical. Since Martha did not have a positive independent sense of self, and because her sense of self was dependent on a reinforcing relationship with her parents, when she moved away and they withdrew support, she became depressed.

One might ask why Martha's parents, and in particular her mother, had such a hard time with Martha's separation. Martha stated that as far as she knew, her mother did not cling so tenaciously to her older brother and sister. Martha eventually came to believe that her mother herself was quite dependent. The mother's relationship with her husband was not close, and it appeared that he was incapable of meeting the mother's dependency needs. As a result, she turned to Martha to get those needs met and had a hard time letting Martha go.

⑥ Chris is a twenty-one-year-old woman who came requesting help with depression. The depression began about four months before coming into treatment, and she stated that the onset of depression correlated with her leaving her parents' home and moving to another city. Symptoms of depression have included sadness, crying spells, increased sleep, decreased appetite, decreased energy, irritability, feelings of inadequacy, low self-esteem, decreased concentration, decreased motivation, and decreased pleasure. She felt that she was losing hope for her future but denied suicidal ideation. Her activity level had decreased to the point where she spent much time in bed or on the couch and was missing several days at work (see Figure 10.4).

Chris described several stressors but felt that the main one had to do with conflicts with her family precipitated by her leaving home. She stated that her parents have reacted negatively to her decision to leave home. According to Chris, her parents see her as sick and don't believe she can live independent from the family. Further, she believes that her mother doesn't want her to succeed, wants her to stay at home with her, wants to keep her sick. She has gotten no encouragement, support, or approval for having gotten a job and moved away from home; she has only gotten criticism.

Another stress relates to Chris's boyfriend. The family has no specific complaints about him as a person, but dislikes the fact that he is taking her away from the family. The family suspects that she has a sexual relationship with this boyfriend and as a result has started calling her a slut and a whore.

Chris described one previous episode of depression, which occurred when she was a junior (age seventeen) in high school. At that point in time, she began a relationship with a boyfriend and began having some sexual feelings toward him. In this context, she began to have memories of a sexual experience at age eleven.

Over Christmas vacation, her family had gone to visit her maternal grandparents for the first week of the break. On the way home, they stopped to see her paternal grandparents. Those grandparents invited her to stay with them for the second week of the break. She did, and the rest of the family went on home. During that week she was sexually molested by her grandfather. When she began to have memories of this molestation in her junior year of high school, she became depressed and was seen in psychotherapy, which she found helpful.

The family psychiatric history is positive for chronic depression in the mother. At times her mother's depression gets worse, to the point where she will not speak for several days. For many years she received no treatment, but in the last few years she has been on Prozac.

There is no history of alcohol or drug abuse either in Chris or in the family.

Her medical history is positive for abdominal pains, which began at age eleven after the molestation. Her parents have taken her to multiple doctors over several years. She has had many GI workups, and nothing was ever found. When she began having memories of the molestation at age seventeen, her GI symptoms went away.

Socially, Chris moved away from home to take a job managing a restaurant. Before that, she had lived at home attaining an AA degree at a local junior college. Since moving she has established relationships with a few female friends who have been supportive. She does have a boyfriend, but that relationship is strained because her parents disapprove of him and he still lives in her hometown.

Developmentally, Chris described growing up in a family that consisted of her mother, father, and two sisters, aged nineteen and seventeen. She did not get along with the nineteen-year-old sister but has been quite close to the seventeen-year-old sister.

She described her mother as a very withdrawn person who shows very little emotion. Chris recalled longing for some affection, support, and acceptance from her mother, but it was never forthcoming. She told the story of how she would hug her mother or tell her that she loved her and would get no response. Her mother was always very negative, making comments like, "You're ugly" or "You're gross." She never had a nice thing to say.

Chris described her father as much more caring and supportive, especially toward the children. The relationship between her father and her mother was troubled for many years. According to Chris, her mother grew up in a very chaotic home environment, and when she was a senior in high school, she became withdrawn and did not speak for a year. Her mother got out of that environment by

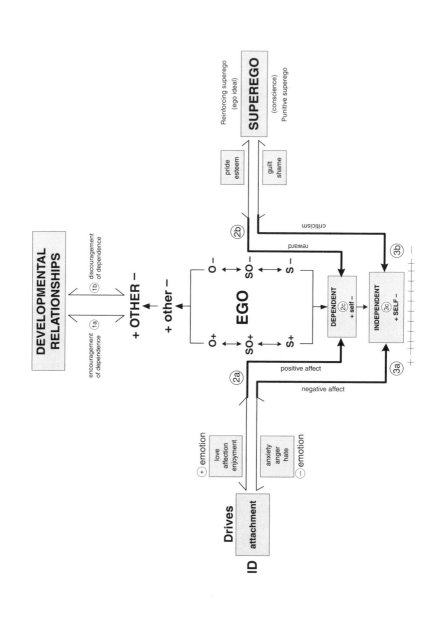

Figure 10.4. Pathology of the Self: Reward for Dependence: Chris

1. Chris's parents encouraged dependence (1a) and discouraged independence (1b).

2. Encouragement of dependence stimulates positive affects such as love and affection from the id (2a) and reward from the superego (2b) but results in Chris's remaining at a dependent level of separation-individuation (2c).

3. Discouragement of independence stimulates negative affects such as anger and anxiety from the id (3a) and criticism from the superego (3b) and prevents Chris from moving on to an independent level of separation-individuation (3c).

Note: The referenced numbers correspond with the numbers on the diagram.

marrying Chris's father just after high school; however, her parents frequently fought. Often her father would get very angry and hit her mother, who would then go hide in a closet. Chris remembered constantly being on the alert for flares of her father's temper, and when they occurred, would try to get between her father and mother to prevent any violence from happening. Though Chris could remember several times when her father hit her mother, there were no episodes of violence toward any of the children.

Chris remembered as a child feeling like it was her job to keep the family together and that she had to work very hard at being the mediator in her parents' relationship. Even though she never had a close relationship with her mother, she wondered if the reason her mother has had such a hard time letting her go is that she fears the loss of Chris's role as a go-between in the parents' marital relationship. Since she has left home, her mother has called her every day. Though she has never been supportive in any of these phone conversations, she has given the clear message that she wants Chris to return home.

Chris remembered very little family life. They rarely did things together as a family other than going to church on Sunday. When she was quite young, they did go on some family outings and vacations, but they just ended up with her parents fighting, so they stopped doing that.

Chris recalled her grade school years as the happier years of her life. She enjoyed school, did well, and had friends. She was not, however, allowed to participate in extracurricular activities, and because friends lived some distance away from town in the country, interactions with them were limited.

After the molestation at age eleven, life changed significantly for Chris. She became withdrawn and kept to herself to a large extent. She was frequently sick and missed school often as a result. She remembered being called weird or crazy by other students in high school. She did not do that well but did enough to get by. She did develop a couple of girlfriends in high school, one of whom she still keeps in contact with. During her junior year she had a boyfriend; she feels she was very dependent on him. It was in the context of this relationship that Chris began to have memories of the molestation. She eventually got into some therapy, which she found beneficial.

After high school she attended a junior college and worked part-time while living at home. She was able to function adequately in school and at work. It was after she finished at the junior college that she moved away from home to take a job that she felt she had prepared for in college.

After coming a couple of times for evaluation, Chris called and stated that she didn't feel that she could make it on her own; she had decided to quit her job and return home.

How do we understand her decision? She explained that being on her own was too depressing; therefore, she needed to return to the security of her parents' home. We might conceptualize this in terms of a failure of separation-individuation.

One aspect of this failure in separation likely relates to her parents not allowing her to separate for at least two reasons: (1) Chris's role in the family has been to keep it together. They were dependent on her to keep the family together. Her separating from the family puts the family at risk for falling apart. (2) Not only is the family dependent on her, she, at least from the family's perspective, is dependent on them. That is, after the molestation, the family developed the belief that they couldn't allow her to separate from them because something bad would happen again. They had to keep a close eye on her. Also, after the molestation, she developed these chronic gastrointestinal symptoms. This resulted in the family seeing her as fragile, weak, and sick and thus in need of protection. This then exacerbated their belief that they shouldn't let her separate because something bad would happen.

Thus, as a result of these two factors, Chris had difficulty separating. That is, her parents tended to reinforce dependency. When Chris tried to separate, they became critical of her; they withdrew whatever support they had given her, and she became depressed.

This leads to the second major aspect of Chris's difficulty separating. She was dependent on a close relationship with her parents to support her emotionally. In other words, she had no stable sense of self that was cathected with positive emotion. The failure to develop any positive internal self is likely related to her mother's rather detached manner of relating, as well as the molestation by the grandfather. Had she developed a more positive sense of self, she might have been able to sustain herself even after the separation and withdrawal of her parents' support. Since she was so dependent on the support of her parents, when that support was withdrawn, she became depressed. To overcome this depression, she defensively moved back to a closer relationship with her parents. This, however, was at the expense of psychological separation and individuation.

DEVELOPMENT INTERACTIONS OF OVER-INVOLVEMENT

At first glance, the issue of over-involvement may not appear to be different from what was discussed in the last section. Certainly the significant others of the persons described were over-involved in that they did not allow separation to occur. What will be discussed here is a little different in the sense that the main issue has less to do with the failure of separation and more to do with the failure of individuation.

To be more specific, the developmental interactions to be described here are typified by interactions between a child and a parent in which the parent directs and controls what the child will become. That is, the child becomes what the parent wants her to become because the child becoming that person meets some need for the parent. The emphasis here is on the child becoming what the parent wants her to become; what is missing in the child's development is the individuation of a self-structure that is based at least in part on activities, interests, and abilities that the child is invested in. Rather the activities, interests, and abilities that the child develops are ones that the parent is interested in.

We have all probably heard the term *stage mother.* Here I will use that term to refer to the mother of a child who performs on stage. This is not necessarily a pathological interaction. The pathology comes in when the child's performance is more important for the mother than it is for the child. The child is performing because that activity has been encouraged by the parent and meets a need for the parent. The parent's self-esteem, for example, is tied up in the child's performing. This situation is especially problematic when the child is not emotionally invested in the activity. The result for the child can be that he invests significant amounts of energy developing skills that he is not emotionally invested in. The development of skills that someone is not emotionally invested in does not help in the growth of an emotionally well-balanced self-structure. The other part of this dynamic is that the time the child invests in meeting the parent's needs is time that is not available for self-development.

Besides performing on stage, another form of performing is via participation in sports. The following case vignette describes an interaction between a father and his daughter that centered on his interest in sports.

Heather is a young woman in her late teens who came in with a complaint of depression. She stated that she has always been depressed, even as a small child.

Heather gave a history of growing up in a family in which her father placed a tremendous emphasis on sports. He himself had been an excellent athlete who competed on a collegiate level. He was not, however, good enough to compete on a professional level as he had hoped to. He aspired for his daughter to be in the Olympics as a gymnast.

Heather described her childhood as one that revolved around gymnastics and her relationship with her father. He would get her up early to take her to a gym for practice before school and would take her back after school for another session. She noted that if she was sick she did not go to school, but she still went to gymnastics practice. On weekends her father would take her to meets throughout the state, photographing and videotaping her performances. He would later study the tapes to be able to give her advice on how to improve and would show off the tapes to his friends.

Heather remembered that gymnastics took precedence over all other activities. She was not involved in any school extracurricular activities and only rarely played with other girls. She stated that she never had a best friend, and if she was invited to parties or outings, wasn't allowed to go because she had to go to practice. She noted, "I never once went to a slumber party." She did not date in high school. Again, her life revolved around gymnastics.

All of this changed suddenly when she was injured during her junior year of high school. It soon became clear that the goal of competing on an Olympic level was no longer realistic. Her father dropped any interest he had in her and began paying all his attention to a younger sister, interacting with the sister in much the same manner he had with Heather.

Heather reported being left without an identity. Gymnastics was the only identity she had ever had. She described having no friends and no social skills. As a result, attempts to interact with others did not go well. She didn't feel that she had anything that she was interested in or enjoyed; she felt uncertain about who she was as a person and uncertain about where to go with her future.

The point of this vignette is to demonstrate the failure of the development of an identity based on over-involvement by a parent. In this case the child must perform in gymnastics to meet the father's needs. What is not allowed is the development of a self based on interests and activities that Heather becomes emotionally invested in. Instead, her life is dominated by an activity that her father is interested in. Thus, when she is injured and no longer able to participate in gymnastics, we see the results of the failure of self-development; she is left without a sense of self and experiences a sense of depression and hopelessness about the future.

DEVELOPMENTAL ISSUES RELATED TO LOSS

Loss is one aspect of development that certainly needs to be mentioned. The issue of loss has been part of many of the case vignettes already presented, though we have not emphasized loss in these presentations. Loss may take many forms. Certainly the loss of a parent through death during the developmental years is one of the most significant losses one can suffer. Loss can also occur when a parent abandons a family (see figure 10.5).

Probably one of the more common forms of loss today is the loss that a child suffers when a family breaks up in a divorce. Even if the child is able to maintain some degree of contact with each parent, the quality and quantity of those interactions are likely to change. The interactions may potentially change for the better and may then foster self-development. On the other hand, the quality and quantity of the interactions may change in ways that do not foster self-development, and in these situations, the person may develop some degree of self pathology.

Another aspect of divorce, besides loss, that may affect self-development is the formation of new relationships that occur. For example, one's parents may remarry, and then there may be a stepfather or stepmother, step-siblings, or half-siblings to relate to. These relationships may have a salutary effect on development in some circumstances; in others they may have a deleterious effect.

A few case vignettes will be presented to illustrate the effects of loss on self-development. In a general sense, we can think of two divergent effects of the loss of an emotionally positive relationship on the emotional balance of the self. First, loss leads to the termination of the positive emotional supplies that were received in the relationship. Loss may also stimulate negative emotions such as sadness or anger. Loss of positive emotional supplies, along with the addition of negative emotional factors, may serve to upset the emotional well-being of the self.

Ingrid is a thirty-year-old woman with a complaint of mood lability. She described that her moods fluctuated frequently, from periods during which she was relatively calm to periods in which she was depressed (and at times suicidal) to periods in which she was anxious. She dated her problems back to age nine, at which point her mother had died of cancer.

Since the death of her mother, she described her life as having been quite chaotic. Her father remarried when she was ten, and she experienced her stepmother as controlling and perfectionistic. She remembers frequently being yelled at by her stepmother and said that her stepmother scapegoated her, always blaming her for anything that went wrong. They constantly fought. She did not do well in school but did manage to barely graduate from high school. During her twenties, she held multiple low-level jobs, frequently moving from one to another. She has on several occasions attended college but has not completed a degree program. She has been involved in numerous relationships; they have all been tumultuous and short-term.

Ingrid described that over the years, she has learned to deal with her mood difficulties in two ways. First, during her late teens and early twenties, she drank heavily to escape from anxiety and depression. Second, she described that she would often dress provocatively in order to precipitate a sexual encounter, "so I could feel loved and cared for."

In Ingrid's memory, everything was fine up until her mother's death. She described a very close relationship with her mother, whom she experienced as warm, giving, caring, understanding, and thoughtful. Her mother was strong and open-minded, and would talk things out if there were conflicts.

Ingrid described various feelings surrounding the loss of her mother. First she described the sense of loss of the very positive relationship she remembered having with her mother. Along with this sense of loss was much sadness. She also described a feeling of being abandoned by her mother, and associated with this sense was much anger.

In summary, we have described a young woman who lost her mother at age nine. She has had significant difficulty in life maintaining a positive emotional balance, maintaining a relationship, or settling on a career direction. If we look at the loss of her mother in terms of Ingrid's emotional balance within her sense of self, we can enumerate a couple of parameters that might have been significant. First, we see the loss of a very emotionally positive relationship. The loss of the influx of positive emotion is significant. Before her mother's death, the influx of positive emotion associated with this relationship was a significant factor in self-growth. With the death of her mother, that positive influx ceased and was replaced by sadness over loss and anger

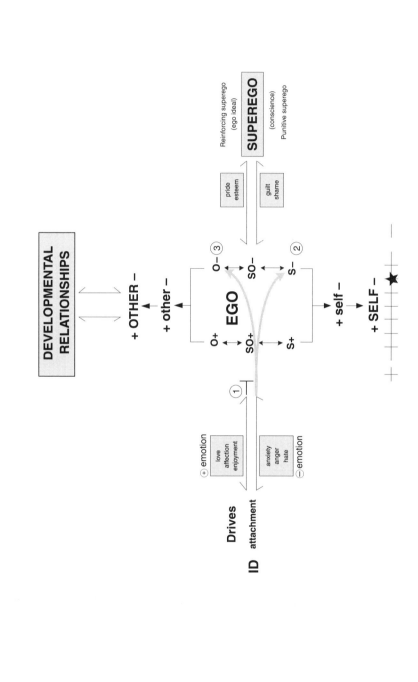

Figure 10.5. Pathology of the Self: Reaction to Loss

Loss may affect a person's inner affect balance via the following:

1. The loss of the positive affective influx that had been associated with the relationship
2. The simulation of sadness over what the self has lost
3. The simulation of anger at the other for leaving

Note: The referenced numbers correspond with the numbers on the diagram.

over abandonment. Thus the positive emotional influx was replaced by a negative emotional influx, which had a deleterious effect on self-growth. In addition, her relationship with her stepmother was negative and only compounded the negative emotional influx related to the loss of her mother. Had the relationship with the stepmother been more positive, this relationship might have mitigated some of the negative impact of the loss of the mother.

⑥ Janice, a twenty-two-year-old woman, presented a somewhat different history of loss. She was born in a foreign country and raised there by her parents until she was two or three. At that point her parents moved to the United States, leaving her to be cared for by a grandmother. She described having a very close relationship with her grandmother and a very happy childhood, which included many positive interactions with other relatives who lived near her grandmother.

She did not see her parents again until she was fourteen when she came to visit. At this time, the parents decided that she should not return to her grandmother but instead stay with them. She described this as a very difficult transition for her, not only because of the sudden change in her family situation, but also because she had to learn a new language and a new culture.

She described her relationship with her mother as much different from the one she had with her grandmother. Her mother was negative, had a bad temper, and always put her down. In addition, she described her mother as intensely jealous, especially of any interaction Janice had with her father. In fact, at one point, her mother accused Janice of having an affair with her father.

Whereas Janice had experienced herself as quite happy prior to age fourteen, she stated she had become chronically depressed since coming to live with her parents. We can look at this from the perspective of the effect of loss on the emotional balance within her sense of self. In actuality, we can conceptualize two layers of loss: one when her parents left when Janice was age two or three and one when she moved to the United States and lost the relationship with her grandmother and other relatives.

It is difficult to speculate what effect the early loss had; obviously she had no memory of it. She did seem to recover from it in the sense of having a happy childhood up until age fourteen. Perhaps the significance of the loss of her parents was lessened by the fact that her grandmother was involved in her care from birth.

The loss of the relationship with the grandmother can, from an emotional perspective, again be conceptualized in terms of the loss of positive emotional influx and the addition of negative emotional influx. The loss of positive obviously refers to the loss of the positive emotional relationship with her grandmother and other relatives. The addition of negative is twofold: (1) the sadness at the loss of the grandmother and (2) frustration and anger over the relationship with the mother. This loss of positive and addition of negative emotional input made it difficult to maintain a positive emotional balance, and as a result she became depressed.

⑥ Kevin is a twenty-six-year-old man who gave a history of witnessing the murder of his brother (who was ten years older), ten years previously when Kevin was sixteen. One morning Kevin's brother drove him to school and then stopped at a store across the street from the school. As he walked toward the store, a truck drove by, and a person in the truck shot and killed Kevin's brother. Kevin, who was outside on the school grounds, saw this occur. Despite the traumatic nature of this incident, Kevin denied symptoms of post-traumatic stress disorder (PTSD) and in fact felt that he had denied the loss of his brother and never mourned the loss. Recently, however, he had become depressed and had been thinking about his brother. He denied any acute stress in his life or any event that had precipitated thoughts of his brother. He did feel that it was significant that he had now reached the age at which his brother had died.

Prior to the murder of his brother, there was nothing especially traumatic in Kevin's development. He grew up in a loving, intact family in which he was the youngest of four boys. He did feel that his relationship with the brother who was murdered was an especially important one to him. He regarded this brother as a mentor, a motivator, a father-like figure, and as such a significant identification figure. His brother was especially important to him as a father figure because his biological father was quite ill from the time he was a small child. Thus, while he experienced his father as very loving, his father was not physically capable of participating with him in the activities of growing up. His brother filled this role.

Again we can look at this in terms of loss of positive emotions and the addition of negative emotions. Kevin lost an ongoing emotionally positive relationship with his brother. This occurred in the context of what appears to have been pretty solid self-development before the murder. Kevin lost a significant identification and idealization figure, but appeared to be far enough along in development so as to be able to find replacement identification/idealization figures in his environment. He did this largely by getting involved in sports, playing football on both a high school and collegiate level.

It appears that for ten years, he dealt with any negative emotional input (sadness, anger) by denial. When the denial broke down, he began to experience these emotions, his emotional balance shifted toward the negative side, and he became depressed.

OTHER TYPES OF DEVELOPMENTAL INTERACTIONS

Many other types of developmental interactions may have been experienced by given individuals. One that comes to mind is a pattern in which an individual assumes an adult role very early in development. Examples might include (1) a child who assumes the role of caring for the house after the mother becomes ill or dies, (2) an older child who is placed in the role of taking care of younger siblings in a large family, or (3) a child who goes to work very early because of economic necessity. In any of these situations, we may see a child or adolescent who is assuming an adult role before he or she has had a chance to develop an adult identity. These situations may serve as maturing stimuli. On the other hand, for some, they may be forces that stymie development of the self. Because the child is spending so much time in an adult role, he or she does not have the time to fully participate in the age-appropriate experiences (school, relationships with peers, extracurricular activities) that could potentiate self-development.

A person may experience many other types of developmental situations, or he or she may certainly have experiences from more than one of the categories mentioned previously. The point is not to try to categorize a person's developmental experiences under one heading or another; the point is to learn about a given individual's unique developmental experience and understand the person from that perspective.

SUMMARY

This chapter focused on pathology of the self and described several developmental pathways via which a person may fail to develop an inner world of self and other representations that are predominantly cathected with positive affect, resulting in an overall positive affect balance within. This chapter emphasized development of the self. Each of the individuals in the case studies also had significant problems with interpersonal relationships, and that is the issue that I will discuss in the next chapter.

11

Disorders of Interpersonal Relationships

This chapter will focus on a discussion of interpersonal relationships. Our goal will be to try and understand why some people have difficulties in interpersonal relationships. The previous chapter focused on persons who have difficulty with their sense of self. Persons with sense of self problems will generally also have difficulties with interpersonal relationships. People who have these difficulties with sense of self and interpersonal relationships would be included in the categories that are traditionally called personality disorders or characterological disorders. For other persons, the predominant problem is with interpersonal relationships. They generally have a healthier sense of self and would be more likely called neurotic traditionally. The format of this chapter will include a brief discussion of (1) persons with combined difficulties in sense of self and interpersonal relationships and (2) persons whose problems are predominantly in the area of interpersonal relationships; this will be followed by (3) a discussion of attachment patterns.

PERSONS WITH DIFFICULTIES IN SENSE OF SELF AND INTERPERSONAL RELATIONSHIPS (PERSONALITY DISORDERS)

The American Psychiatric Association's (APA) *Diagnostic and Statistical Manual* (*DSM*) (2000) includes a long list of personality disorders. In general, persons with personality disorders have difficulty maintaining a cohesive, positive sense of self and have difficulties with interpersonal relationships. Since the focus in this chapter is on interpersonal relationships, I will give a few examples of the relationship problems that those with personality disorders experience.

A person with borderline personality disorder "fears abandonment in relationships and tends to form multiple, intense, short term relationships." A person with dependent personality "seeks nurturance and support from others, needs others to assume responsibility for their care, fears being left to care for themself and urgently seeks another relationship as a source of care when a close relationship ends." Persons with avoidant personality disorder "avoid interpersonal relationship because of fear that they will be shamed or ridiculed, because of fear that they will not be liked or because of feelings of inadequacy." Persons with narcissistic personality disorder are "interpersonally exploitative, lack empathy in relationships and expect to be recognized as superior." Those with paranoid personality disorder "suspect that others are exploiting or deceiving them and have difficulty trusting others." A person with schizoid personality "neither desires nor enjoys close relationships," and a person with schizotypal personality "lacks close friends or confidants other than first degree relatives." Those with antisocial personality "show disregard for and violation of the rights of others." A person with a histrionic personality disorder "is attention seeking in relationships, may be inappropriately sexually seductive or provocative and considers relationships to be more intimate than they actually are." A person with obsessive-compulsive personality disorder "may try to control others in relationships or may be so devoted to work that relationships are excluded from their lives." (All quotes APA *DSM* 2000)

What has been emphasized in the previous discussion are the difficulties that those with personality disorder have with interpersonal relationships. Again, these persons also have significant difficulties with their sense of self.

PERSONS WHOSE PROBLEMS ARE PREDOMINATELY WITH INTERPERSONAL RELATIONSHIPS

Some persons, despite having a quite well-developed sense of self, still have problems with interpersonal relationships. In these persons, the deficits in sense of self described in chapter 10 are not present or are not present to such a degree as in persons with self disorders. In other words, the persons to be described now generally have completed the separation-individuation process and have a cohesive, mostly positive sense of self and other. As a result, they have an ability to modulate affects (i.e., affects are neither all positive or all negative; they are capable of experiencing a wide spectrum of affects). In addition, they have a well-developed ability to control impulses (i.e., they are able to repress drives from entering the ego). They also have an ability to repress affect so that the ego is not overwhelmed by negative affect. In fact, as opposed to many persons with self disorders who have difficulty repressing drives and affects, patients with disorders of interpersonal relationships may repress drives and affects to such an extent that this repression interferes with the development of interpersonal relationships.

As a result of good development of the ego, these persons function very well in most areas. They may function very well in school, work, and various recreational activities, and even relate very well with other people in general. The specific problem is often with intimate relationships. They may have problems forming close interpersonal relationships or sexual relationships or both. Classically, persons with problems in interpersonal relationships are thought of as neurotic, as opposed to those with disorders of the self who are thought of as having personality disorders.

If we examine the developmental histories of those with interpersonal relationship problems, we frequently do not see the degree of pathology that we see in the histories of those with self disorders. We do not usually see histories of abuse, neglect, criticism, and molestation. In fact, the histories of those with disorders of interpersonal relationships usually include histories of very good mothering, which is what leads to good development of the sense of self. Usually, however, there is a history of some problem in interpersonal relatedness that sets up an attachment pattern that inhibits intimacy in relationships, even though relationships in general may go very well. As a result, these persons may come to therapy requesting help with intimate relationships specifically, as opposed to persons with disorders of the self who have problems with relationships in general including intimate relationships. Since we generally form our most intimate relationship with members of the opposite sex, we may find in the past of a person with an intimacy problem, a history of some difficulty with a significant other of the opposite sex.

This difficulty with the significant other in the past sets up a pattern so that forming intimate relationships in the present is problematic. This pattern is sometimes referred to as a repetition compulsion. In this formulation, patterns of unhealthy relationships from the past are repeated in current relationships with the hope that they will work out in the present. We will look at this issue of repetition of patterns of relating from the perspective of attachment theory.

Earlier I described persons with significant problems with both their sense of self and their ability to relate to others (personality disorders). I also described those with a healthy sense of self, but difficulty with interpersonal relationships. We might think of these two as being end points of a spectrum. In between these two end points would be persons who have difficulty with relationships and some difficulty with sense of self, but not to the degree of those with a personality disorder. The case of Roberta, presented later in this chapter, falls into this middle category.

PATTERNS OF ATTACHMENT

Chapter 7, Attachment Theory, described how attachment patterns or internal working models are learned in development. Unhealthy (insecure) patterns of attachment persist because they have been reinforced and because healthy patterns of attachment have not been modeled and learned. As a result of the persistence of unhealthy patterns of attachment, a person has difficulties with interpersonal relationships (see figure 11.1).

The degree of difficulty a person has in interpersonal relationships is proportional to the degree of healthy versus unhealthy attachment patterns he or she has learned in development. We all interact with a variety of people throughout development (e.g., mother, father, siblings, grandparents, aunts, uncles, teachers, coaches, etc.). They all relate to us in a somewhat different manner. Thus, we learn a variety of attachment patterns. If healthy attachment patterns are reinforced (as a result of healthy, gratifying interpersonal relationships), then we can continue those healthy attachment patterns throughout life and relate well to people. If unhealthy attachment patterns are reinforced (as a result of unhealthy, frustrating relationships characterized by abuse, neglect, emotional unavailability, molestation), then we may have significant difficulty with interpersonal relationships.

If some of the attachment patterns we learn are healthy and some are unhealthy, we end up with a situation in which we may be able to relate well under certain circumstances but not relate well under other circumstances.

These attachment patterns are the models through which attachment drives are expressed. So, for example, if someone has grown up with mostly gratifying relationships that have gone well, then the attachment pattern that he has learned includes the expectation that relationships will go well. Attachment drive is then expressed via this pattern and in this situation may be expressed rather exuberantly.

If, on the other hand, someone has grown up with mostly frustrating relationships, then the attachment patterns that she has learned include the expectation that relationships won't go well. Attachment drive is expressed via this pattern and may be expressed rather cautiously. Again, someone may have learned a variety of attachment patterns, some healthy and some not so healthy, so that he or she relates well in some situations and not so well in other situations.

A series of attachment patterns are listed next. With respect to each of the attachment patterns, we can describe three possible outcomes: (1) repression of attachment drive because expression of attachment drive via that specific attachment pattern is associated with anxiety; (2) expression of attachment drive via the attachment pattern (i.e., repetition of the attachment pattern); or (3) expression of the attachment drive via the attachment pattern but with the self and other roles reversed (i.e., reversal of the attachment pattern).

Controlling/Restrictive Parent ⇐ *Child Who Is Compromising and Tries to Please*

In this pattern, the parent is very restrictive and controlling of the child's social activities, dress, and so on and demands compliance with the parental rules. Deviations from the parent's wishes are met with anger/punishment; compliance is rewarded directly (praise) or indirectly (lack of anger/punishment).

In the face of this type of developmental environment, possible outcomes might include the following:

Repression. Attachment drive is repressed and relationships are avoided to avoid repeating the negative aspects of this pattern.
Repetition. Attachment drives are repeated along this attachment pattern. The person gets involved with others who are controlling and repeats *the positive aspects of the pattern (i.e., receiving reward for complying with and pleasing the other).*

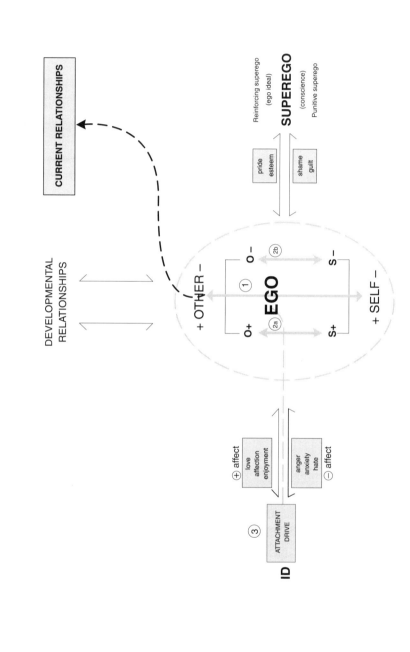

Figure 11.1. Attachment Patterns

1. An attachment pattern is an internalized self-other pattern of relating that has been learned on the basis of actual relationships between a person and his or her significant developmental others. A self-other attachment pattern is represented by the large bold arrow in the diagram. The arrow is shown centered between bold +OTHER− and +SELF−. For some people, the arrow may be more to the left of center, indicating their tendency to relate in a positive manner (likely a result of having internalized a more positive attachment pattern from the experience of positive, healthy, nurturing relationships in development). For other people, the arrow may be more to the right of center, indicating their tendency to relate in a negative manner (likely a result of having internalized a more negative attachment pattern from the experience of negative, unhealthy, abusive relationships in development). This bold arrow indicates a whole self-other attachment pattern, meaning an attachment pattern that exists within a person with whole, integrated self and whole, integrated other representations.

2. Also represented by the arrows labeled 2a and 2b are part self-other attachment patterns. These occur in persons with split (unintegrated) self representations and split (unintegrated) other representations. Persons who relate on the basis of split part self-object attachment patterns tend to relate in a very polar fashion (i.e., they relate in either a very positive manner or a very negative manner). Those who relate on the basis of whole self-object attachment patterns have a continuum of patterns available from positive to negative with many gradations in between.

3. Attachment drives may be expressed via learned attachment patterns in relating to others in our environment. Expression of an attachment drive along a certain attachment pattern stimulates the emotion associated with that attachment pattern. If those are pleasant emotions, the probability of expressing the attachment drive may be increased. If the emotions are unpleasant, the probability of expressing the attachment drive may be decreased.

As discussed in the text, attachment drive may be expressed along a certain attachment pattern that either repeats that attachment pattern or reverses that attachment pattern (self and other roles are reversed). Alternatively, if the attachment pattern is associated with significant negative emotion, attachment drives may be repressed.

Note: The referenced numbers correspond with the numbers on the diagram.

Reversal. The pattern is repeated, but the roles are reversed. That is, the person adopts the controlling role and seeks out others whom they control.

Dependency-Inducing Parent ⇐ Dependent Child

This pattern reinforces dependency and discourages separation-individuation. The child may remain dependent to receive parental reinforcement, but this is at the expense of separation-individuation.

Possible outcomes as a result of this type of developmental environment might include the following:

Repression. Attachment is repressed because of fears of engulfment—that is, for fear that others will not allow the person to individuate.
Repetition. The person repeatedly gets involved with others who reinforce dependency in others to obtain that reinforcement.
Reversal. The pattern is repeated, but the roles are reversed such that the person seeks out others who are dependent on them.

Abusive, Rejecting Parent ⇐ Devalued, Unworthy Child

In this pattern, the parent may be physically abusive, emotionally abusive, sexually abusive, or verbally abusive, telling the child things like, "You are worthless," "I wish you had never been born," and so on. The result is that the child feels worthless and undeserving.

Possible outcomes might include the following:

Repression. Attachment drive is repressed in order to avoid further abuse.
Repetition. Attachment drive is expressed along this same attachment pattern perhaps because the person feels unworthy and undeserving of a different kind of relationship or perhaps because he or she maintains the hope that the other will change and become rewarding instead of abusive.
Reversal. The attachment pattern is repeated, but the roles are reversed. That is, the person becomes involved in relationships in which he or she abuses and/or rejects others.

Unresponsive, Aloof Parent ⇐ Attention-Seeking Child

In this pattern, the parent may be present and may provide for the basic needs of the child but may be unresponsive to any of the child's accomplishments, thus not meeting the child's psychological needs. The child strives to accomplish to get recognition, but to no avail.

Possible outcomes might include the following:

Repression. Attachment drive is repressed to avoid further disappointments.

Repetition. The person strives to find a relationship in which someone will bestow recognition for his or her accomplishments.

Reversal. The person adopts an aloof, unresponsive pattern of interacting with others.

Demanding/Perfectionistic Parent ⇐ Striving to Succeed/Please Child

In this pattern, the parent is very demanding of performance, sometimes to very perfectionistic standards. The child strives to succeed to please the parent.

Possible outcomes might include the following:

Repression. Attachment drive is repressed to avoid such high-pressure types of relationships.

Repetition. Attachment drive is expressed along this pattern to receive the reward that goes along with achievement.

Reversal. The attachment plan is reversed. The person develops relationships (perhaps with his or her own children) in which he or she becomes demanding of the other.

Over-Gratifying Parent ⇐ Special Child

In this pattern, the parent is over-gratifying and treats the child as special. Possible outcomes include the following:

Repression. Attachment drive is repressed because in adult life the person cannot find anyone who is as gratifying as the parent was.

Repetition. The person repeatedly seeks out a relationship in which he or she is treated as special.
Reversal. The attachment pattern is reversed, and the person treats others as if they are special.

These are but a few examples of potential attachment patterns. It is important to emphasize that these are just examples. What is significant is to understand the specific attachment patterns that have developed in the persons we are treating.

These attachment patterns may occur in the development of both persons with self disorders as well as persons with interpersonal disorders. We can perhaps think of the difference in quantitative terms. In other words, in persons with self disorders, most of the attachments have been of a pathological or frustrating nature. In persons with interpersonal disorders, many of the developmental relationships have been healthy, but a quantity of them have been unhealthy.

Another aspect of the difference between those with sense of self disorders and those with disorders of interpersonal relationships relates to their level of anxiety. Persons with disorders of the self tend to experience anxiety when they are not in a relationship because they need the relationship to stabilize their sense of self. Persons with disorders of interpersonal relationships may tend to be more anxious when they are in a relationship. That is, when they are not in a relationship, they are relatively anxiety free because they have a good sense of self. When they are in a relationship, if the relationship activates attachment patterns that are associated with negative affects, then they may experience those negative affects (such as anxiety) in the context of this relationship.

In this context, Kohut's (1971) concept of self-object relationships versus object-object relationships may be helpful. In patients with disorders of the self, the predominate form of relationship is the self-object relationship. In this form of relating, the object (other) meets a need for the self, such as helping the person stabilize his or her self-system. In object-object relationships, there is much more mutuality. Each person is capable of giving (emotional supplies) to the other as well as receiving them. Each person can meet the self needs of the other. The problem here is not so much needing the relationship to stabilize the self-system. Rather, the problem, if there are unhealthy attachment patterns, is that when the person gets into a relationship based on unhealthy attachment patterns, the negative affects associated with those patterns may destabilize the emotional balance of the self.

A person who has developed unhealthy attachment patterns may deal with them in one of three ways: (1) he may repress attachment drive related to the attachment pattern, or he may express either via (2) repetition or (3) reversal attachment drive related to the attachment pattern. The more neurotic person (disorder of interpersonal relationships) has more choice. He may repress attachment drive and thus avoid the anxiety (or other negative affect) associated with expression of the attachment drive along a given attachment pattern. The problem with this is that the desire for fulfilling attachments goes unmet. If the person then expresses the attachment drive along unhealthy patterns of attachment, he risks experiencing the negative affect associated with that attachment pattern. Obviously, the goal is to learn healthy patterns of attachment so that the person can go on and form healthy attachment relationships.

The person with a disorder of the self may have less appealing choices with respect to the expression of attachment drive. Since the sense of self is unstable, the tendency is to try to form a positive attachment so as to stimulate the influx of positive affect into the self-system. The problem is that the attachment drive is likely expressed along unhealthy attachment patterns so the person then experiences the negative affect associated with the unhealthy attachment pattern; this then has a destabilizing effect on the emotional balance of her sense of self and perhaps on the relationship. The other alternative to the person with a self disorder is to repress attachment drive (avoidant personality.)The problem with this alternative is that it leaves her with her baseline emotionally unstable sense of self.

The final topic to discuss here is that of the distinction between whole object relationships and part object relationships. A whole object relationship attachment pattern is one between a whole (cohesive) self and a whole (cohesive) object. This type of attachment pattern is illustrated with a large arrow between self and other in figure 11.1. A whole object relationship obviously implies that separation-individuation has progressed to the point where self representations are integrated and other representations are integrated.

Whole object relationship patterns may vary significantly in degree from those that are more positive, rewarding, and fulfilling to those that are negative, unrewarding, and unfulfilling. In figure 11.1, imagine the large arrow moving from its current center position to either the right or the left. An arrow to the left of center would represent a more positive attachment pattern and one to the right of center a more negative pattern.

Part object relationship attachment patterns are those between a part self representation and a part object representation. This implies that separation-individuation is not complete, that self and other representations are not integrated, that self and other representations exist at a split level. In figure 11.1, two part object relationship attachment patterns are illustrated. The first is a part object relationship attachment pattern between a positive part self representation and a positive part other self representation. The second is a part object relationship attachment pattern between a negative part self representation and a negative part other representation. These part object relationship patterns tend to be very polar (i.e., all positive or all negative).

Figure 11.2 illustrates two other possible part object relationship attachment patterns. One is between a positive part self representation and a negative part other representation. This might be seen in a narcissistic person who overvalues himself and sees those he relates to as worthless. Another example is between a negative part self representation and a positive part other representation. This might be seen in a person with borderline personality who sees himself as worthless and his partner as all positive.

The goal of this chapter so far has been to further discuss the concept of attachment patterns and to describe how unhealthy attachment patterns can lead to problems in interpersonal relationships. Next, two clinical cases, Roberta and Suzanne, will be presented to further illustrate the concept of attachment patterns and the problems of forming interpersonal relationships.

The major goal of the following case is to illustrate the concept of attachment patterns in interpersonal relationships. Issues related to sense of self will also be mentioned.

⑥ Roberta is a twenty-two-year-old soon-to-be college graduate who came in after a fight with her fiancé. She wanted help with the way she related to her boyfriend and the way she felt about herself. Roberta had recently been to visit her fiancé, who lived in another state. While there, they had a fight. She stated that she can't even remember what started the fight but says that it ended with her being verbally abusive toward him, shouting obscenities toward him, and throwing dishes across the room at him. Since this has occurred several times in their relationship, Roberta's boyfriend suggested that they see a couples counselor. They

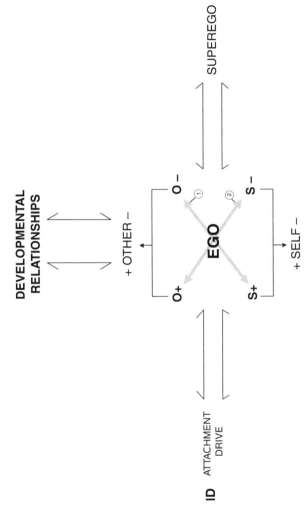

Figure 11.2. Attachment Patterns

This diagram illustrates a part object relationship attachment pattern between

1. a positive part self representation and a negative part other representation.
2. a negative part self representation and a positive part other representation.

Note: The referenced numbers correspond with the numbers on the diagram.

did, and the couple counselor told her she needed help on her own, and thus she came in requesting therapy.

Roberta has been in a relationship with her fiancé for the last three years, and they have lived in the same town most of that time. Several months ago, however, her fiancé was transferred to another state. They have maintained a long-distance relationship and plan to get married after Roberta graduates from college. For the most part, she feels it has been a good relationship that has had a stabilizing effect on her life. They do have frequent arguments, and while she doesn't see that as unusual, she is concerned about her rather violent reactions to these arguments.

The other problem that Roberta mentioned was chronic mild depression, which she believes dates back at least to sixth grade. Symptoms of depression include frequent crying spells, feeling as if she's always wrong, feeling she's not loved, feeling negative, low self-esteem, feeling she's always being put down, and uncertainty as to why she exists. She has had some transient suicidal ideation but maintains hope that things will get better. In general, she has not had trouble with her sleep, appetite, energy, concentration, or libido, but for a period of several weeks after her fiancé was transferred, her depression did deepen, and she developed all of these symptoms. The depression improved when she was able to visit him during a school break. For the most part, she feels that her depression varies with the degree of harmony versus disharmony in the relationship with her fiancé. If things are going well she is less depressed; if they are not, she is more depressed.

Other than what's just been mentioned, there is no history of any treatment. There is no history of alcohol or substance abuse. She believes that her mother may have been treated with antidepressants one time many years ago, but other than that, there is no known family history of psychiatric illness, though two of her mother's brothers have had legal problems and spent time in prison. Roberta is currently healthy and has no past history of medical problems.

Roberta's developmental history included relationships with a variety of people. She grew up on a farm near a small rural town. The immediate family consisted of her mother, father, and a younger brother. Her paternal grandmother lived next door. Her paternal aunt, along with the aunt's husband and children, lived across the street. Her maternal grandmother lived in the nearby town.

Her relationship with her mother was complex. She experienced her mother as verbally abusive, critical, and controlling. She remembers her mother telling her that she hated her, that she wished she had never been born, that she wasn't good enough, or that she should be ashamed of this or that. During the frequent arguments between Roberta and her mother, Roberta's mother would throw things at her, frequently the family dishes. The mother also often argued with Roberta's father and during these arguments would throw things at him and then blame the argument on Roberta.

Of note is the history that Roberta's mother had an especially close relationship with her own mother, Roberta's grandmother. When Roberta's grandmother died, during Roberta's sixth grade of school, Roberta's mother tried to get closer to Roberta. She remembers resisting this but in some ways feels she is very dependent on her mother. Though she had moved away from home to go to college, she still talked to her mother on the phone three to four times a day. Roberta characterized those conversations as ones in which her mother is critical and controlling, telling her what she should do about this or that on a daily basis. Though Roberta experiences this as very negative, she fears that she is too dependent on her mother and is concerned about how well she is going to do when she marries and moves away to another state.

Her relationship with her father was much different. She described him as calm, peaceful, even-tempered, mellow, and reserved. He would stand up for her in conflict with her mother, but advised that she should do as he does with the mother—that is, try to avoid conflict and placate her if conflict arises. In general, Roberta felt that she had a good relationship with her father.

She has fond memories of interactions with her aunt's family across the street. Her aunt had children who were around her own age and who were her major playmates as she was growing up.

She was also close to the paternal grandmother next door but was especially close to her maternal grandmother. She recalls that after school each day, rather than riding the bus home, she would walk over to her grandmother's house. She has many positive memories of doing things with her grandmother (e.g., baking cookies, going to the park, etc.). She would return home in the evenings with her father, who worked in town. This grandmother died when Roberta was in sixth grade, and this loss was experienced as very significant to her. It is interesting that when describing her depression, she dated it back to sixth grade, though she did not initially make the connection between the onset of her depression and the death of her grandmother.

Grade school was generally a good time for her. She did well and had a circle of girlfriends. During one period she grew fast and was rather tall and skinny, and she got teased for her appearance. She, however, matured into an attractive young woman and was popular in high school. She had several girlfriends and boyfriends, got good grades, and was involved in a number of extracurricular activities such as student government, speech, debate, basketball, and an agricultural club.

She remembers that she strove to accomplish to please her parents. Her father was always complimentary. Her mother would initially be positive, but then when they got into their next fight, she would tell Roberta that her accomplishments meant nothing to her.

After high school she went to college. She also did well in college and was involved in a number of clubs and extracurricular activities. It was in college that she met her fiancé, whom she planned to marry after graduation.

I will briefly discuss issues of depression and dependency and then move on to discuss attachment patterns.

Depression

Roberta's chronic depression involves several factors.

Internalized self representation. Roberta's internalized self representation was cohesive but contained significant negative elements. This may relate to the internalization of some of her negative interactions with her mother in which her mother told her she hated Roberta, wished Roberta had never been born, or that Roberta was not good enough. The negative elements of her internalized self representation were manifest by her chronic negative feelings and low self-esteem. There were, however, significant positive elements of her internalized self representation. She could, for example, see herself as competent and accomplished in school. The positive aspects of herself may have been internalized from her positive relationship with her father, her grandmothers, her aunt, and cousins, as well as the positive aspects of her relationship with her mother.

Internalized other representations. Roberta's internalized other representation was complex. Again, she described several positive relationships that contributed to a positive other internalization (e.g., father, grandmothers, aunt, etc.). The loss of her grandmother in sixth grade was a significant loss for her, and it is this period to which she dates the onset of her depression. The loss of her grandmother may have led to the loss of significant amounts of internalized other representation. It certainly led to the loss of an ongoing sustaining, nurturing relationship for her.

Her relationship with her mother was very dichotomous as has been described—at times quite positive, at times intensely negative. This relationship led to the internalization of both some positive as well as significant negative elements into her internalized other representation. This negative element must have been very significant, as she often said, "I grew up feeling that no one loves me."

If we view her internalized self representations and internalized other representations, we find a sense of self with a fairly tenuous emotional balance. There are significant positive elements, but the amount of negative makes it difficult to maintain a positive emotional balance, and thus she is usually depressed.

Superego factors. The already precarious self-system balance is made worse by a superego that has significant punitive elements and a paucity of rewarding elements. Roberta talked of growing up always feeling blamed, always put down, always made to feel inferior. She can remember praise from her father and grandmother, but the predominant memories were the critical ones leading to an imbalance of punitive over rewarding superego, which further made it hard to maintain any positive emotional balance within the ego. Also, during arguments her mother would tell her that her accomplishments meant nothing. The internalization of such statements into the superego structure tends to negate any positive feelings she may have had about her accomplishments.

Id factors. Because of significant amounts of frustration during childhood, Roberta harbored much anger and aggression. When she was frustrated in the present, repression would break down, and the ego would be flooded. Her ego had limited ability to bind negative affect, and so any influx of negative affect had a very destabilizing effect on the system, making her more depressed.

Interpersonal relationships. Because of the tenuous affective balance within the ego and the tendency for it to be further imbalanced by superego and id forces, Roberta was quite dependent on external sources of positive affect to keep her in balance. Her boyfriend was a main source of this positive affect. She reported feeling good when things were going well between herself and her boyfriend. However, if things were not going well, she became depressed. These intra- and interpsychic factors that predisposed Roberta to depression are diagrammed in the accompanying figure 11.3.

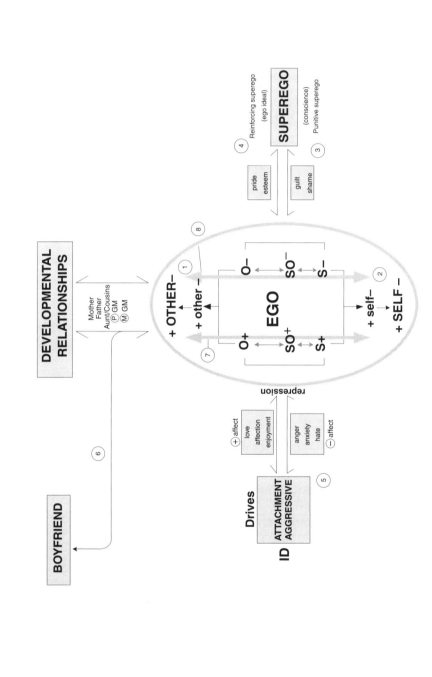

Figure 11.3. Attachment Patterns: Roberta

Roberta's internal emotional balance was somewhat tenuous due to the following:

1. Internalized other: Though there were significant positive internalizations (father, P GM, M GM, aunt), there was also a significant negative element to the internalized other representation as a result of some of the negative interactions with her mother.

2. Internalized self: While there were significant positive elements in her internalized self, there were also some negative elements (likely resulting from the negative interaction with her mother). There appears also to be an issue of dependency (i.e., an issue of failure of complete separation-individuation of the self into a mostly positive, cohesive structure, likely based on her mother's dependency on Roberta, which hampered separation and individuation).

3. Punitive superego: The internalization of criticism from others (especially mother) led to the development of a rather critical superego that served to destabilize her already tenuous emotional balance with the infusion of guilt and shame.

4. Rewarding superego: She did have a rewarding superego, which likely developed on the basis of reinforcement received from significant others. One problem, however, was her tendency to discount her accomplishments, as her mother often did during their arguments.

5. Id factors: Frustrating relationships may have led to significant anger and aggression, which she tried to repress. When the repression broke down, the anger and aggression flooded the ego, destabilizing her emotional balance and at times (as in her arguments with her boyfriend) leading to the acting out of that anger and aggression.

6. External supports: Because of her tenuous emotional balance, Roberta tended to rely on external supports such as her relationship with her boyfriend to maintain a positive emotional state.

   Attachment patterns: We might understand Roberta's relationship with her boyfriend in terms of attachment patterns (i.e., internalized self-other models of relating) (see text for more detail).

7. Positive attachment patterns: Roberta had learned positive attachment patterns (patterns associated with the expression of positive affect) via her relationship with her father, grandmother, aunt, and, at times, her mother.

8. Negative attachment patterns: She had also internalized some negative attachment patterns as a result of some of the angry, critical interactions with her mother.

With her boyfriend, she was able to interact on the basis of positive attachment patterns much of the time. When stressed, she quickly became anxious and in need of support. If her boyfriend was able to meet her needs, her emotional balance was restored and she became calm. If he was not able to meet her needs, she became frustrated and angry. This anger was expressed via the more negative, critical attachment pattern.

Note: The referenced numbers correspond with the numbers on the diagram.

Dependency

The previous discussion has already alluded to the fact that Roberta was quite dependent on external sources of nourishment in order to sustain herself. Another interesting aspect of her dependency was her relationship with her mother. Though she described frequent negative interactions, she talked with her on the phone three to four times per day. It appeared as if Roberta's mother was quite dependent on her. Recall how Roberta's mother tried to latch on to her after Roberta's grandmother (the mother's mother) died. Roberta also expressed the concern that she was not independent enough and feared how stable she would be when she moved out of state away from her mother. In part, her dependence is related to the imbalance of positive and negative representations as described earlier. This leaves her overly dependent on external relationships to maintain stability. In part the dependence may relate to the failure of the separation-individuation process in that she failed to individuate characteristics that she felt positive about (though she did have many positive characteristics). In part her dependence may be related to her mother's dependence. That is, she appears to have been given the message that she should not separate.

Attachment Patterns

Attachment patterns refer to internalized patterns of relating that have been set up in the ego between the internalized self and internalized other representations. Within the ego we develop an internalized sense of self and an internalized sense of other. An attachment pattern refers to the pattern of relating between self and other that has been learned throughout development. In development we may learn a number of different attachment patterns on the basis of the various significant relationships we have experienced. Attachment drive, along with various associated emotions, is expressed along one of these attachment patterns. The attachment pattern one uses may shift according to the circumstances. For example, someone may use a certain attachment pattern at work while interacting with superiors, another pattern with his or her spouse, and another pattern with friends. In addition, the attachment pattern may shift over time with the same person. For example, if things are going well in a relationship, one pattern may be used; if the relationship is stressed, another pattern may be used.

In Roberta's case, we can enumerate various attachment patterns based on her significant developmental relationships (figure 11.3). The attachment pattern that she described with her maternal grandmother was that of a fun-loving, eager-to-learn young girl and a nurturing, supportive grandmother. The problem with this pattern was that it ended when she was eleven years old. Her attachment pattern with her father was that of a successful, accomplished student and a rewarding, though somewhat uninvolved, father. Her attachment pattern with her mother was more complicated and shifted, sometimes rather rapidly, from one point in time to another. At times the relationship between them was close, though in the present at least Roberta feared that it was too close. That is, it seemed to Roberta that her mother was and wanted to be dependent on her, especially after the death of Roberta's grandmother. As stated earlier, Roberta resisted this closeness. A more age-appropriate attachment pattern would have been for Roberta to be dependent on her mother rather than the other way around.

The other predominant attachment pattern between Roberta and her mother was the more negative one described earlier where she and her mother would get into fights during which her mother would be verbally abusive and would throw things at Roberta. We might think of this as a pattern between an angry, critical mother and a weak, dependent child seeking approval. A problem for Roberta in her relationship with her boyfriend was that she tended to repeat this pattern with her fiancé. In her relationship with her fiancé, however, instead of being in the child role, she was in the mother role and would be verbally abusive to her fiancé and throw things at him. In fact, as Roberta described her relationship with her fiancé, it became apparent that she shifted into different attachment patterns at different times. At times when they were engaged in activities that they mutually enjoyed, she felt much as she did in her relationship with her maternal grandmother. At other times, if she felt stressed (as she did on several occasions during school), she enacted a pattern of an anxious, dependent person seeking approval. As long as her fiancé was able to meet her needs, she felt calm and reassured. If, however, he frustrated her needs, she rapidly became angry and shifted into her critical, abusive pattern. Roberta's shifts into this pattern were frequently quite abrupt. This may relate to a limited ability to tolerate frustration and a limited ability to control impulses and bind affect. That is, when frustrated she became angry. She was already, at baseline, repressing significant amounts of anger. The addition of some more anger made it difficult for her to continue the repression, and anger and aggression flooded her ego. This flooding of the ego may have been a result of not only the excess in anger but also a limited ability to repress impulses and affects. Once these entered the ego, Roberta had a limited ability to bind affects and impulses. In part this was a function of the intensity of the anger and aggression. In part it was a function of an ego that had a tenuous affective balance to begin with. As a result, the anger and aggression were expressed. In her relationship with her fiancé, the anger and aggression were expressed toward him using the same pattern that she had learned in her relationship with her mother.

Summary

This case presented Roberta's history, including that of her current problems and that of her developmental history. Her symptoms of depression along with the psychodynamic factors discussed make it clear that there are problems with the emotional balance of her sense of self. The main point of this chapter, however, is to illustrate how the attachment patterns she learned in development affect her current relationship with her boyfriend.

Ⓖ The goal of this case presentation is to further illustrate the concept of attachment patterns, especially as it applies to problems in interpersonal relationships. We shall discuss developmental relationships that occurred in the life of Suzanne, attempting to discern what attachment patterns she might have internalized as a result of those developmental relationships. We will then look at her adult relationships, trying to illustrate how attachment drives are expressed (repeated) along those attachment patterns, reversed along those attachment patterns, or repressed.

Suzanne is a twenty-eight-year-old single woman who worked for a museum in a large city, having recently completed a Ph.D. in art history. She came requesting help because she was dissatisfied with her relationships with men. Besides the relationship problems she also experienced self-doubt and low self-esteem and saw herself as clingy and needy. These latter sense of self problems, though present, were not pervasive, she did not suffer from chronic depression or anxiety, and in general, she was able to maintain a positive emotional balance, a sense of inner well-being. In the context of a relationship, this inner well-being might be toppled, and she would then experience episodic anxiety and depression.

In terms of relationships with men, she complained, "Men will not accept me for who I am." She was able to see herself in positive terms, as an intelligent, sensitive woman. She believed, however, that if she is herself, she won't be accepted. She felt subordinated by men and treated like an object. She believed that in a relationship with a man, it was her job to meet the man's needs, but she felt angered by this belief. On the other hand, she experienced feelings of guilt if she made her own needs known.

Suzanne began dating in high school and has had a series of relationships with men since then. Most of the relationships have lasted anywhere from a few months to a year. In these relationships she feels unaccepted for the person she is and subsequently angry and guilty. These feelings interfered with the development of emotional and physical intimacy in the relationships, and usually the man left her. She felt that part of the problem was likely related to the types of men she was picking—that they were men who had problems with closeness. At the same time, she believed that she had feelings within herself that were interfering with these relationships and that somehow these feelings were related to her earlier developmental relationships.

In terms of those developmental relationships, she described her dad as a very self-centered person. He was mostly interested in himself and his money and was not especially interested in other people, particularly women. He was always negative toward women and belittled women, including Suzanne and her mother, his wife. He saw Suzanne as an expense, a debit on his ledger sheet. He had always wanted a boy and made it known that he was unhappy with a daughter. Suzanne had a male cousin who lived nearby, and though her father spent no time with her, he would spend time with the cousin, taking him to sports events, and so on.

One somewhat extraordinary feature of Suzanne's family was that several generations back, a significant family fortune had been amassed. This had been handed down from generation to generation, and control of it now resided with Suzanne's grandmother. Suzanne remembers that throughout her childhood, her father frequently expressed concern about what was going to happen to the family fortune. He obviously wanted to gain control of it, and this seemed likely since he was an only child and the heir apparent. He seemed to fear that his mother would leave the money, or a portion of it, to a charity, and therefore spent much of his time catering to his mother so as to stay in her good graces. Suzanne believed that her father and grandmother had never gotten along and that he maintained a rather duplicitous relationship with her because of the issue of the inheritance; in her presence he was pleasant and polite and catered to her every desire; in her absence he denigrated her as he did all women.

Suzanne described her mother as a rather quiet, shy, passive woman who never questioned her husband but maintained a largely subservient relationship to him. She felt emotionally close to her mother but experienced her as somewhat overprotective. Suzanne believed that her mother was more protective of her than of her sister and that this protectiveness was related to the fact that Suzanne had experienced a childhood illness. Her mother tended to shelter and protect her for fear of recurrence of the illness.

Suzanne's mother and father were the two major adult figures she interacted with during her developmental years. She did not have significant interactions with any other relatives or adult figures in the home in these early years. Thus, much of what she learned about relationship patterns resulted from her interactions with her father and her mother and what she observed in the interactions between her mother and father. Let us examine these attachment patterns more closely in an attempt to understand why her current adult relationship patterns were problematic.

Let us define what appear to be the two major attachment patterns learned in her relationships with her father and mother. With her father, we might characterize the attachment pattern as one between a nonaccepting, rejecting father and a trying-to-please little girl. The affects associated with this pattern are anger at not being accepted and fear of future rejection. The predominant attachment pattern learned in Suzanne's relationship with her mother was that between an anxious, overprotective mother and a defective child. The associated affect is fear of engulfment.

Some quotes from Suzanne help us to understand more specifically how she experienced these relationships:

"I felt like my father didn't care for me; he was negative towards every aspect of me, my appearance, my sexuality, my personality. I am very angry at him; I have a ball of emotion inside of me that needs to be lanced."

"I tried to please my father so he would accept me; no matter what I did, he was rejecting."

"In relationships now I try to please men so I won't be rejected. I don't show them who I am for fear they won't accept that; I put my light under a bushel basket."

"When I'm not in a relationship, I'm able to feel like a mature, competent, adult woman. When I'm in a relationship I begin to fear rejection and develop self-doubt and low self-esteem and become dependent and clingy."

"I feel that if I am myself, an intelligent, successful woman, no one will accept me. To be myself is to be a spinster."

"I fear that if I am myself, I'll be rejected. So, I put on an act and get rejected anyway."

"I believe the rejection from my father got worse as I matured as a woman. He seemed to have a hard time with my emerging sexuality. I've never been able to enjoy sexual relationships with men; I never felt like it's a shared or equal experience. I end up feeling like an object."

"In relationships with men I expect that my role is to meet their needs; that makes me angry. I want to make my needs known but I end up feeling guilty about that."

"I felt that my mother loved me very much, but she was very protective of me. I had to struggle to gain some independence from her. Now I fear that if I do develop a close relationship, I will lose my individuality."

Let us now look at some of Suzanne's relationships in terms of the issues of attachment drives and attachment patterns. Previously we outlined three different possibilities: (1) one might repress attachment drives; (2) one might express attachment drives along established attachment patterns, repeating those patterns; or (3) one might express attachment patterns along established attachment patterns, reversing the roles so that one now assumes the role that the parent was in during development and puts the significant other in the role of the child.

Let's look more closely at these three patterns.

Repressing Attachment Drives

One option is to repress attachment drive altogether and not get involved in relationships. This, in general, was not a pattern that Suzanne used, though there were periods of time during which she did try to not get involved in relationships because of her negative experiences in relationships; she did not want to again experience the pain of a relationship.

Another way to deal with attachment drives, other than complete repression, would be to partially repress attachment drives. A person may do this and get involved in limited relationships. If she can limit the relationship, she can decrease the chance of getting hurt. Suzanne described two types of limited relationship. In one type she got involved with a man who lived in another city about three hundred miles away. They would see each other on weekends about once a month. She described that these weekend encounters would often be very pleasurable. The distance limited the possibility of getting hurt but also limited the growth of intimacy in the relationship.

We might call the previously described relationship a distance-limited relationship. Suzanne described another form of partial repression, a time-limited relationship. She once got involved with a foreign exchange student who was going to be studying at her university for only one quarter. The fact that the end of the relationship was dictated by a time that he had to return, rather than by his rejection of her, seemed helpful in decreasing anxiety.

Expressing Attachment Drives along Established Patterns

Expressing attachment drives along learned attachment patterns repeats the role relationships that were laid down in the development interactions with parental figures. We might consider three subsets of this mechanism:

1. Establish a relationship with someone who is like a developmental figure. In Suzanne's case, this meant getting involved with rather narcissistic men (like her father), trying to please them but ending up feeling subordinated and eventually rejected. Suzanne felt that there were many such narcissistic men in her field, and she described various relationships of this type.

2. A second subset of the repeat mechanism might be to establish a relationship with someone who really is not like a developmental figure, but experience them as if they were like the developmental figure. Suzanne described one such relationship like this in which, in retrospect, she believes the man was, in fact, caring and accepting, but she came to experience him as rejecting.

3. A third subset might be to repeat a relationship with someone like a developmental figure in an idealized manner. In this scenario one enters a relationship with someone who is like a developmental figure but experiences him or her in an idealized manner. Suzanne described relationships like this, which she called "Prince Charming" relationships, relationships in which

she fantasized that the man would meet all of her needs. The problem in these relationships was that there was obviously a discrepancy between her fantasy of what the man was like and the way they actually were. She even maintained the fantasy that her father would eventually change and become accepting, a fantasy that she eventually worked through so that she could view him in a more realistic manner.

Expressing Attachment Patterns along Established Patterns, with Role Reversal

The third mechanism mentioned was the reversal mechanism. In this mechanism, attachment drive is expressed along established attachment patterns with the roles reversed. The person is in the parental role and the significant other in the role that the child was in during development. Suzanne described one brief relationship like this with a younger man. In this relationship, she was in the dominant role and the man in the trying-to-please role.

We have discussed the previous mechanisms from the perspective of the attachment pattern that Suzanne had learned in her relationship with her father. The major anxiety associated with this pattern is the fear of rejection. The other attachment pattern was that learned in her relationship with her mother: the anxious, overprotective mother and the defective child. The anxiety associated with this pattern was the fear of engulfment. Suzanne did describe that there were periods of time in some of these relationships during which she felt secure; that is, the fear of rejection diminished. Unfortunately, at that point the fear of engulfment emerged, and she began to fear losing individuality.

The case of Suzanne has been presented with the goal of further illustrating the concept of attachment patterns learned in development and how those patterns have affected adult relationships. A diagrammatic representation of the case is presented in figure 11.4.

SUMMARY

This chapter has discussed disorders of interpersonal relationships. Via developmental interactions, a person internalizes various self-other attachment patterns. Numerous examples of attachment patterns were described. At-

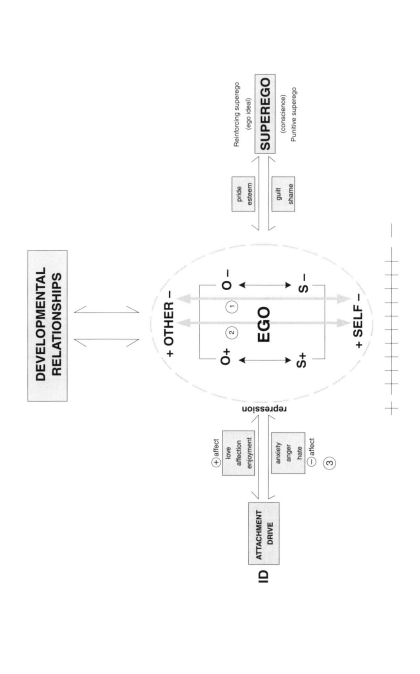

DEVELOPMENTAL RELATIONSHIPS

SUPEREGO

Reinforcing superego (ego ideal)

(conscience) Punitive superego

pride esteem

guilt shame

+ OTHER –

O –

S –

① EGO ②

O+

S+

+ SELF –

repression

(+) affect love affection enjoyment

anxiety anger hate (–) affect ③

ID ATTACHMENT DRIVE

Figure 11.4. Attachment Patterns: Suzanne

The two bold arrows represent the two major self-other attachment patterns that Suzanne learned:

1. One attachment pattern, based on her relationship with her father, was between a nonaccepting, rejecting other and a trying-to-please self. The emotions associated with this pattern were anger and fear of rejection. In the text I described how attachment drive in conjunction with this attachment pattern might be repressed, repeated, or reversed.

2. A second attachment pattern, based on her relationship with her mother, was between an anxious, overprotective mother and a defective self. The emotion experienced with the attachment pattern was fear of engulfment.

3. A problem with both of these attachment patterns is that they are associated with negative emotions. Note: The referenced numbers correspond with the numbers on the diagram.

tachment drive may be expressed along an internalized attachment pattern either by repeating the original self-other attachment pattern or by reversing the roles of self and other. Alternatively, if expression of attachment drive along a certain attachment pattern is associated with significant negative affect, then attachment drive may be repressed, leading to an avoidant interpersonal style. Two cases were discussed to illustrate the previous concepts.

┌─────────┐
│   │
│   12   │
│   │
└─────────┘

Combined Problems with Self & Relationships

Having discussed problems with sense of self (chapter 10) and problems with interpersonal relationships (chapter 11), I now turn to a
discussion of both of these problems together. In reality, most people present with problems in both areas. This discussion will occur in the
context of the presentation of a clinical case.

CLINICAL PRESENTATION: STEPHANIE

Stephanie is a single, white professional woman in her mid-thirties who
came in requesting help with relationships. She had just terminated a relationship with a man she had been dating for about nine months; she was beginning to wonder if a relationship would ever work out for her. She was
concerned especially because she hoped to eventually have a family but saw
time as running out.

⟳ Stephanie reported a history of a troubled childhood that left her with many
feelings of insecurity and inferiority. In her late teens and twenties, she had been
involved in a series of relationships with men that she characterized as "dependent." She felt so insecure that she needed to have someone with her to establish a
sense of well-being. She was frequently left in these relationships and often told
that she was too clingy and needy.

As a result, Stephanie went into therapy for a number of years during her
twenties. She found the therapy very helpful in improving her self-esteem. During that time, she completed college and obtained a master's degree. For the last

three years, she has worked in a job that she finds very fulfilling; she is quite satisfied with the career aspect of her life.

Relationships, however, are another matter. Stephanie felt that the association between anxiety and a relationship had reversed as she had come to feel better about herself as a person. Whereas in the past, she felt anxious if she was not in a relationship, now she felt anxious when she was in a relationship and more secure if she was not. She described that previously she feared rejection and being alone. Now, in more recent relationships, the fear is more that she'll lose her individuality. Because of this fear, she believes that she often precipitates arguments that create distance and hamper closeness in the relationships.

Besides her fear of losing her identity, her other anxiety is around sexuality. She described that she usually didn't enjoy sexual intercourse, often found herself crying during it, and usually felt guilty afterward.

Her most recent boyfriend was a white male approximately her own age whom she had met at church and who was thus of the same religion. This boyfriend was different from most of her previous boyfriends, as will be described later. He was quite attracted to her and wanted to spend much time with her. While there were many things about him that she found attractive, she found it hard to invest in him emotionally. She experienced his desire to spend time with her as intrusive and controlling and again began to experience fears of losing her autonomy. In retrospect, while she believes that in reality there was a controlling element in him, it was not as great as she experienced it. The more he pursued her, the more distant she became until the relationship eventually terminated.

Still, despite the fact that this relationship did not work out, Stephanie did feel that there were some positive aspects of the experience. She had picked a man this time with whom she had several things in common; they were of the same race and religion, approximately the same age, shared common recreational interests, and were at about the same level professionally.

As alluded to previously, this type of boyfriend was atypical. She said that picking boyfriends such as described earlier would have caused her much anxiety in the past because they resembled people from her developmental past with whom she had had negative experiences. Most of her previous boyfriends were of different races, ethnic backgrounds, and religions. A couple of them were married to other women. Most of them had some problems in their lives: unsteady jobs, drugs, alcohol, legal problems. Some of them were emotionally abusive, but none were physically abusive.

She generally experienced these men as very controlling but in her younger years clung to these relationships for fear of being alone. In more recent years, she has been more able to terminate these types of relationships and is hoping to seek better object choices. One of the problems in these relationships was that she had very little in common with these men. Besides the fact that she was avoiding a relationship with a man more similar to her, the one bond she felt in these relationships was that these men often come from troubled backgrounds as she had. She recalled one other time in the past dating a man who was similar to her in age, race, and religion and who came from a stable family. While there was a part of her that wanted to marry this man so as to experience the stable family she never had, there was another part of her that had a hard time feeling a kinship with him and his background. She ended up feeling unworthy in the relationship and developed a sense that she didn't deserve to be part of this family.

At the present time, Stephanie was requesting help with her ability to form a lasting relationship. As noted previously, she had been in therapy in her twenties and found it helpful. Prior to that time, she had problems with anxiety and depression, which she felt has improved significantly. She was hoping to achieve similar results in the area of interpersonal relationships.

Besides the past history of psychotherapy treatment, there was no other past psychiatric history, no history of alcohol or drug abuse, and no formal family psychiatric history of diagnosis or treatment. She was physically healthy at the time of presentation and had no history of significant health problems. She worked for a large firm in a professional position and was quite satisfied with that. She belonged to a church and attended several church functions. Since breaking up with the previously mentioned boyfriend, she had not established a new relationship with a man. She did have one close girlfriend, whom she had known for a number of years.

In terms of developmental history, Stephanie grew up in a family that consisted of her parents, an older brother, an older sister, and a younger brother. The family moved often due to her father's work instability, and by the time she graduated high school, the family had lived in four different states. She recalls frequently being the new kid in school and feeling like she didn't fit in. Despite this, she always did well academically.

She felt that there was little closeness, little nurturing in the family, little in the line of good relationships in the family. As a result, she often turned to animals as companions and to this day keeps several cats and dogs at her home. She stated that there were so many restrictions at home that "being at home was like being in a prison." She summarized her childhood as "a nightmare I couldn't get out of." Let us take a little closer look at her developmental relationships to see why she reacted so negatively to her childhood.

She described her father as tyrannical, authoritarian, chauvinistic, controlling, emotionally labile, critical, verbally abusive, angry, demanding, mean, and hurtful. He was physically abusive toward her mother and brothers but not toward her or her sister. She remembered scenes of him physically beating up the boys, scenes of him holding a handgun to her mother's head, or threatening the whole family with a shotgun. She had no memories of sexual abuse in relation to her father.

He ruled the home with an iron fist. When she was in grade school, he became ill and was placed on disability. This meant he was around home most of the time and led to his increasing domination of everyone in the family. He was very strict. The children were not allowed to make or receive phone calls, to have friends over, or to go over to friend's houses. The children were made to dress in very conservative clothes that were not in style. Extracurricular school activities were not allowed. Once, Stephanie was chosen as a high school cheerleader; she had to turn down the opportunity, as her father would not allow it. She was not allowed to date until she was eighteen. Stephanie recalled going out on her first date at age eighteen with a boy her father picked. When they came back a few minutes past the proscribed time, her father was out in the driveway threatening the boy and his family.

Stephanie's feelings as a result of the relationship were "diminished, unsubstantial, dirty, guilty, ashamed, inferior, less, than. He totally dominated everyone. You couldn't have any autonomy or independence. The only escape was to retreat to my room or out back with the animals." Stephanie's feelings toward her father now include anger, sadness, and resentment. The major feeling as a child was numbness.

The one memory that contradicted the preceding was the memory of the sporadic occasions when her father would rather suddenly seem to change and want everybody in the family to be loving. He would gather everyone around him and hug them and tell them he loved them. Stephanie learned, however, that this mood was always short-lived and in a little while he would revert to his old way of being. To this day, Stephanie has a hard time trusting someone who is nice to her; it is hard to believe that it is genuine or that it will last.

Stephanie's relationship with her mother was more positive; she recalls her mother as kind and loving. Her mother worked, however, to try to help support the family; she often worked evenings, and so frequently wasn't around. This left the children at home with the father. When she was home, there were frequent fights between her parents. Her mother's approach to these conflicts was to be compromising and to try to please him.

Stephanie feels that she has tended to do this in her relationships with men, try to please them. This leads to anger and resentment because she never expresses or gets her needs met. This has been especially problematic in the area of sexual relationships. She will get involved in a sexual relationship with a man because she believes that's what he wants even though it is not what she wants. She ends up frustrated with feelings of resentment.

Stephanie did describe some feelings of resentment toward her mother; this related to the fact that she kept them in the abusive relationship with her father and didn't do anything to protect them or get them out of it. Her mother always said, "Things will get better." Stephanie described staying in bad relationships longer than she would have because she clung to this hope that "things will get better."

The relationship between Stephanie's father and mother was an abusive one. Several of Stephanie's relationships with men were at least verbally and emotionally abusive. She wondered if there was any hope for a better relationship and noted, quite appropriately, that she had no model for a happy relationship.

The other significant relationship to describe is that with her older brother. She was not particularly close to her sister or younger brother, but described her older brother as kind, understanding, empathetic. He was someone whom she could talk to, who would do things with her, and who would stick up for her in conflicts with the father (sometimes to the point where the father would beat him up). He is the one person she felt close to as a child.

However, when she was about ten and he eighteen, her brother engaged her in some sexual exploration. No sexual intercourse took place, but there was mutual touching. She described very mixed and confused feelings of anger, anxiety, enjoyment, and guilt over these episodes. To the present, she has been plagued by disturbing nightmares of these episodes. She still has very mixed, confused feelings toward her brother over these episodes, especially since even after these episodes, he continued to be her friend, confidant, and protector. Here was the one person she felt so close to, and now she also had some very negative feelings toward him. Now, in adult relationships with men, it is hard to experience feelings of closeness without also experiencing the feelings of anger, anxiety, and guilt. This is especially true when the relationship with a man progresses to the point of becoming sexual. Besides the mixed feelings, her relationship with her brother has also raised significant issues of trust. "How could I trust him after he had violated me in such an intimate manner; how can I trust any man now?"

To round out the history, I will add that after high school, Stephanie received a scholarship and was allowed to leave home to attend a Christian junior college. She did well and graduated with an AA degree in two years. For the next ten years, she attended a university part-time and worked part-time, eventually obtaining a bachelor's degree and subsequently a master's degree. During this time, she had experienced periods of anxiety and depression and was involved in some of her more chaotic relationships. It was also during this time that she received the therapy that she believed was helpful in bring some emotional stability to her life.

This is an interesting case to discuss from the perspective of both the issue of sense of self and the issue of interpersonal relationships. If we look at Stephanie as she described herself in her twenties before her first therapy, she appeared to be having difficulty in both of these areas. She described very problematic relationships, frequent periods of anxiety and depression, and an inability to develop a sense of emotional well-being unless she was in a relationship. After her first therapy, she reported feeling much more emotionally stable, autonomous, and independent. She no longer needed a relationship to establish and maintain her emotional equilibrium. She still had problems with interpersonal relationships and now, in fact, felt more stable outside of a relationship than inside.

It appears that her therapy had been helpful for her in developing a more emotionally stable, independent sense of self. How did this happen? It seems this occurred in part because she was able to resolve some of the negative feelings she had about developmental figures in the past and to build up positive feelings about herself in the present. As she progressed through school and entered a profession, she took significant steps in the separation-individuation process and consolidated a more positive, independent, cohesive sense of self. She did not appear to have internalized effective models for healthy interpersonal relationships and so continued to function on the basis of maladaptive attachment patterns. These maladaptive attachment patterns carried with them significant negative affect, and so, when she would enter a relationship along one of these patterns, the stimulation of negative affect associated with this pattern would serve to dysregulate the emotional stability of her sense of self. Let us look at these two issues of sense of self and inter-personal relationships in more detail.

Sense of Self

I will begin with a discussion of id, ego, and superego forces that are relevant to this issue of sense of self. As I do that, I will discuss how those id, ego, and superego forces changed over time so that Stephanie could change from a person who had a fairly emotionally unstable sense of self to a person with a more stable sense of self (i.e., from a person with a negative emotional balance to a person with a positive emotional balance).

Ego Factors

I will start out looking at internalized self and other representations as they developed as a result of interactions with significant others in her childhood. I have already described the very negative interactions with her father. He frequently referred to her as "You little bitch!" Clearly the self and other in-teractions resulting from these interactions would both be rather negative. Her interaction with her mother had many positive elements. Unfortunately, her mother was frequently away at work, and so there was a significant sense of being abandoned and unprotected in this relationship. We might hypoth-esize the introjection of positive self and other representations from the inter-actions with the mother when she was present but the internalization of nega-tive representations as a result of the times when she was away. Her relationship with her brother had many positive elements but was contami-nated by the sexual aspects of this relationship. This relationship also likely resulted in the introjection of both some positive and some negative self and other representations.

Where does this leave us, then, in terms of the balance between positive and negative self and other representations? It would appear as if we have some positive representations but also a significant quantum of negative rep-resentations to deal with. Where does this leave us in terms of the separa-tion-individuation process? It has left us somewhere short of completion of that process. That is, as a result of development and before her therapy, Stephanie had not consolidated a mostly positive cohesive sense of self and other (see figure 12.1). Where, then, is she at this point along the separa-

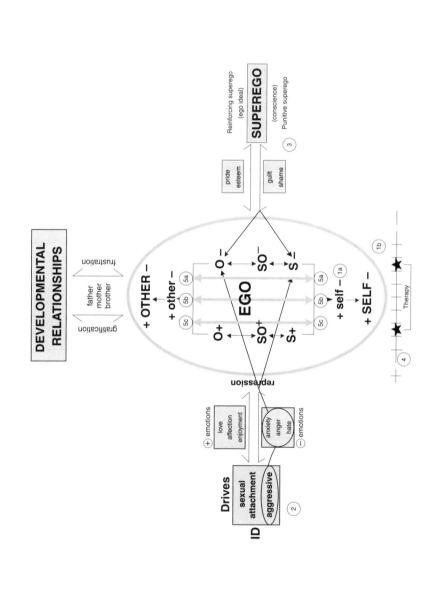

DEVELOPMENTAL RELATIONSHIPS

frustration

gratification

father
mother
brother

SUPEREGO

Reinforcing superego
(ego ideal)

(conscience)
Punitive superego

3

pride
esteem

guilt
shame

O⁻   SO⁻   S⁻

+ OTHER −

+ other −

5a   5b   5c

EGO

5a   5b   5c

+ self −

+ SELF −

1a

O⁺   SO⁺   S⁺

1b

Therapy

4

repression

+ emotions

love
affection
enjoyment

anxiety
anger
hate

− emotions

Drives

sexual
attachment

aggressive

ID

2

Figure 12.1. Stephanie: Issues of Sense of Self and Interpersonal Relationships

SENSE OF SELF

1. As a result of the negative aspects of developmental relationships, Stephanie had internalized significant negative self and other representations, leaving her at the depressive level (1a) with a negative emotional balance (1b) and an inability to take the next step toward the formation of a cohesive positive sense of self and other.

2. Aggression and negative emotions from the id could, when stimulated further, destabilize her emotional balance.

3. Similarly, the critical aspects of the superego could induce shame and/or guilt and still further destabilize her emotional balance.

4. Therapy helped her deal with her balance of positive/negative representations, her anger and aggression, as well as her tendency to be self-critical. As a result, she was much more able to maintain a positive emotional balance.

INTERPERSONAL RELATIONSHIPS

5. We can understand some of Stephanie's problems with interpersonal relationships by understanding some of the predominant attachment patterns she learned during her developmental years.

   a. Father pattern: Controlling, critical, abusive other interacting with a frightened, inferior self. The emotions associated with this pattern were anger and anxiety. If she repeated this pattern in relating to a man, the anxiety and anger that were evoked would have a destabilizing effect on her emotional balance. She might deal with this by repressing attachment and stopping the relationship.

   b. Mother pattern: Nurturing, but compromising and often absent other interacting with a loved, but unprotected self. The emotions associated with this relationship were mixed feelings of affection and resentment. If operating on this pattern in a relationship, Stephanie would tend to be compromising and meet the man's needs but not get her own needs met. The mixed feelings of affection and resentment would come up, making it hard to maintain a meaningful relationship.

   c. Brother pattern: Nurturing but inappropriately sexual other interacting with a nurtured but violated self. Again, there were mixed feelings associated with this pattern, including love and affection on the one hand, but also anger, anxiety, repulsion, and guilt on the other hand. This caused problems in relationships with men, especially as those relationships became more intimate. It was hard to feel positive emotions toward the man without also feeling negative emotions.

Note: The referenced numbers correspond with the numbers on the diagram.

tion-individuation continuum? It would seem that she's at a point we've called the depressive position, the step prior to the consolidation of a healthy sense of self and other. She does not appear at the less separated borderline position because we do not see the typical defenses (splitting, projective identification, etc.) characteristic of the borderline level of development.

Id Factors

I now turn to a discussion of id factors pertinent to her sense of self. The major factor to point out here is the anger, aggression, and resentment that would have been stimulated as a result of her frustrations in her relationships with her father, mother, and brother. One hypothesis is that to the degree possible, she dealt with this by repression, but if the repression broke down, negative affects such as anger could enter the ego, further destabilizing it. I will reserve a further discussion of other id factors, attachment drives, sexual drives, and positive emotions until later.

Superego Factors

If we look at what sort of rewarding/punitive superego balance would have been internalized on the basis of Stephanie's development relationships, we would likely conclude that there were significant punitive elements within her superego. The constant criticism from her father would have been a major factor leading to the internalization of a punitive superego. There may have been some more reinforcing elements derived from her interactions with her mother and brother.

Summary

In summary, then, we find a person with a rather tenuous emotional balance within her ego. That ego is poised between an angry, aggressive id and a punitive, guilt-inducing superego that may further destabilize it at any time. Thus, again, there was a paucity of inner mechanisms to maintain any sense of inner well-being. How did Stephanie deal with this? As a child she described withdrawal as one mechanism. She would retreat to her room and be alone. This would at least prevent the influx of more negative emotions from, for example, interactions with her father. She also described that sometimes she would "go numb" and not feel anything. This might be effective in stabilizing the ego if what gets numbed out are any potential negative inputs, either from her father, her angry id, or her guilt-inducing superego. Another mechanism she described was her interactions with her animals. "A dog will love you unconditionally," she said. These interactions, as opposed to her human interactions, allowed for the generation of positive emotional influx.

When she left home, a major mechanism by which she tried to stabilize herself was via the formation of relationships, with the hope that this would lead to the influx of positive emotion. Because she did not possess any positive patterns for interpersonal relationships, this mechanism, more often than not, led to further frustration, which led to destabilization of her emotional balance in two ways: (1) there was the negative emotional influx from the frustrating relationship itself, and (2) the stress of the current relationship would frequently lead to a breakdown of repression, which would then precipitate the influx of anger and aggression from past relationships.

Because of her unhappiness, Stephanie, in her twenties, got into therapy and seemed to work through some of these issues and develop a state of greater emotional well-being. When she began therapy she described herself with the following terms: "Irritable, agitated, angry, critical, judgmental, anxious, scared, uncertain, sensitive, inferior, a failure." After the therapy, she was able to see herself in a much more positive light. Some of the words she used included the following: "kind, generous, loving, happy, secure, accepted, considerate, thoughtful, friendly, caring, sincere, worthwhile, confident, and trustworthy."

How did this change come about. Referring to figure 12.1, I will discuss this in terms of changes in id, ego, and superego factors. Starting with ego factors, Stephanie felt that the therapy had helped her deal with some of the negative conscious feelings she had about her mother, father, and brother. That is, it helped her decrease negative representations. She also became more able to look at positive aspects of herself and, as she went through school, to add new positive aspects of herself that she felt good about. Thus, along with decreasing negative representations, she also increased positive representations and seemed to get to the point of developing a more positive balance of representations so that she could take the next step in the separation-individuation process and develop a healthier internalized sense of self and other (move from the depressive position to a more positive cohesive position).

In terms of id factors, as she spoke more of her early development, she became more aware of repressed angry feelings and was able to express them and work through them and thus discharge much of the anger and aggression that previously had been able to destabilize her ego anytime the repression broke down. In addition, besides decreasing her tendency to trigger anger from the id, she began to develop means to stimulate positive emotions from the id. She enjoyed her work and her church activities. The positive emotion, enjoyment, from these activities infused the ego and helped maintain a healthier emotional balance.

Finally, the therapy seemed to help her modify her superego functions so that she could be more rewarding and less critical. Thus, for example, she not only enjoyed her work but was proud of it. This increased ability of the superego to infuse the ego with pride, as opposed to guilt, certainly also helped in the maintenance of a more positive emotional equilibrium.

What seemed to change in therapy was (1) the balance of positive over negative representations within the ego, (2) the ability to stimulate positive over negative emotions within the id, and (3) the shift from a more punitive to a more rewarding superego. The result was a more positively balanced ego along with an id and superego that had significant potential to infuse positive emotion to further stabilize the ego. As a consequence, Stephanie was a happier, healthier person; her therapy had helped her deal with her sense of self problem.

Interpersonal Relationships

Stephanie left her therapy because she graduated from college and received a very good job offer in a distant city. Once she moved, she felt happy with herself and content in her work. Relationships with men, however, did not go so well. She believed she was picking healthier, more appropriate men to relate to, but somehow these relationships did not seem to be working out. Three years after ending her therapy, she decided it was time to see if therapy could help her with her problems in interpersonal relationships. To try to understand this problem with interpersonal relationships, let us look at the patterns of attachment that likely were internalized as a result of her interactions with her father, mother, and brother.

Father

The predominant pattern with her father was between a controlling, critical, abusive other and a frightened, inferior self. Significant feelings of anxiety and anger were associated with this pattern, along with significant fears of both rejection and engulfment.

This pattern was repeated many times in relationships with men. In her twenties, she described relationships with men who in fact appeared to be quite controlling. Even though these relationships would trigger much anxiety and anger, she would stay in them for fear of rejection (which meant being alone).

In recent years, she felt that the men she picked were less controlling but that she still tended to experience them as controlling. Her major fear now was loss of her hard-won autonomy and independence. Thus, any sense of control in a relationship triggered negative feelings which she often dealt with by repressing attachment drive and stopping the relationship. This repression of the attachment drive shut off any emotional investment in the relationship and stifled the growth of the relationship. Thus the attachment pattern that she learned from her father was not useful in forming healthy adult relationships with men.

Mother

The two aspects of relating that I previously discussed with respect to Stephanie's mother were her tendency to be compromising and pleasing in relationships and her tendency to believe that "things will get better." These two aspects of relating were characteristic of Stephanie's earlier relationships, but were not particularly helpful in the formation of healthy relationships. Increasingly she held (1) the belief that she should not be the only one doing the pleasing in a relationship (i.e., there should be mutuality) and (2) the belief that things will get better did not necessarily always apply to relationships.

Brother

As already mentioned, Stephanie's relationship with her brother was mixed. There were many positive aspects to the relationship, at least early on. It was a relationship between a nurturing father figure and a young girl in need of nurturance. This relationship was, however, tainted by the sexual involvement. Had it not been for that, her relationship with her brother might have provided a model for healthy relationships. As it was, it provided a conflicted model. In recent years, Stephanie did seem to be picking healthier, less controlling men with whom she had more in common and with whom she shared activities and ideas in conversation. These relationships often went well in the early stages, but as soon as they started to become sexual, the positive feelings Stephanie had toward the man turned to anxiety and anger. At that point, she seemed to shut off further emotional investment (repress attachment drive), thus stifling the relationship. In these relationships, she appeared to be operating on a pattern derived from her relationship with her brother. She was unable to invest the relationship with positive emotion without the relationship also stimulating significant negative emotion.

Interestingly, Stephanie described that she, over the years, has often had male friends. In some ways, as she described these men, they seemed like some of her healthier object choices. She often felt quite close to these men but did not become sexually involved with them. Thus, as long as the relationships remained platonic (as a relationship with a brother should and as her early relationship with her brother had been), she was able to invest in the relationship in an emotionally positive manner.

She was feeling, however, that it was the time in her life to try to develop relationships that might be able to combine the elements of friendship and companionship as well as sexual and emotional intimacy. The brother pattern of relating was not helpful in this regard.

She had via her first therapy gotten to the point of feeling significantly better about herself as a person. She now wanted to deal with the issue of interpersonal relationships. She realized that relationships were not working out because getting close emotionally brought up lots of negative feelings such as anxiety and anger. Neither the father, mother, nor brother patterns of relating were adequate patterns for forming a healthy adult relationship. The goal of the second therapy became to identify the attachment patterns that were not working for her, work through the negative emotions associated with those patterns, and then move on to learn new attachment patterns associated with more positive affects.

SUMMARY

The goal of this chapter has been to present a case and discuss issues of sense of self (the emotional balance of the inner world) and issues of relating to others in a person's outer world. I have attempted to describe how these problems evolve throughout early development and how they manifest in adulthood. The next question is how to help a person with these problems, and so now we turn to part III of the book and discuss treatment.

☙ III ❧

Psychotherapy

Part III focuses primarily on psychotherapy. Chapter 13 discusses the process of taking a history that can lead both to a descriptive *DSM-IV-TR* diagnosis and to a psychodynamic formulation. The second half of this chapter goes over treatment. Treatment of a descriptive diagnosis is discussed briefly, and then psychotherapy is discussed in more detail. Both general and specific psychotherapeutic techniques are described. Examples of general interventions include empathy, experiencing, and explanation. Specific interventions include those aimed at (1) helping a person improve the affective balance within his or her sense of self, (2) helping a person develop healthier patterns of relating to others, (3) helping a person with any existing issues of adult development, and (4) helping a person with any cultural, religious, or spiritual conflicts that may be present.

The remainder of the chapters in part III present clinical cases and discuss the therapy of the various types of problems described above. Chapter 14, Bob, discusses the treatment of a person presenting with symptoms of anxiety and difficulty in interpersonal relationships. Gwen, in chapter 15, presented with depression, psycho-physiological symptoms, problems with sense of self, and relationship difficulties, as well as issues related to her phase of adult development and her religious beliefs. Terry, in chapter 16, presented with symptoms of anxiety and dissociation as well as problems with her sense of self and difficulty in relationships. Finally, chapter 17 presents the treatment of Rosilyn, who came in with multiple symptoms as well as issues related to sense of self, relationships, adult development, and spiritual beliefs. The goal in each clinical presentation is to illustrate the use of the psychotherapeutic techniques outlined in chapter 13.

13

History, Diagnosis & Treatment

The goal of this chapter is to attempt to illustrate how the previously outlined concepts of psychodynamics and development can be used in psychotherapy. The goal is not to provide a detailed and comprehensive discussion of all aspects of psychotherapy; for that type of presentation, please see Malan (1979), Sifneos (1979), Basch (1980, 1988, 1995), and Kernberg et al. (1989).

An underlying assumption of this discussion is that currently, most therapy is once a week and short-term. Certainly more long-term and more in-depth therapies may achieve more thorough and long-lasting results. Unfortunately, these more comprehensive therapies are not available to most people. As a result, our discussion will focus on therapy that is once a week for approximately ten to twenty-five sessions.

HISTORY

We begin with a thorough history and examination including the history of the person's current problems, symptoms and situation, any past psychological history, history of psychological problems in the family, alcohol and drug history, medical history, social history, mental status exam, and, where applicable, physical exam and laboratory/radiologic evaluation. The goal of the above assessment is to arrive at a *DSM-IV* diagnosis. A *DSM-IV* diagnosis is a descriptive diagnosis, a diagnosis of a particular symptomatic syndrome that may be manifest in a person (e.g., an anxiety disorder, depressive disorder, psychotic disorder, substance abuse disorder, eating disorder, etc.).

This level of diagnosis may lead us to a very specific treatment for our patient's problem (e.g., medication for a depressive disorder, desensitization for post-traumatic stress disorder, a twelve-step program for alcoholism, behavioral therapy for bulimia). A *DSM-IV* diagnosis, however, does not tell us anything about the person's underlying psychodynamics. If psychodynamic psychotherapy is to be considered, we must obtain additional history that will allow us to formulate the psychodynamic issues that are in need of treatment; to do this we obtain a developmental history.

The type of developmental history described here is one that aims at understanding the development of the inner world of the self (ego strength, affect balance within the ego, dynamic interactions between the id, ego, and superego), as well as the development of a person's ability to relate to others (what attachment patterns does a person have in his or her repertoire, are they functional or dysfunctional, does he or she repeat these patterns, reverse them, or repress interacting with others). We will also be interested in how development of the self and his or her ability to relate to others progresses across the various phases of the life cycle from childhood through adulthood. Some of the questions that can be used to generate a discussion of a person's development are listed next.

Early Family

1. Where are you from? Did you grow up in the same place? Did you move frequently? If so, how did you adapt to these moves? Were they major sources of stress, or were they interesting adventures?

2. What was the makeup of your nuclear family (i.e., parents, siblings)? What words would you use to describe your mother, your father, brother, sister, etc.? How would you describe your relationship with your mother, your father, brother, sister, etc.? Was this a stable family, a happy family? Did your parents get along, were there separations, divorces? Were there stepparents, step-siblings, half-siblings present in the family? How would you describe them and your relationship with them?

3. Were there extended family members—grandparents, aunts, uncles, cousins— present in your life as you were growing up? Were you particularly close to any of them, or did you have particular problems

with any of them? Did the extended family get along with your nuclear family, or were there conflicts?

4. Did you experience any losses of key family members?

Elementary School Years

1. How did school go for you in general? What sort of grades did you get? Were you involved in extracurricular activities, clubs, organizations within the school or outside the school (religious/scouts, etc.)?
2. How did relationships go for you, with teachers, with peers? Did you have a circle of friends, a best friend? Did you do things with friends outside of school?
3. Were there any major stresses that occurred in your life during these years— divorce, death in family, move to new city, etc.?

High School Years

1. Again, in terms of your self-development, how did things go in school in both academics and extracurricular activities? If you were involved in activities outside the school, how did those work out?
2. How did relationships go during the high school years—with family, friends, teachers, and other authority figures? Asking about relationships with members of the opposite sex is important: Did you begin to date? Did you have a steady boyfriend or girlfriend? How long did these relationships last? Were any of these relationships sexual relationships; if so, how did that go? How did you feel about yourself as a sexual person (i.e., your sexual identity)?
3. Again, did you experience any major stresses or traumatic events during these years?

College Years

1. In addition to asking about academics and extracurricular activities, we should ask the following questions: Have you considered a career path, a vital interest in life, an activity that you find both enjoyable and

rewarding? In addition to a career path, have you maintained or developed recreational interests that stimulate pleasurable affects?

2. In terms of relationships, besides those with family, friends, peers, colleagues, and superiors, we are interested in monitoring the development of intimacy in relationships: Have your significant other relationships become closer and more long-lasting? Have you found a partner to whom you are going to make a commitment of a lifelong relationship?

3. Did you experience any major stresses, losses, or traumas during these years?

Early Adult Years (Beyond College, Approximately Age Twenty to Forty)

1. In terms of self-development, has your chosen career path worked out? Is it enjoyable and rewarding? Did this turn out to be the wrong direction? Have you switched directions? Have you been able to maintain recreational interests outside of work?

2. In terms of relationships, have you been able to develop a major significant other relationship? How is that going? Do you have children? How are you adjusting to the role of parenthood? How are your relationships outside the immediate family going?

3. Did you experience any major stresses, losses, or traumas during these years?

Middle Adult Years (Age Forty to Sixty)

1. How has your career direction worked out? Have you continued to evolve within the context of that career? Is it still rewarding, fulfilling? Have you stagnated in your career? Have you switched to another career path? Do you have some fulfilling recreational interests?

2. How are relationships going with your significant other, children, family, peers, colleagues, superiors, and friends? Have you experienced any major losses of relationship (i.e., divorce, death of parent)? Are there any significant new relationships in your life?

3. Did you experience any major stresses or trauma during these years?

Late Adult Years (Age Sixty to Eighty)

1. Have you retired from your career, or have you continued in some capacity? If you have retired, have you found some new vital interest(s) in your life?
2. What is the status of relationships with spouse, parents, children, grandchildren, peers, and colleagues? Have relationships continued, or have there been losses, breakups, estrangements?
3. Did you experience any major stresses or trauma during these years?

In summary, we seek to understand how things have gone in each major life period with respect to the development of sense of self and also relationships.

DIAGNOSIS

Descriptive Diagnosis from DSM-IV

As stated previously, our evaluation may lead us to a *DSM-IV* diagnosis and to a specific treatment that is associated with that diagnosis (exhibit 13.1).

Psychodynamic Formulation

Our expanded evaluation with a developmental history may lead us to underlying psychodynamic issues that could be addressed via psychodynamic psychotherapy. We will want to put the information we have gathered into a psychodynamic formulation. A psychodynamic formulation is a summary of the underlying psychological makeup of an individual. We tend to focus on those psychological issues that are problematic, but we should also look at a person's psychological strengths.

We will begin to develop a psychological formulation by asking four basic questions: (1) How can we describe the inner psychological world of this person? (2) How does this person with this psychological makeup relate to others in the world around him or her? (3) Besides whatever issues this person may be dealing with as a result of his or her early development, is this person grappling with issues from adult developmental phases? (4) Are there specific cultural, religious, or spiritual issues that may be unique to the person and which we need to understand in order to understand this per-

---

Exhibit 13.1 Diagnosis

I. Descriptive diagnosis

Is there a *DSM-IV* diagnosis present?

II. Psychodynamic formulation

A. How can we describe the inner psychological world of this person?

1. Ego development

a. What is the degree of separation-individuation within the ego?

b. Describe this person's internalized self representation

c. Describe this person's internalized other representation

d. What is the level of affective balance within the ego?

2. Superego development

a. Does this person have a rewarding superego that can help him or her experience pride and esteem?

b. Is there an ego ideal that helps him or her set realistic goals?

c. Does the punitive superego induce excessive amounts of guilt and shame?

d. Is this person's conscience consistent with his or her sociocultural environment?

3. Id development (drives and affects)

a. What are the affects associated with the expression of attachment and assertive drives?

b. To what extent are these drives and affects expressed or repressed?

c. How do these drives affect the affective balance of the ego?

B. How does this person with this psychological makeup relate to others in the world around him or her?

1. What are the attachment patterns that this person has learned via interactions with developmental figures?

2. How are these attachment patterns used in current relationships and in the therapy relationship? (repeat, reverse, repress)

C. Besides early developmental issues, are there issues from adult development to be considered?

1. What stage of adult development is this person in?

2. Is there an interaction between this stage of development and any of the above psychodynamic issues?

D. Are there specific cultural, religious, or spiritual issues that may be unique to this person and which we need to understand in order to understand this person?

son's inner world and relationships to others? These questions are summarized in the accompanying exhibit 13.1 and will be discussed in more detail next.

How Can We Describe the Inner Psychological World of This Person?

In addressing this question, we will look at (1) ego development, (2) superego development, and (3) id development and the dynamic interactions between the three. In particular we will try to understand the affective balance of the ego and how the id and superego may have a beneficial or deleterious effect on the ego's affective balance.

Ego development

1. What is the degree of separation-individuation within the ego? We want to try to understand whether the person has completed the separation-individuation process to the point of having a cohesive mostly positive sense of self and other or whether there has been an arrest at an earlier level of separation-individuation (e.g., the depressive, borderline, or psychotic). A person with a mostly positive cohesive sense of self will be emotionally stable most of the time, though he or she may have episodic symptoms such as depression or anxiety. A person at the depressive level of separation-individuation will tend to have more chronic emotional symptoms (e.g., depression, anxiety). A person at the borderline level will tend to vacillate between the extremes of positive mood and negative mood. A person at the psychotic level will have problems with ego boundaries and may manifest symptoms such as delusions or hallucinations.

2. Describe the person's internalized self-representation.

3. Describe the person's internalized other representation.

We will address 2 and 3 together using the accompanying figure 13.1 along with some of the information we obtained from the developmental history. If we draw our attention to the top of the diagram (developmental relationships), we want to list the significant others who were present during development (mother, father, etc.) as well as the positive and negative aspects of the interactions between the patient and his or her significant developmental others. These interactions will be perceived at the level of the ego, which will process the cognitive aspects of these interactions. These interactions will also be processed at the level of the id, which will add the affective components and then send them to the ego to form a combined cognitive-affective perception of the other and the interaction between self and other. From multiple of these interactions over time, a person develops an internalized image of other and an internalized image of self. At this point, we are particularly interested in the affective components of these representations. Has the person internalized an affectively positive or negative representation of others? Has he or she internalized an affectively positive or negative representation of self?

4. What is the level of affective balance within the ego? From our understanding of the affective components of the internalized self and other representations discussed earlier, we can get an idea of the affective balance with the ego. We can graphically represent the affective balance within the ego using the scale below the ego in figure 13.1.

Superego development

Having established a general idea of the person's affective balance, we next want to understand how his or her superego structure can affect the ego's affective balance in either a positive or a negative manner (also illustrated in figure 13.1).

1. Does this person have a rewarding superego structure that can help him or her experience pride and esteem? Infusions of pride and esteem from the superego to the ego can help maintain and/or improve the ego's affective balance.
2. Is there an ego ideal that can set realistic goals for the ego to accomplish? If the ego can accomplish goals set by the ego ideal, then the rewarding superego can supply the ego with pride and esteem, improving the ego's affective balance.
3. Does the punitive superego induce excess feelings of guilt and shame? If the person tends to be unrealistically self-critical, it may be hard for the ego to maintain a positive affective balance.
4. Is the person's conscience consistent with his or her sociocultural environment? Or does the person come from a culture or subculture that has a significantly different value system from the one he or she is living in, making it hard for the person to experience positive affects

from the environment and increasing the probability of experiencing negative affects from the superego.

Id development (Drives and affects)

1. Is this person able to express attachment drives associated with positive affects, thus helping to maintain the ego's affective balance? Or have attachment drives become associated with negative affect, leading to either imbalancing of the ego or repression of these drives?

2. Are assertive drives to act on the environment associated with positive affects, thus helping to maintain the ego's affective balance? Or have assertive drives become associated with negative affect, leading to either imbalancing of the ego or repression of these drives?

How Does This Person with This Psychological Makeup Relate to Others in the World around Him or Her?

What are the attachment patterns that this person has learned via interactions with developmental figures? In the previous section we identified internal self representations and internalized other representations. Now we want to define the relationship between those self and other representations. The self-other pattern of relating, along with the associated affect, is what we are calling an attachment pattern—for example, a nurturing other relating to a valued self with the associated affect of love, or an abusive other and a worthless self associated with the affect of anxiety.

How are the attachment patterns learned in developmental relationships used in current relationships and in the therapy relationship? Does the person express attachment drive repeating the learned pattern? Is the pattern reversed (i.e., self put in the other role and other put in the self role)? Is attachment drive repressed because expression of attachment drive along any of the available attachment patterns leads to the experience of negative affect?

Besides Early Developmental Issues, Are There Issues from Adult Development to Be Considered?

Is the person, for example, dealing with early, middle, or late adult developmental issues (e.g., difficulty deciding on a career path in early adulthood,

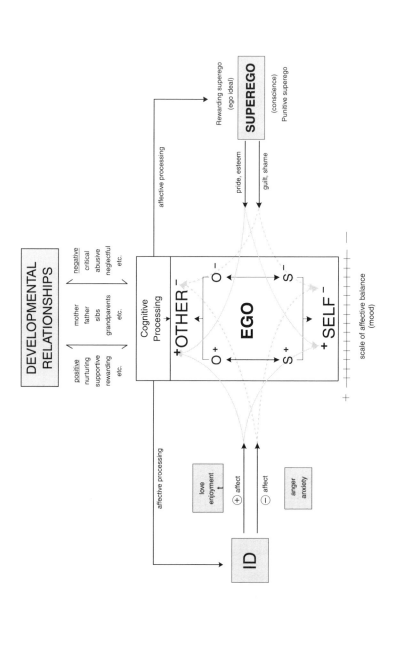

DEVELOPMENTAL RELATIONSHIPS

positive
nurturing
supportive
rewarding
etc.

mother
father
sibs
grandparents
etc.

negative
critical
abusive
neglectful
etc.

Cognitive Processing

⁺OTHER⁻   O⁻
                 O⁺
EGO
       S⁻
⁺SELF⁻
       S⁺

affective processing

SUPEREGO

Rewarding superego
(ego ideal)

(conscience)
Punitive superego

pride, esteem   guilt, shame

affective processing

love
enjoyment

⊕ affect

⊖ affect

anger
anxiety

ID

scale of affective balance
(mood)

Figure 13.1. Psychodynamic Formulation

The relationship between a child and significant developmental others (parents, sibs, etc.) may be positive (nurturing, supportive, rewarding) or negative (critical, abusive, neglectful). The interaction between the child and significant others is perceived at the level of the ego, leading to an inner cognitive representation of self and other in that interaction. Further processing of the interaction occurs at the id and perhaps also the superego, which add affective elements to the perception of the interaction. The affective elements may be generally positive (love, enjoyment, pride, esteem) or negative (anger, anxiety, guilt, shame). Affective elements combine with cognitive elements of the perception to form combined cognitive-affective representations of self and other, some of which will be affectively positive and some of which will be affectively negative. The degree of positive versus negative cognitive-affective representations determines the person's overall affective balance or mood.

anxiety over time running out in middle adulthood, death of a spouse in late adulthood)? Are the problems he or she is having with adult development partly related to unresolved early developmental issues?

Are There Specific Cultural, Religious, or Spiritual Issues That We Need to Understand in Order to Understand This Person?

Does the person come from a culture different from that of the therapist, or does he or she have a religious or spiritual belief system unfamiliar to the therapist? An example would be a young divorced woman I saw who came from another country. In her culture, much more shame is associated with divorce than in American culture. Understanding this was important in understanding her distress.

Another example might be a person who is caught in a clash of cultures. Consider a young man who came to this country as a child with his parents. Conflicts may arise between the value system he learns at home and the one he learns in school.

After answering these four questions, the therapist is now prepared to present a formulation. Treatment cases and a discussion of the formulation will be presented later. For now, suffice it to say that a formulation might look something like the following.

A twenty-four-year-old man comes in with chronic symptoms of depression and anxiety. He grew up in a home in which he was abused by his father and constantly criticized by his mother. He has just dropped out of college for the third time and has no particular goals or direction in his life. He has experienced only a few brief relationships with women; relating tends to increase his anxiety.

Within the ego, his chronic anxiety and depression suggest a failure to complete the separation-individuation process to the point of having a mostly positive cohesive sense of self. From his developmental interactions we might hypothesize an excess of negative self and other internalizations, leading to a negative affective balance.

His superego seems to be overly punitive with a tendency to be guilt-inducing and little ability to be rewarding. His ego ideal is poorly developed; he has no concept of what he wants to do with his life; he has no goals.

Within the id attachment drives tend to be repressed because they have become associated with anxiety. Similarly, assertive drives are not associated with positive affect. Thus, we have an ego with a baseline negative affective balance in between an id and a superego, neither of which have an ability to induce positive affects to help with the chronically negative ego balance.

In terms of adult development, he is in the early adult phase and is failing to negotiate the two main tasks of this stage: (1) finding a life direction and (2) forming an intimate relationship. These failures seem most likely related to failures of earlier development rather than any new stress that is ongoing in the present.

The patient and the therapist do not appear to have any major cultural differences, though the patient's lack of any involvement in religion or spirituality may be an issue.

The previous formulation suggests several areas that are in need of treatment; treatment is the topic to which I will turn next.

TREATMENT OF A *DSM-IV* DIAGNOSIS

Introduction

The position taken here is that treatment should have a goal(s) and the goal(s) should be agreed upon by the patient and therapist. In the sections on history and diagnosis we made the distinction between a descriptive *DSM-IV* diagnosis and a psychodynamic formulation. The first decision then is whether the goal is to work on one or the other or both. Let us try to clarify this with an example.

Suppose a person comes for treatment with all the symptoms of major depression in the present and a history of many stresses and losses in their early developmental years. It may be clear to the therapist and to the patient that there is some connection between the current depression and the early developmental conflicts. Nevertheless, there are different treatment options. For example:

1. The patient may decide that he is interested in taking an antidepressant medication or receiving another treatment (e.g., supportive psychotherapy) that is aimed at current symptom relief of his major depressive episode, but is not interested in or ready to address the underlying psychodynamic issues. In this situation, the goal of treatment is the relief of the symptoms of major depression.

2. The patient may decide that he is not interested in taking medication but that he is interested in dealing with the stresses of his early developmental years and in dealing with how these past stresses are related to his current depression. In this situation the goals are to deal with the underlying psychodynamic issues (to be discussed more thoroughly later) in order to relieve the symptoms of depression and hopefully decrease the likelihood that depression will return. This approach may potentially lead to an increase in symptoms initially before symptoms improve. Certainly part of this approach may involve therapy that takes into consideration not only past psychodynamic issues but also current stresses that may be dynamically linked to past stressors.

3. The patient may decide that he is interested in both medication and psychotherapy. This combined treatment may have the advantage of improving the present symptom picture while the patient is dealing with psychodynamic issues that may bring up even more emotions for that person.

Treatment Techniques

Below are listed some of the treatment techniques that may be used to treat persons with various diagnoses. A distinction is made here between these techniques and the psychotherapy interventions listed in the next section. The distinction is that the treatment techniques listed below are aimed predominantly at the symptomatic diagnosis, whereas the psychotherapy interventions discussed in the next section are aimed at underlying psychodynamic issues that are thought to be related to the symptomatic diagnosis.

1. *Depression.* medication, ECT
2. *Schizophrenia.* medication, residential treatment, social skills training
3. *Substance abuse.* twelve-step programs, halfway houses, medications
4. *Agoraphobia.* in vivo desensitization
5. *Social anxiety.* exposure, medication
6. *Simple phobia.* systematic desensitization
7. *Obsessive-compulsive disorder.* exposure and response prevention, medication
8. *Generalized anxiety disorder.* relaxation, biofeedback, stress inoculation

9. *Adjustment disorder.* crisis intervention
10. *Borderline personality.* dialectic behavioral therapy

PSYCHOTHERAPY

The therapy described below is short-term, ten to twenty-five sessions, and carried out once a week (exhibit 13.2). The focus of the therapy is not on transference, the reenactment of object relationships within the therapy between the patient and therapist. Rather, the focus is on the examination of the inner world of self and other, and self-other relationships as they evolved in developmental relationships and as they are enacted in current relationships. In examining the inner representational world of a person, the goal in therapy is to improve the affective balance of self and other representations and to develop self-other attachment patterns that are associated with more positive affects than older patterns.

Ground Rules of Therapy

Next I will move on to a discussion of the ground rules of psychotherapy; this is also referred to as the psychotherapy contract or the frame of psychotherapy. These are simply the guidelines, agreed to by the therapist and patient, that govern the process of therapy. The ground rules of therapy are discussed in more detail elsewhere (Mackinnon and Michels 1971; Weiner 1975; Langs 1989; Gabbard 1994) and will be outlined briefly here:

1. The setting: Where is the therapy to take place?
2. Time and frequency of sessions
3. The fee
4. Issues of attendance
   • Responsibility for attendance
   • Missed sessions policy
   • Vacation policy
5. Phone policy
6. Therapist anonymity
7. Patient privacy and confidentiality
8. Mode of communication: honest and open, free association, etc.

Exhibit 13.2 Therapy Interventions

I. General interventions
  A. Empathy
  B. Experiencing
  C. Explanation
II. Specific interventions
  A. The inner world of the id, ego, and superego
    1. Ego
      a. Increasing the positive affective balance within the ego
      b. Decreasing the negative affective balance with the ego (mourning)
    2. Superego and its relationship to the ego
      a. Increase pride and esteem from the rewarding superego
      b. Decrease guilt and shame from the punitive superego
    3. Id and its relationship to the ego
      a. Increase positive affective influx to the ego via activities and relationships
      b. Decrease negative affective influx
  B. Relationships
    1. Diminish negative attachment patterns
    2. Develop and/or enhance positive attachment patterns
  C. Adult development
    1. Assess a person's progress in negotiating the tasks associated with his or her stage of adult development
    2. If there are problems mastering tasks of adult development, design strategies to deal with those problems
  D. Cultural, religious, spiritual issues
    1. Identify cultural, religious, or spiritual issues that may be interacting with any of the above categories
    2. Develop techniques to resolve these issues

---

9. Goals of therapy: If the decision is made to embark on a psychodynamic treatment, we can move on to formulate psychodynamic goals. These are the goals that aim at changing underlying psychodynamic structures and relationships so that ultimately symptoms are relieved and the overall well-being of the patient improves. Examples of psychodynamic goals might include (a) helping the person resolve very negatively cathected internalized self and other representations,

(b) helping the patient develop positively cathected self and other representations, (c) improving the patient's rewarding superego and diminishing his or her tendency to be self-critical, and (d) learning healthier internalized attachment patterns so as to be able to develop more fulfilling relationships.

General Interventions

I will divide my discussion of psychotherapy interventions into general interventions and specific interventions. General interventions address the process of therapy, the overall pattern or style of interaction between the therapist and the patient. Next I will discuss three general interventions: empathy, experiencing, and explanation.

Empathy

The term *empathy* is used here to refer to the ability of the therapist to emotionally understand the patient sitting across from her and to convey to that person that they understand him. Those familiar with the work of Heinz Kohut (1971, 1977) and the self-psychologists know that they placed much importance on the development of an empathic relationship between the therapist and the patient. In self-psychology therapy, a person's problems are thought to be a result of empathic failures on the part of significant development figures. These empathic failures lead to an arrest in development with attendant symptom formation. Therapy, in part, consists of the formation of an empathic relationship between the therapist and the patient so that the arrest can be undone and development can proceed.

Carl Rogers was another person who put a lot of emphasis on empathy. In a series of papers dating back to 1954, he explored empathy in the psychotherapeutic relationship (Rogers 1961; Kirshenbaum & Henderson 1989). Rogers described empathy as the ability of the therapist to sense the feelings and personal meanings that the patient is experiencing at any moment and to communicate to the patient that he, the therapist, understands the patient's inner state. Rogers described several other factors that he felt were important components of the psychotherapeutic relationship; they are listed next. I would like to include these components as part of what I mean by the general intervention, empathy.

1. *Acceptance.* The ability to accept the person as she is; to accept her various facets.
2. *Genuineness.* The ability of the therapist to be himself in a relationship without front or facade. A manifestation of this is that the therapist's words match his internal feelings.
3. *Warmth.* The ability to convey a caring, interested attitude toward the patient.
4. *Sensitivity.* An ability to understand the patient's needs, feelings, and attitudes.
5. *A nonjudgmental attitude.* The ability to convey to the patient the sense that she is free from the threat of external evaluation.
6. *Unconditional positive regard.* The ability of the therapist to positively care for the patient no matter what feeling is going on in the person at that moment.
7. *Trustworthiness, dependability, and consistency.*

Rogers believed that a psychotherapeutic relationship made up of these characteristics would facilitate growth in the patient, would allow her to actualize her potential.

The term *empathy* is used here to describe the formation of a type of relationship that helps a patient (1) undo negative from the past and (2) develop positive in the present and the future. With respect to the past, the empathic relationship establishes a secure base for the patient from which she can express her past negative emotion and hopefully put those emotions behind her. With respect to the present and future, the goal of the empathic relationship is to undo developmental arrest and begin to grow by cathecting herself and those around her with positive emotion. Thus, the goal of the empathic relationship in affective terms is to help the person decrease her negative and increase her positive affective valence.

Experiencing

In therapy, a patient experiences a relationship between himself and the therapist. The position taken here is that the quality of that experienced relationship is critically important. Can this be the type of relationship described earlier between a warm, nonjudgmental, validating therapist and a patient who can feel valued, worthwhile, and secure? Many of the people who come to us as therapists have not experienced this type of relationship. In therapy can we provide the patient with a qualitatively different form of relationship experience than he has had in the past?

One might ask how experiencing is different from what was described earlier in the section on empathy. I would say that it is simply the other side of the empathy coin. In other words, the therapist strives to create this empathic relationship and the patient experiences this relationship. Separating empathy and experiencing in this way allows me not only to focus on the empathic relationship I am trying to create, but also to pay attention to what the patient is experiencing. Hopefully, this empathic experiencing relationship will help the patient grow as a person and will enable her to learn a new pattern of relating that she can use in relationships outside of therapy.

Empathy and experiencing address the process of the therapy as opposed to the content of the therapy (to be discussed in the next section, Specific Interventions). In any interaction between two people there is always process and content, always a process that underlies whatever the content of the conversation is. Placing emphasis on these process elements, empathy and experiencing, reminds me to maintain focus on process in the context of the ongoing content of the therapy. Without a therapeutic process, content interventions are not likely to be successful.

Explanation

In discussing psychodynamic psychotherapy, we often use the term *interpretation*. Interpretation refers to the process by which the therapist makes the patient conscious of something that was previously repressed in the unconscious. In this sense, interpretation is a specific intervention in that it addresses a psychodynamic issue that is specific to that person. The term *explanation* is used here in a much more general sense. Explanation is used here to describe a process by which the therapist explains to the patient some aspect of his problem or some aspect of the therapy. This could be explaining to the patient his negative affective balance and the goal of improving that affective balance.

For example, a therapist might say to a depressed, anxious patient who has come from an abusive environment, "Given the fact that others were always critical of you and you were always made to feel worthless, I can understand why you have always been anxious and depressed, why it has been hard for you to maintain any sense of emotional well-being. Hopefully, we can work on helping you decrease all the negative feelings you are carrying around and help you develop some positive feelings about yourself and others so that you can have a sense of emotional well-being instead of chronic feelings of depression and anxiety."

In this explanation there is no process of making the unconscious conscious (i.e., the person is aware that she comes from an abusive environment, she is aware of the feelings she has about that, and she is aware of her own feelings of worthlessness). The therapist is using his understanding of this person's inner affective world to explain her chronic negative emotional imbalance and is suggesting that to correct this imbalance, he and the patient have to work on resolving these negative feelings as well as work on developing more positive emotional representations with the inner world of this person.

Before moving on to talk about specific interventions, I would like to add a little more emphasis to the importance of general or nonspecific factors in psychotherapy. Many studies have shown that psychotherapy is effective (Luborsky et al. 1975; Smith et al. 1980; Lambert et al. 1986, Langs 1989). What is less clear is what makes psychotherapy effective. Studies comparing psychotherapies have failed to show that one type is more effective than another (Gabbard 1994). This suggests that the more general or nonspecific factors in psychotherapy are of significant importance. Work by Docherty (1985) focused on the importance of the therapeutic relationship. Kay and Kay (in Tasman, Kay & Lieberman 2003) in their discussion of psychoanalytic psychotherapy discuss a shift from a focus strictly on insight to a more balanced focus that emphasizes that rapport between the therapist and the patient within the therapeutic relationship.

My point here is to suggest that we keep these general interventions in mind and maintain focus on the quality of the relationship between the patient and the therapist. Sometimes, in learning psychotherapy and in trying to master specific therapeutic techniques, it is easy to forget these general interventions. However, since these general factors may be the most important part of the therapy, it is important to keep them in mind.

Specific Interventions

In this section I will address more specific interventions following the same outline used in the section on formulation focusing on (1) the inner world of

the id, ego, and superego, (2) relationship issues, (3) adult developmental issues, and (4) cultural, religious, and/or spiritual issues.

The Inner World of the Id, Ego, and Superego

Ego. From our history and formulation we have a pretty good idea of ego
development. We can think of two interacting axis of the ego, a vertical axis
and a horizontal axis. The vertical axis addresses the degree of separation-individuation, and the horizontal axis addresses the degree of affective balance
within the ego. From what we know about the patient, we should be able to
get a pretty good sense of her level of separation-individuation and her degree of affective balance. It may be useful at this point to get a little better
sense of our patient's inner experience.

The following exercise is often illuminating. Ask the patient to make a list
of her positive self-characteristics and her negative self-characteristics. You
can also ask her to list the positive and negative characteristics of significant
developmental others. Next to each characteristic, ask the patient to write an
emotion word that describes how she feels about that characteristic. A table
such as table 13.1 may be used.

What is often interesting is how long the negative list of characteristics is
and how short the positive list of characteristics is. As one would probably
expect, the emotions associated with the negative characteristics tend to be
negative emotions, but what is surprising is that often even characteristics
that the person considers positive are associated with negative emotion. A
goal of therapy is to decrease the list of negative characteristics and to increase the list of positive characteristics, as well as to increase the frequency
of positive emotions associated with positive characteristics.

One could approach this material with cognitive therapy principles. The
negative list the person has generated can be viewed as negative self-thoughts
and negative thoughts about others in the world around her. A cognitive approach would challenge the negative thoughts and would strive to replace
them with more positive thoughts. For a detailed discussion of cognitive
techniques, please see Beck (1981) and Beck (1995).

A more traditional psychodynamic approach would focus more on emotion than thoughts. A goal is to decrease the negative emotion associated
with internalized self and other representations and increase positive emotions associated with internalized self and other representations. Dealing

Table 13.1 Positive and Negative Self and Other Representations

Positive Other Characteristic	Associated Emotion	Negative Other Characteristic	Associated Emotion
Positive Self Characteristic	Associated Emotion	Negative Self Characteristic	Associated Emotion

with the negative internalized representations is often difficult for a person because it brings up painful memories of past developmental interactions. Sometimes it seems helpful to suggest a mourning model to a patient. The stages of grief are something that many people are familiar with. For some people, viewing the childhood as the loss of something that might have been is a useful metaphor that helps them work through sadness, anxiety, and anger and arrive at some level of acceptance and resolution. This can help them put negative self and other representations behind them, shift their affective balance toward the positive, and possibly also aid in the separation-individuation process.

Besides decreasing negative representations, increasing the positive emotional valence of positive representations can help shift one's overall emotional balance toward the positive. A person may have positive characteristics that he has not learned to value because these characteristics were not valued in his interactions with his parents. Pointing out the value of a person's positive characteristics may be an important step in helping him cathect his positive characteristics with positive emotion. In the therapeutic experiencing interaction, the therapist demonstrating to the patient that she values the patient's attributes and characteristics is another important manner via which a patient can internalize positive affect associated with his positive characteristics. (For a clinical example of this, see the case of Rosilyn in chapter 17.)

In summary, the goal here is to help the patient decrease negative and increase positive within the ego so as to improve his overall affective balance and to facilitate personal growth via the separation-individuation process.

Superego. Next we turn our attention to the superego and in particular the superego's interaction with the ego. The superego may interact with the ego, approving or disapproving of various ego attributes and/or characteristics; or by approving or disapproving of various id impulses that the ego allows expression of.

One problem is that of the overly critical superego that may have been internalized from overly critical others during development. The person is very critical of herself, inducing guilt and shame, which has a deleterious effect on the emotional balance of the ego. She may criticize herself for things others would not be self-critical of, or her self-criticism may be far in excess of that which would be experienced by the average person in the same situation.

The first step in treating this guilt-inducing superego is often that of making the person aware of how self-critical she is. Her self-criticism may be so long-standing and automatic that she is unaware of it. Working with a self-critical statement in a cognitive manner by challenging its validity may help the person develop a more modulated punitive superego. The hope is that the person can decrease the intensity of these self-critical statements and eventually replace them with self-reinforcing statements.

Within the process of the therapy (experiencing), maintaining a nonjudgmental relationship in the interaction with the patient provides her with a different form of interaction from the critical form that led to the overly punitive superego in the first place. The hope is that the patient can internalize this nonjudgmental style into her superego and become less self-critical, punitive, and guilt/shame inducing.

The other side of the superego coin is the rewarding superego. Oftentimes the person who is overly punitive has very limited ability to be rewarding. Certainly part of helping a person deal with an overly punitive superego would be to help him balance it with a rewarding superego. Again, one can cognitively work on this development of the rewarding superego by teaching a person to make rewarding superego statements (e.g., "I am proud of what I accomplished at work this week."). Also, in the process of the therapy, the therapist can demonstrate a sense of pride in the patient's accomplishment (e.g., "It's great that you were able to do that."). The hope is that the patient will be able to internalize this rewarding superego pride-inducing function and use it to improve and maintain a positive affective balance within the ego.

Next we turn to the ego ideal and will discuss two problems: (1) the lack of an ego ideal and (2) the overly perfectionistic ego ideal. The person with a lack of an ego ideal may not have had any idealizing figures in her life, persons with whom she could identify so as to internalize goals. The therapist may be an idealizing figure for the patient, or as the patient improves with therapy, she may be able to find an idealizing figure in her environment, someone with whom she can identify and internalize goals (i.e., "I want to be like that person.").

The other ego ideal problem is the perfectionistic ego ideal. This is the person who has goals but who must accomplish them to perfection in order to be satisfied, in order for the rewarding superego to kick in. Since perfection is an elusive goal; these people rarely reward themselves and frequently criticize themselves. The therapist demonstrating reward for accomplishments by the patient at a level less than perfection may allow the person to develop a more modulated ego ideal (i.e., "It's wonderful that you got a B on your exam."). However, it is often necessary to look at the developmental origins of his perfectionism. Did the parents reward perfect performance and make acceptance contingent upon it? Were the parents uninvolved and unloving so that the child developed the hope that if he were perfect, he would be loved? In either situation it is obviously important to demonstrate in the therapy relationship that the patient does not have to be perfect to be accepted and loved.

Finally, I will say a word about the conscience, one's internalized sense of right and wrong. One situation to be discussed here is the person whose conscience is significantly out of sync with most of those around her—for example, an action that most people feel is wrong and which would cause guilt if performed is seen differently by this person. She may not see it as wrong, and if she performs the act, does not feel guilty. An example might be a person who does not believe it is wrong to steal, a belief not generally held by the majority of people. These may be people with sociopathic tendencies, and unfortunately we do not have any great treatments for this problem.

The other side of this coin would be the person whose conscience is excessively moralistic compared to the society around them. Here we are not talking about someone who belongs to a certain group that has a different system of moral standards compared with the rest of society. We are talking about the person who everyone would agree is excessively concerned about the rightness or wrongness of every act. He may be so concerned that some action on his part will be wrong that he becomes paralyzed and has limited ability to act on or interact in the world. Helping this person see the discrepancy between his moral system and that of the world around him may free him to function in the world.

Exhibit 13.3 is a summary of the superego issues just discussed.

Id. We now turn our attention to the id, its drives and affects, and its relationship to the ego and superego. The following are four circumstances for consideration:

1. Assertive drives to act on the environment and attachment drives to interact with others are associated with positive affect and expressed in a manner that leads to adaptive behavior. In this circumstance, the expression of drives and associated positive affects leads to an influx of positive affects into the ego, thus maintaining and/or improving the affective balance of the ego. For example, a person learns how to paint pictures, an activity that brings them a sense of pleasure and pride maintaining their affective balance.

2. Assertive drives to act on the environment and/or attachment drives to interact with others are associated with positive affect and expressed in a manner which, though it may improve the ego's affective balance, leads to maladaptive behavior. An example of this would be the person who expresses drives impulsively because of a lack of ego strength to control those drives. A dependent or borderline person with limited ego strength and poor affective balance may act impulsively (form an immediate liaison with another, drink, take drugs, cut on himself) in order to decrease tension and stimulate some positive affect so as to improve his affective balance. While this expression of drive and affect may improve the ego's affective balance, the behavioral component is self-destructive (drug abuse, self-mutilation).

> **Exhibit 13.3 Psychotherapy Issues of the Superego**
>
> Punitive Superego
> 1. Is the punitive superego excessively punitive (i.e., guilt and shame inducing)?
> 2. Is the punitive superego balanced at all by a rewarding superego?
>
> Rewarding Superego
> 1. Is the person able to be self-rewarding, to experience a sense of pride?
> 2. Is the degree of reward commensurate with the accomplishment? Too little? Too much?
>
> Ego Ideal
> 1. Is there an ego ideal present that can generate meaningful goals for the person?
> 2. Are the goals of the ego ideal overly perfectionistic?
>
> Conscience
> 1. Does the person lack the moral value system of the society around him?
> 2. Is the person's value system excessively moralistic compared with the society around him?

If the impulsivity leads to very destructive behavior, then the therapy may be behavioral (i.e., limit setting, a more structured environment, or hospitalization). In less self-destructive situations, an approach would be to help the person improve coping skills; that is, instead of acting impulsively, he might call a friend (or perhaps AA sponsor), exercise, do relaxation exercises, or listen to music. From a more psychodynamic perspective, the treatment involves the therapy of the ego described earlier, which is aimed at improving ego strength via improving the affective balance of the ego so that the need to act impulsively diminishes, and so the ego has more control over impulses.

3. Assertive and attachment drives have become associated with negative affect and are repressed, or

4. Assertive and attachment drives have become associated with negative affect but continue to be expressed.

In 3, the repression limits the flow of negative affect into the ego, but also prevents the flow of positive affect and prevents the person from acting on the environment or forming relationships. In 4, drive expression is accompanied by the flow of negative affect into the ego with the resultant imbalancing of the ego's affective balance. Drive expression may be maintained because of the hope of potential positive experience or because at least intermittently the person does have a positive experience.

Therapy here involves trying to understand why drive expression has become associated with negative affect. What experiences has the person had that have led to the association of assertive and attachment drives with negative affect? For example, does the person repress the expression of assertive drive because she was always criticized? Does she repress the expression of attachment drive because she was abused? Can the patient talk about these experiences, express her feelings about these experiences, and hopefully put these experiences behind her? This may include the use of the mourning model described previously. At the same time, can we use the process of the therapy, the experiencing relationship, to give the person a more positive experience as she interacts with the therapist so that she can begin to associate drive expression with positive affect?

Another aspect of this problem may be that the person never learned to experience positive affect in any activity she participated in. When a child learns a new skill (walking, throwing a ball, playing Candyland), the parent participates in the child's joy. If parents are not able to express joy with their child or if they can only express negativity, the child may learn to not experience joy in her actions. In therapy it may be helpful to encourage the patient to find some activities that she enjoys, to give her the message that it is okay to experience enjoyment, and when she does engage in the activity, to participate in her joy with her.

Relationships

The previous section touched on the issues of relationships in the discussion of attachment drives. There, we were interested in how the expression of attachment drive and associated affects affected the person's inner affective balance; here we are interested in how that expression of attachment drive and affect influence their external relationships with others. I want to discuss relationships further because patients often seek help not only because they are having a hard time maintaining their inner emotional balance but also because they are having problems in relationships. That is, expression of attachment drive, associated with negative affect, has a deleterious effect not only on one's inner emotional balance but also on one's ability to form relationships.

First we want to define the problem: is it a problem in sexual relating or interpersonal relating or both? If it is a sexual problem, what is the nature of the problem? If it is a problem of interpersonal relating, is the person relating in a dependent self-object mode, or is he capable of object-object relating but experiencing some barrier to intimacy?

Next we want to move on to an understanding of this person's attachment patterns. From our developmental assessment we should have a good idea of what self-other attachment patterns were learned in early development. Our other two sources of information are what the patient describes to us about his pattern of relationships in the present and what relationship pattern we experience in the interaction between the patient and the therapist.

The attachment pattern will consist of an internalized relationship between a self representation and an other representation, along with a certain affect. The patient may express attachment drive along this attachment pattern, putting another person in the other role and herself in the self role (repeating the pattern). Or she may put the other in the self role and herself in the other role (reversing the pattern). Some people will go back and forth between repeating and reversing the pattern. A third option would be to repress attachment drive, since expression of attachment drive along existing patterns stimulates the negative affect associated with that attachment pattern.

I said earlier that this form of therapy is not primarily based on transference, but certainly transference may come up (i.e., the patient may repeat an attachment pattern in the therapy, putting the therapist in either the self or the other role). The advantage of the attachment pattern being expressed in the relationship between the patient and the therapist is that it is being manifested in real time, allowing us to examine it in the here and now. We can look at the adaptiveness versus maladaptiveness of the pattern, we can look at the affects associated with the pattern, and we can look at the distortions inherent in the pattern. For example, if the attachment pattern is between a critical judgmental other and an insecure self with the associated affects of anxiety and anger, the patient may put the therapist in the role of the critical judgmental other and express anger at him. Assuming the therapist has maintained his nonjudgmental stance, he will be able to point out the distortion. Alternatively, the patient may place themself in the critical, judgmental role and heap criticism on the therapist. If there is really nothing to criticize the therapist for, the therapist can again point out how the patient distorts aspects of an interpersonal relationship. For a more detailed discussion of transference in the therapeutic situation, please see Basch (1980, 1988, 1995), Kernberg et al. (1989), and Gabbard (1994).

One can look at these attachment patterns in the context of the therapy relationship as well as the person's current interpersonal relationships and the person's developmental relationships. By going back and forth between these three sets of relationships, the patient comes to understand their maladaptive attachment patterns, but, more importantly, can work through and resolve the affects associated with the interactions that led to these patterns in the first place. At the same time, the hope is that the patient can use the relationship with the therapist to learn and internalize a new, healthier attachment pattern, which he can then use in relationships outside therapy.

In the previous section, I talked about using the mourning model to help patients work through affectively negative self and other representations. We can use that same mourning model to help a person deal with negatively cathected attachment patterns. In fact, because these two issues are so intimately related, we are frequently working on both simultaneously. One way to conceptualize this is that the patient needs to mourn the loss of a relationship that never was or might have been better. This will involve dealing with the negative aspects of the relationship that were present but also the lost, longed for positive aspects that were not present.

Adult Development

So much of what we tend to deal with in psychotherapy has to do with early development. This section is included to remind us that development continues throughout the life cycle, and a person may come to treatment because he or she is having difficulty negotiating one of the tasks of a certain phase of adult development.

I cannot here discuss all of the potential issues that may come up in the adult years. It is useful, however, to try to differentiate between a problem that is specific to a phase in adult development and a problem that represents an interaction between an adult developmental issue and an early developmental issue. Let me try to make this distinction with the following examples.

Two women came to therapy, each requesting help in relating to men. The first was thirty-three and had come from a rather traumatic childhood. She had never had a long-term relationship with a man but had not sought treatment previously. She was now seeking treatment out of a sense that "time is running out." She wanted to marry and have children but obviously saw the lack of a relationship as an impediment to that goal. She had in the past dealt with her anxiety over relating to men by avoiding relationships, but now the early adult task of forming an intimate relationship and having a family was in conflict with her avoidant pattern propelling her into therapy.

The second woman was twenty-four and, as opposed to the first woman, described a very happy childhood development. She had up until recently enjoyed rewarding relationships with men. This changed several months before coming to therapy as a result of a sexual assault. She experiencing symptoms of post-traumatic stress disorder, one of which was difficulty getting close to men. People who have coped well all of their life may experience a significant stress during one of the adult development phases, develop symptoms, and come to us for treatment.

Besides the experience of a trauma in the adult years, there are also issues that are related to the developmental tasks associated with each of the phases of adult development. For example, a person in the early adult years may come in with anxiety because she is unable to decide on a career path. A middle-aged person may come in with depression after the death of an elderly parent, or with anxiety because he has realized that he has already lived one-half of his life and has a sense that time is running out. A person in the late adult period may come in because she has recently retired and now has no sense of meaning in her life.

Cultural, Religious, or Spiritual Factors

Some patients may be from a different culture from the therapist and have different cultural belief systems. Or patients may come from a different religious or spiritual background from the therapist. Understanding the person's cultural, religious, or spiritual belief system may be key to understanding a person and their conflicts.

As an example, a twenty-two-year-old woman came in with severe anxiety after she began to have sexual intercourse with her boyfriend. This history might suggest that she had had some bad experiences with sex in her past;

however, there was no such history. What she described was that she grew up in a small town and with a religion that had very strong beliefs against premarital sex. When she moved to a larger town, that belief system was not so prominent. Understanding this background was important in understanding her anxiety over the sexual relationship with her boyfriend. Sometimes it is difficult to help people in situations like this who are caught between a religious belief they grew up with and a different belief system that they move into. This young woman said, "I don't want to give up my religion, but I don't want to give up my natural urges." Therapy did not resolve this issue for her but did give her a forum in which to discuss the issue and to express her feelings. It was suggested that she talk to some members of the religious community to which she now belonged. She did do this and eventually came up with a compromise with which she was comfortable. She came to the conclusion that having sex with her boyfriend did not mean she had to give up her religion, but it did mean she had to modify her views on premarital sex.

I do want to mention one other thing about religion and spirituality that relates back to the previous discussion on finding ways to stimulate this influx of positive affect. For some people, becoming involved in a religion may be an activity that they find intrinsically enjoyable and which stimulates positive interactions with others. Of course, we do not want to be in the position of proselytizing, but in exploring activities that may be meaningful to a person, which may be positive affectively, this is one possibility.

SUMMARY

In this chapter I have discussed history, diagnosis, treatment, and psychotherapy. The history can lead us to both a symptomatic diagnosis and a psychodynamic formulation. A psychodynamic formulation describes the underlying psychological problems of a patient. Treatments of a symptomatic diagnosis were briefly discussed; psychotherapy of the underlying psychological problems was discussed in more detail.

The book's last four chapters consist of detailed case presentations that illustrate the previous points. In the cases we will be looking at the inner representational world of each person. I will discuss the negatively cathected components of each person's inner world and describe attempts to diminish those negative elements, replace them with positive affective cathexis, and improve the person's overall emotional balance.

14

Clinical Presentation: Bob

Bob, a twenty-nine-year-old man, came to me seeking help for his feelings of anxiety and anger. He described constant feelings of nervousness and anxiety of about four months' duration. The anxiety began to interfere with sleep and the ability to concentrate at work. The acute stress was the breakup of his relationship with his girlfriend after he found out that she was having an affair with his best friend.

In retrospect, Bob recalled that prior to the breakup, his girlfriend had been going through a stressful time and turned to him for support. He experienced her as needy, and he withdrew. It was then that she turned to his best friend. Since the breakup Bob has been anxious and has had questions about his own insecurities and abilities to form a relationship. Bob sees the breakup of the relationship as a major stress, but at the same time is surprised at the length and intensity of his reaction to it.

Bob had had some periods of anxiety during past stressful periods of his life, but it had never been as severe or long lasting, and he had never been treated before. He'd never been treated for any other emotional difficulties and had never had a problem with alcohol or drugs. There was no family psychiatric history and no history of any medical problems.

Developmentally, Bob grew up in a family that consisted of his parents, a brother who is three years older, and a sister who is two years younger. His parents got along; there were never any major tensions between them. His father was a businessman; Bob described him as kind and giving. He feels that they have had a rather close relationship.

He described his mother as cold, nonempathic, unemotive, critical, and judgmental. He experienced her as having a hard time giving acceptance or recognition. "If you went to her with a problem, you didn't get understanding, but an analysis of the problem along with what she thought you should do about it." He felt that his mother favored his sister and gave her more attention, leaving him feeling neglected, rejected, and left out. He tended to deal with that by belittling his younger sister, which then made him feel better about himself. His behavior would evoke an angry reaction from his mother, which left him feeling even more excluded. As a result there was always tension in his relationships with both his mother and his sister.

Bob reports feeling quite close to his older brother, and sometimes they had mutual friends. His brother also got less attention than their sister but seemed less bothered by it. He was quite intellectual, spent much time reading, and developed relationships outside the home through school.

In grade school Bob did generally well, obtaining mostly A's and B's with an occasional C. He had friends and played several sports. High school also went well scholastically and athletically. He had a circle of male friends, some of whom he is still close to. He dated one girlfriend for a couple of months, but he feels he drove her away by being too judgmental.

After high school, Bob attended college and graduated in four years. He then worked for a couple of years before going back and obtaining a master's degree. For the last two years he has worked in a job that he enjoys very much.

Relationships, however, have not gone as well for him. He believes that he is somewhat insecure, and that is especially true in relationships with women. As a result, he has tended to shy away from relationships with women he perceives as secure and has tended to pick women who are less secure like himself.

After high school, his first relationship was with a young woman he met in college. He got along well with her, but she also had a boyfriend back in her hometown, and she did not want to give up that relationship. Bob felt angry and excluded by that situation, so in retaliation he started dating his girlfriend's best friend. This caused much stress among all parties involved, and he ended up losing both relationships.

In his first job after college, and before going to graduate school, he met and developed a relationship with a woman who worked at the same place. He described her as a very high-energy, passionate woman who was rather insecure and had lots of problems related to the fact that she had grown up in an abusive home. Bob, however, felt very close to this woman. After about a year, however, she left town to pursue higher educational opportunities. They tried to maintain a long-distance relationship, but it gradually fell apart because of the distance and because she developed a new boyfriend relationship. He again ended up feeling excluded.

While he was at graduate school, other than a brief sexual liaison, Bob didn't have any long-lasting relationships.

About a year prior to coming to treatment, Bob met and began dating his most recent girlfriend, the one who eventually had an affair with his best friend. She, like some of his previous girlfriends, was rather insecure and demanded much support from him. Bob says he's always had a hard time giving in relationships with women but has, as this and other girlfriends have told him, tended to be judgmental, critical, and condescending. In retrospect, he feels that when she couldn't get the support she wanted from him, she turned to his best friend, and Bob again ended up feeling excluded.

DIAGNOSIS

Descriptive Diagnosis

From a *DSM-IV-TR* perspective, a diagnosis of Adjustment Disorder with Anxiety is most consistent with the clinical findings. Anxiety was a prominent symptom; it was excessive in the sense that it lasted longer than expected and was not getting better with time. It was also interfering with functioning by causing sleep difficulty and problems concentrating at work.

Psychodynamic Formulation

How Can We Describe the Inner Psychological World of This Person?

Ego. Bob seemed to have achieved a high degree of separation-individuation and to have developed a mostly positive, cohesive sense of self and other. He did describe some negative elements in his self representation (insecurity) and other representation (critical), but for the most part, up until the present, has been able to maintain a positive affective balance; that is, he has been a happy person most of his life. In the context of this relationship he developed symptoms of emotional imbalance, anxiety, and anger.

Superego. Bob possessed a pretty healthy superego structure with a good balance between rewarding and punitive elements, an ego ideal that was very capable of goal formation, and a conscience that was commensurate with his environment.

Id. In general, Bob was very capable of expressing assertive drives of self-expression and attachment drives toward others along with positive affect leading to maintenance and strengthening of the positive emotional balance of the ego. He did, however, have problems with intimate relationships.

How Does a Person with This Inner Psychological Makeup Relate to Others in the World around Him?

Bob described two different attachment patterns that he had learned in development. The first was between a loving, supportive other and a valued, worthwhile self with associated affects of affection and pleasure. He identified this as the pattern that he had experienced in his relationship with his father and brother. He was able to use this pattern in many relationships, especially with men, to establish fulfilling, long-lasting relationships. He still maintained relationships with some of the guys he grew up with. The second pattern was that of a critical, judgmental other and an insecure, excluded self with the associated affects of anxiety and anger. Bob identified this as the pattern he experienced in his relationship with his mother. He did not repeat this pattern in relationships with women by picking women who were critical and judgmental. He did, however, repeat the pattern by reversing the roles; he became the critical, judgmental one and put the women in the role of the insecure, excluded one. Rather than anxiety and anger, the affect associated with this pattern was security.

From the history, one can see that Bob used this reversal pattern from a very young age in his relationship with his sister. He was critical and judgmental of her, and this was associated with a feeling of security in him, at least until his mother discovered what was going on and reversed the roles back again, assuming herself the critical, judgmental role and putting Bob in the insecure, excluded role.

In his attempts to form intimate relationships with women, Bob described picking women he perceived as insecure and shied away from secure

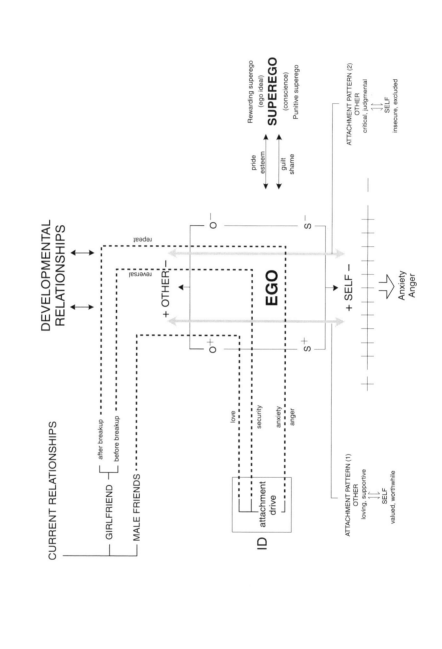

Figure 14.1. Psychotherapy: Bob

ATTACHMENT PATTERN 1 (bold arrow between +other and +self)

As a result of his experience with his brother and father, Bob learned a rather positive attachment pattern (supportive, loving other and a valued, worthwhile self). The affects associated with this pattern were love and security. He was able to express attachment drive along this pattern and to establish and maintain long-term rewarding relationships with men.

ATTACHMENT PATTERN 2 (bold arrow between −other and −self)

As a result of his experience with his mother, Bob learned a more negative attachment pattern (critical, judgmental, belitting other and an insecure, excluded self). The affects associated with this were anxiety and anger. Bob dealt with this by reversing the attachment pattern, first in his relationship with his sister and later in his relationship with other women. He (self) became the critical, judgmental, belitting one and the woman became the insecure, excluded other. For Bob, the affect associated with reversal of the pattern was security.

As long as the pattern was reversed and not repeated, Bob maintained a sense of security in the relationship. When his girlfriend had an affair with his best friend, she effectively switched the pattern back to a repeat pattern. She became the critical, judgmental other and Bob became the insecure, excluded self. The affects associated with this pattern were anxiety and anger, the affects Bob presented with for treatment.

women. He then related in a critical, judgmental manner, which obviously did not foster the development of intimacy. Also, as described with his last girlfriend, his tendency to put her in the excluded role and not respond to her needs was not a prescription for the growth of intimacy in a relationship. As Bob thought about it, Bob realized that he had interacted in the previously described pattern not only in this relationship but also in past relationships with women. When his girlfriend had an affair with his best friend, she effectively reversed the self and other roles back to their original positions; she assumed the critical, judgmental role and put Bob in the insecure, excluded role, stimulating the affects associated with this pattern, anxiety and anger, the affects that Bob presented with. It is hypothesized that the reason these affects were so intense and persistent was that the affects that were triggered were related not only to the present relationship but also to past relationships as well. These dynamics are illustrated in figure 14.1.

Adult Developmental Issues

Bob was in the early adult years of development; as stated previously, the two main goals of this period are (1) to establish a career, life goal, or purpose that makes life meaningful and (2) to form an intimate relationship. In terms of the first goal, Bob was well satisfied with the career that he had chosen and enjoyed his work very much. In terms of the second goal, an intimate relationship, Bob had some concerns. A lasting intimate relationship had not developed for Bob, and he was concerned that if he didn't find someone pretty soon, he might not ever find a mate. Whereas in past years he had seen the problem as one of just not meeting the right person, now he was thinking that the problem was more within himself. His most recent girlfriend had complained that he was critical and judgmental; as he looked back on past relationships, other girlfriends had made the same complaint. Bob wanted to change so that he could go on and form a fulfilling relationship; his desire and willingness to change was an important motivating factor in the psychotherapy.

Cultural, Religious, and Spiritual Issues

There were not any issues in any of these areas that came up in either the evaluation process or the treatment.

GOALS OF TREATMENT

The Inner World of the Self

Bob possessed a pretty healthy ego structure along with an id and superego that were capable of helping him maintain the emotional balance of the ego. He became imbalanced in the context of intimate relationships, and it was to the area of relationships that the attention of the therapy was directed.

Relations

Bob was very capable of forming relationships in general, but he had problems with intimate relationships. The psychotherapy was directed to the task of understanding and working through maladaptive attachment patterns and replacing them with healthy patterns so that Bob could go on and form a meaningful, lasting intimate relationship.

TREATMENT

Treatment Based on the DSM-IV Descriptive Diagnosis

Shortly after the breakup of his relationship with his girlfriend, Bob had received an anxiolytic (Xanax) from his primary care physician. While this was very helpful for him in controlling his anxiety, Bob did not want to be on medication and did want to try to do something about his problems with relationships.

Psychotherapy

Bob was seen on a weekly basis for ten sessions. During the first two sessions, he related the history that was described earlier. As he did, it became clear that Bob had been a pretty emotionally stable person all of his life but was having trouble with intimate relationships. As a result, the therapy was less involved with building emotional stability within the inner world of the self and more involved in how he related to others.

In these early sessions, Bob recounted the history of the breakup of his relationship along with his anxiety, anger, and feeling of being excluded. He felt that he had overreacted to this breakup, that this breakup had brought up feelings of being excluded in past relationships with girlfriends and feelings of being excluded within his family. He recounted the history of how he didn't get along with his sister, how this led to conflicts in the relationship between himself, his sister, and his mother, and how he ended up feeling excluded and insecure. Bob would put his sister down, which made him feel better, but then there was the inevitable backlash when his mother found out.

Much of the therapy went back and forth between the recent relationship between Bob and his girlfriend and past relationships, either with old girlfriends or with his family.

Session 3

BOB: I feel very angry about the way things turned out with my girlfriend; it's that same feeling of being excluded. It's the way I felt growing up, excluded and unwanted.

THERAPIST: That sounds pretty lonely. (empathy)

BOB: Yeah, and back then I dealt with it by being mean to my sister; I never had anything positive to say to her. I'm realizing that with my girlfriend I had a hard time giving, being positive, but being critical and negative comes naturally.

THERAPIST: It's hard for a relationship based on the exchange of negative emotions to be a growth relationship. (explanation)

BOB: I want to change that part of me that is so negative and critical.

Session 4

BOB: My girlfriend has been wanting to get back together.

THERAPIST: What do you think about that?

BOB: It's hard for me because of my anger at what she did, but with time that's less and less of a factor; there's something more.

THERAPIST: Can you help me understand it.

BOB: Well, it's that she's so needy and dependent, but that's the way all my girlfriends have been. I've shied away from more secure women; I guess I feared they'd be critical of me or that they wouldn't put up with me being critical of them.

THERAPIST: So, you've picked insecure women and been critical of them?

BOB: Yes, being negative just seems to come so natural, but that's not going to work.

THERAPIST: No, that's not a pattern of relating that's going to lead to a fulfilling relationship.

Session 5

Bob started the session with two dreams he had the night before:

1. In the dream I was going somewhere with a friend, his wife, and his ex-wife.
2. I was in a convenience store; someone was in the back room eating ice cream.

Bob thought that the first dream was symbolic of the triangular relationships he tends to get into (i.e., his mother, sister, and himself or his girlfriend, his best friend, and himself). To Bob the second dream symbolized something going on behind his back (e.g., his girlfriend having an affair with his best friend).

From there he went on to talk about his feelings about his family and childhood.

BOB: Growing up I competed with my sister for attention and lost.

THERAPIST: That must hurt. (empathy)

BOB: Yeah, I've been angry about that for years, but now that I'm talking about it more, it's become more of a sense of sadness. (mourning—moving from anger to sadness)

THERAPIST: As you talk about it, you sound sad. (empathy)

BOB: It is; I think I was angry at my mom for not giving me the attention I wanted and I took that anger out on my sister. But, more and more I am realizing that I come from a very good family. My dad was calm and understanding; and even though I didn't always get along with my mom, in most ways she was a great mom. Those are the memories I have to cling to, not the negative ones. (mourning—moving toward acceptance)

THERAPIST: It seems that you are putting the negative from the past behind you.

Session 6

BOB: I've been thinking back on several of the interchanges between myself and my girlfriend; so many times I would put her down, then she'd get angry and put me down. It's a very familiar pattern.

THERAPIST: You're describing a pattern based on the exchange of negative emotion; maybe it's possible to learn a pattern based on the mutual exchange of positive emotion. (explanation)

BOB: I want to.

Session 7

BOB: I've had a lot of anger at my girlfriend over the affair, but now I see that I'm part of the problem.

THERAPIST: How do you see it?

BOB: When she needed support I not only withdrew but became critical. Now that I see it, I feel bad abut the way I acted. I want to be more supportive in relationships.

THERAPIST: It seems to me that you are really working hard on changing.

Session 8

BOB: I've had lots of feelings of sadness lately.

THERAPIST: Can you tell me what you have been sad about?

BOB: I've been thinking a lot about this relationship with my girlfriend; mostly it's sad thoughts, sadness that it didn't work out. (mourning-dealing with sadness)

THERAPIST: That does sound sad. (empathy)

BOB: At the same time I'm feeling more optimistic about the possibility of being able to relate in a positive way and feeling better about my ability to relate to someone who is more secure.

Session 9

BOB: I began seeing someone new.

THERAPIST: How is it going?

BOB: So far so good; I'm working hard on relating in a positive manner.

THERAPIST: That sounds great.

BOB: In some ways it's not so hard; I've related that way in other situations, but usually not with girlfriends.

THERAPIST: I hope it goes well.

Session 10

BOB: I went out again with the woman I mentioned last week.

THERAPIST: How was it?

BOB: It was different.

THERAPIST: How so?

BOB: In the past my focus would have been on how soon we could have sex, now I'm more interested in getting to know her as a person.

THERAPIST: Great, I hope it works out for you.

Later . . .

THERAPIST: Well, this is our last session; how do you feel you are doing?

BOB: I'm feeling good about myself and where I am at in my career; the anxiety and anger are gone. I feel good about the prospects of a relationship; I am at the stage of my life when I would like to get married and have a family; I'm hopeful that things will work out.

THERAPIST: Can you say what, if anything, has been helpful for you in this therapy?

BOB: Yes, it's been helpful to have a forum in which to talk about my feelings; it's been helpful to be in a supportive, nonjudgmental relationship; it's a model for me. (experiencing)

THERAPIST: Best wishes for your future.

BOB: Thank you for your help.

SUMMARY

In summary, Bob was a young man who came to treatment with symptoms of anxiety and anger that developed in the context of the breakup of his relationship with his girlfriend. Evaluation showed that the emotional balance of his inner world was generally quite good, but that he had some maladaptive attachment patterns. The focus of the therapy was on helping him put these maladaptive patterns behind him and to learn some new patterns so that he could move on and develop happier, more fulfilling intimate relationships.

Bob was an active, motivated participant in the therapy. The techniques used in this therapy were (1) empathy—empathic understanding was used as a means by which to help Bob express and work through negative emotions from both his past and present; (2) explanation was used to help him understand the concept of attachment patterns and to then identify his own attachment patterns and the associated emotions; (3) experiencing was used to help him experience a supportive, nonjudgmental therapy relationship, which he could internalize as an attachment pattern and use in the formation of new relationships; and (4) mourning was used to help him with the loss of his relationship with his girlfriend as well as negative aspects of developmental relationships.

Bob seemed to respond well to these interventions and by the end of therapy was no longer experiencing any emotional dysregulation, had put the loss of his previous relationship behind him, and had started a new relationship with a woman who appeared quite emotionally healthy; he was trying to relate to her using a more positive attachment pattern.

I wished him well.

In this chapter, the case of Bob was discussed in order to illustrate the internalization of attachment patterns via developmental interactions and the subsequent use of those attachment patterns in adult relationships. Negatively cathected attachment patterns made it difficult for Bob to form intimate relationships with women. Therapy helped him deal with the developmental origins of those negatively cathected attachment patterns so as to free him up to use healthy patterns in relationships with women. Techniques used included empathy, explanation, experiencing, and the mourning of negative past developmental relationships.

15

Clinical Presentation: Gwen

Gwen is a white woman in her early forties who was referred for evaluation by her primary care physician. She had gone to her doctor with symptoms including headaches and GI upset for the last two years. His workup was negative, and he thought that her physical symptoms were stress related; she agreed. His diagnoses were tension headaches and irritable bowel syndrome.

Gwen reported that she has had these sorts of physical symptoms on and off all of her life during stressful times, but they have never been as severe or as persistent. The physical symptoms began as she was going through a divorce four years earlier. The divorce had been finalized for over two years, but the physical symptoms have persisted.

One other stress that occurred around the time of her divorce was the death of her grandfather with whom she had been very close since childhood. Another stress related to her current marriage. Gwen has been remarried for about one year. This relationship is going well, but Gwen reports that her two teenage daughters are very loyal to her ex-husband, their father, and are disinterested in forming a relationship with her current husband. This upsets Gwen because she's always had a dream of having a happy family.

Gwen also described her age as a stress. Especially before she remarried, she was concerned that time was running out on her, that if she did not find someone soon, she would never have a happy relationship. She was concerned because she felt she was not as attractive as she had been when she was twenty and because she was not as physically able. She had been an avid rock climber since she was young but, as a result of a number of falls, had developed back and shoulder problems so that she was no longer able to climb.

Besides her physical symptoms, Gwen also reported being depressed around the time of the divorce. The depression has improved but not completely gone away; she does not have symptoms of major depression. Gwen remembered being depressed as a child and related that to the fact that her parents fought all the time. She thought, however, that she was happy during her teenage years and, despite an unhappy marriage, had maintained a good mood in her twenties and thirties up until the time of the divorce. The only treatment she had ever received in the past was some couples counseling during her first marriage.

Family psychiatric history was positive for alcohol problems in her father and possibly her brother. Her mother had physical symptoms similar to hers. Gwen had no history of alcohol or drug abuse. Other than the previously mentioned physical symptoms and physical injuries, she has no other history of major medical illnesses; she was healthy as a child.

Currently, Gwen works as a bookkeeper for a local small business, a job that she enjoys. She has two teenage daughters by her first marriage. She has been remarried for the last year; that is going well except for her concern that her daughters don't seem to want to have a relationship with her new husband. Gwen used to be very involved in rock climbing but has had to give that up in the last few years; since, she has not developed a new recreational interest.

Developmentally, Gwen grew up in a family that consisted of her parents and a brother five years older. They lived in a house on a piece of property owned by her maternal grandparents. The grandparents lived in another house on the same piece of property. She stated that her parents never got along, were always fighting, critical of each other, and mean to each other. Gwen and her brother got along quite well and, even though her parents were always fighting, they were always nice to the children. Still, the constant tension between her parents led to feelings of insecurity within Gwen. She recalled that her greatest fear as a child was that her parents would divorce and she would be abandoned.

A safe haven for Gwen was her grandparent's home; she would often go there because the atmosphere was always very calm there. She spent a lot of time with her grandmother and grandfather and developed close relationships with them.

In grade school she did well academically and had friends. One friend, who lived across the street and who Gwen had played with since she was very young, died at age nine of leukemia. This was a big loss for Gwen, but she was able to go on and develop a relationship with a new best friend.

Her high school years were somewhat more tumultuous. She had a steady boyfriend during high school, and he liked to party. On the weekends they would go out, drink, and smoke marijuana. She, however, limited this activity to the weekends, studied hard during the weekdays, and was always on the honor roll. Extracurricularly, she was involved in gymnastics at school and rock climbing outside school.

After high school she took an office job and began attending classes at a junior college. She met some friends who influenced her to become a Christian. Gwen broke up with her partying boyfriend, joined a church, and became actively involved in that church. Religion has continued to be a very important part of her life.

During her junior college years, she met her first husband, but the relationship deteriorated shortly after the marriage; in fact, she said, "We fought on the honeymoon." She described him as emotionally and verbally abusive, pathologically jealous, always accusing her of having an affair. If she went grocery shopping and was gone longer than he thought she should be, he accused her of having a liaison with someone. He traveled in his job and was often gone for several days at a time. Women would call the house looking for him, but he would always claim that they were just acquaintances, and he would then turn around and accuse her of having an affair.

Despite the problems in her marriage, Gwen found fulfillment in raising her children. She homeschooled them and continued to be very active in her church. Once her children got older, she went back to school, finished her degree, and began working part-time at her bookkeeping job.

Her being away from home more, for school and then work, fueled her husband's jealousy and increased tensions between them. After seventeen years of marriage, Gwen filed for and obtained a divorce. She maintained full custody of the children, and her ex-husband had visitation every other weekend.

DIAGNOSIS

Descriptive Diagnosis

This is a middle-aged woman who presented with depression and stress-related physical symptoms. Her depression did not meet *DSM-IV-TR* criterion for one of the diagnoses in the mood disorder category; a diagnosis of Adjustment Disorder with Depressed Mood was made. The psychiatric diagnosis related to her physical symptoms would fall into the *DSM-IV-TR* category entitled Psychological Factors Affecting Medical Condition. The specific diagnosis in that category would be Stress-Related Physiological Response Affecting tension headaches and irritable bowel syndrome.

Psychodynamic Formulation

How Can We Describe the Inner Psychological World of This Person?

Ego. Gwen appeared to have attained a good degree of separation-individuation and to possess a cohesive sense of self and other (figure 15.1). Her internalized self and other representations contained positive elements but also a significant number of negative elements. She described an affective balance that had been generally positive much of her life. However, in the last few years, as a result of several stressors, including the breakup of her marriage and the death of her grandfather, she experienced an influx of negative emotion that shifted her affective baseline toward the negative end of the scale, leading to symptoms of depression and anxiety (which were manifested in physical symptoms).

Superego. Gwen possessed an ego ideal that was very capable of setting goals and a conscience that was consistent with her sociocultural environment. As will be discussed further in the next section on treatment, she did have a tendency to be quite self-critical (punitive superego) and a limited ability to be self-reinforcing (rewarding superego).

Id. Gwen was able to express (not repress) both attachment and assertive drives. Her attachment relationships with her current husband, daughters, other family members, friends, and colleagues were generally positive; her relationship with her ex-husband continued to stimulate lots of anger, which had a destabilizing effect on her affective balance. Assertive drives of self-expression associated with positive affect were expressed via work, helping to maintain some emotional stability within the ego. One important form of past self-expression, rock climbing, had been lost and had not been replaced.

How Does This Person with This Psychological Makeup Relate to Others in the World Around Her?

If we look at learned attachment patterns, we can define at least two; one she experienced in her relationship with her parents, and one she experienced in her relationship with her grandparents. The first might be characterized as a pattern between a mean, critical other and a neglected, undervalued self with associated emotions of anger and fear. The second might be characterized as a pattern between a loving, supportive other and a valued, worthwhile self with associated emotions of pleasure and affection.

Gwen felt that the pattern of her first marriage followed very much the pattern of her parents' relationship. To the extent that she still related to her ex- husband around visitation and other issues with her daughters, the negative emotions associated with this pattern were triggered. She seemed to be able to use the healthier second pattern in her relationships with her daughters, second husband, and others, leading to happier interpersonal interactions.

Adult Developmental Issues

Gwen was at the beginning of the middle adult years of life, her early forties. She described some typical midlife concerns including (1) decreased physical ability to do some of the things she used to be able to do, (2) changes in her physical appearance with age, and (3) concern about time running out. Her concerns about time running out were most acute after her divorce and were related to a fear that time would run out before she was able to find a new relationship. This anxiety had decreased significantly since her remarriage. Her relationship with a reassuring husband had helped decrease her concerns of bodily aging. Her inability to do physically what she once could was still of concern; she missed her rock climbing very much and had not found anything to replace that.

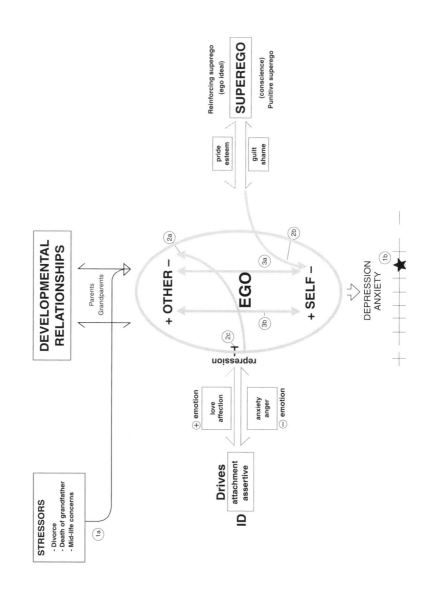

STRESSORS
- Divorce
- Death of grandfather
- Mid-life concerns

DEVELOPMENTAL
RELATIONSHIPS

Parents
Grandparents

SUPEREGO

Reinforcing superego
(ego ideal)

(conscience)
Punitive superego

pride
esteem

guilt
shame

+ OTHER –

EGO

+ SELF –

DEPRESSION
ANXIETY

Drives
ID   attachment
      assertive

+ emotion
love
affection

anxiety
anger
– emotion

repression

Figure 15.1. Psychotherapy: Gwen before Therapy

1. Though Gwen had maintained a generally positive affective balance most of her life, several stressors (1a) had stimulated the influx of negative affect that upset her affective balance, leading to symptoms of depression and anxiety (manifested in physical symptoms) (1b).

2. One of the affects stimulated was anger (2a) with her ex-husband, and another was guilt (2b) over the divorce. Besides the addition of these negative affects, there was the loss of positive affect, which had previously been stimulated by her relationship with grandfather and her ability to rock climb (2c).

3. Gwen described two different attachment patterns:

   a. Mean, critical other interacting with a neglected, undervalued self with associated emotions of anger and fear

   b. Loving, supportive other interacting with a valued, worthwhile self with associated emotions of pleasure affection

4. Therapy goals:

   a. Work through her negative feelings of anger toward her ex-husband and continue to invest positive affect in her relationship with her current husband.

   b. Resolve the feelings of loss she experiences over the death of her grandfather and replace those with happy memories of their interactions together.

   c. Express her feelings about no longer having the ability to pursue her rock-climbing interests and find a new interest that is associated with positive affect.

   d. Help her balance her superego by becoming less self critical and more self-rewarding.

   e. Work through the negative self and other affects associated with her early relationship with her parents as well as the affects associated with that self-other attachment pattern (3a), allowing her to experience positive self and other affects that she has and to relate according to her more positive attachment pattern (3b).

Cultural, Religious, and Spiritual Issues

Gwen was a very religious woman and had strong negative feelings about divorce. Though not very aware of it at first, as the therapy proceeded, Gwen became very aware of her own profound feelings of guilt concerning her own divorce. The influx of guilt from her superego made it difficult to maintain a positive emotional balance within the ego.

In summary, Gwen presented with depression and stress-related symptoms. Current stressors that led to a sense of loss and a negative emotional influx included her divorce, the death of her grandfather, and midlife concerns. The divorce and death stimulated negative emotions from the id (anger and sadness). Her inability to continue rock climbing led to the loss of a positive emotional influx. Guilt from the superego exacerbated the negative emotional influx from her id, making it harder to maintain a positive emotional balance. The previously described stresses triggered the experience of negative emotions from her past relationships with her parents, which further complicated her ability to maintain a positive emotional balance. Her remarriage, however, stimulated positive emotions and helped restore her emotional balance to a degree.

GOALS OF THERAPY

1. Help Gwen work through the negative emotions that have been stimulated in the past via her relationship with her parents and in the present via her relationship with and divorce from her husband.
2. Help Gwen work through the memory of the loss of the emotionally positive interactions with her grandfather and to replace the negative memories of loss with pleasurable memories of past interactions with her grandfather. Try to replace these losses with new, positive interactions.
3. Work through the loss of past abilities (rock climbing) and develop new modes of self-expression associated with pleasurable emotion.
4. Help Gwen work through the guilt she has over the divorce and help her to develop more of an ability to be self-rewarding.
5. Work through old maladaptive attachment patterns associated with negative affect so this does not get repeated again and so that she is free to use the positive patterns she has in her repertoire.

TREATMENT

Symptomatic Treatment

At one point, Gwen's primary care physician had started her on a low dose of a tricyclic antidepressant; this had been helpful in quieting down her GI symptoms, but Gwen had stopped it after a short time because she did not want to be on medication. We discussed the possibility of trying a relaxation exercise to see if it would help with her physical symptoms; Gwen was interested in this. During an early session we did deep breathing, muscle relaxation exercises along with some guided imagery of a relaxing scene. The exercise was audiotaped; Gwen practiced the exercise at home and reported that she found it helpful in learning a relaxation response and in decreasing her physical symptoms.

Psychotherapy

Gwen was seen on a weekly basis for eight sessions. The therapy addressed the following four areas, though certainly not in such a sequential manner as is presented (figure 15.2).

Working on Decreasing Negative Emotional Balance

In the early sessions, Gwen spoke often of her interactions with her ex-husband in the present; the interactions mostly revolved around discussions about visitation times and driving her daughters back and forth for visitation with their father. Sometimes these interactions were contentious, often they were not. Still, these interactions almost always brought up many feelings of anger. Consider the following interaction:

GWEN: I saw my ex-husband again last night.
THERAPIST: How did that go?
GWEN: Nothing happened, just the weekly exchange of the kids for visitation.
THERAPIST: Oh, I see.
GWEN: But, afterward, I began feeling angry again; I began thinking of all the past episodes.
THERAPIST: Can you share your thoughts and feelings with me?

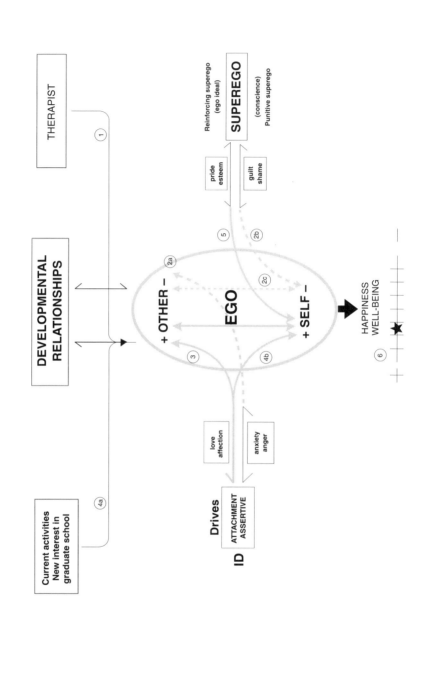

Figure 15.2. Psychotherapy: Gwen after Therapy

1. Via the therapy relationship, the therapist provides Gwen with a secure base from which she can experience various affects both positive and negative.

2. bFrom this secure base, Gwen was able to express and resolve various affects, including
   a. her anger with her ex-husband,
   b. her guilt over her divorce, and
   c. the negative self and other affects associated with early developmental relationships.

3. As Gwen mourned the loss of her grandfather, she was able to replace her feelings of sadness with happy memories of past interactions.

4. Gwen replaced her former interest in rock climbing with a new interest in learning in graduate school (4a), which stimulated positive affects for her (4b).

5. Gwen was able to rearrange her superego so that it was much less punitive and much more rewarding.

6. The effect of the above was to decrease negative affective inputs and increase positive affective inputs, thus shifting her affective balance from its depressive state to one of happiness and well-being.

GWEN: I remember one time he came home after being away for two days on a business trip; three different women had called the house. I asked him about it, but he just got angry and then began accusing me of having an affair. I felt so bad (cries).

THERAPIST: Those must have been really difficult times. (empathy)

GWEN: (crying) Yes, I have lots of sadness over that relationship, but now what I experience more is anger. (experiencing various stages of mourning)

Through multiple such empathic exchanges, Gwen worked through her feelings over the abusive relationship with her ex-husband. Explanation was also used; for example: "Hopefully we can decrease the amount of negative emotions that you walk around with so that you are not so depressed most of the time." As her negative feelings toward her ex-husband diminished, Gwen began to talk more and more about her early family.

GWEN: Whenever I think about my childhood, I cry.

THERAPIST: It sounds like you have lots of sad feelings about that time in your life.

GWEN: My parents never seemed to want to have anything to do with me. I remember one time when I was seven or eight, I ran away from home. I walked two or three miles down the road, but then came to a freeway and was afraid to cross. I hid behind a tumbleweed and waited to see if someone would come looking for me. After about an hour, no one came and I walked back home.

THERAPIST: What happened when you got home?

GWEN: It was getting late so I went to bed (cries); my parents didn't notice that I was gone.

THERAPIST: That's very sad. I can see why you have lots of feelings about your childhood; you are giving me a really good sense of what it was like to grow up in your world. (empathy)

Here is another example:

GWEN: I feel bad that my daughters don't seem to want to have much to do with my new husband.

THERAPIST: Can you help me understand what that feeling is like?

GWEN: I guess it brings up feelings of my childhood; my daughters and husband don't interact, just like my parents didn't interact with me and my brother (cries).

THERAPIST: Those must be very hurtful feelings. (empathy)

GWEN: (sobbing) Yes!

These types of interchanges stimulated a mourning process for Gwen—mourning a loss of a childhood that might have been better. She eventually seemed to be able to put that behind her and then moved on to the issue of her divorce.

GWEN: I have felt bad about my divorce ever since it happened.

THERAPIST: Can you help me understand what that feeling is like?

GWEN: It was just a general bad feeling for a long time, but now I know it's guilt.

THERAPIST: Guilt?

GWEN: Yes, it's the guilt that has made me depressed. Divorce is wrong in my religion; I broke my vows; I failed my family and worse, I failed my God.

THERAPIST: Oh, now I understand why this has been difficult for you. (empathy)

Talking about her divorce in the nonjudgmental context of the therapy relationship seemed to be helpful for Gwen. She also talked to her minister and members of her church, and that was helpful. She was able to get beyond the guilt and get to a point where she felt that she had given her marriage her best try and to accept that it had failed.

I have discussed decreasing the negative within the self, including her anger at her ex-husband, her anger at her parents, and her guilt over her divorce. Next I move on to a discussion of increasing positive.

Working on Increasing Positive Emotional Balance

GWEN: When I was in grade school, I worked hard to get good grades because I thought that would lead to some recognition from my parents, but it didn't.

THERAPIST: That sounds pretty frustrating. (empathy)

GWEN: (sadly) Yeah.

THERAPIST: Are you able to feel good about any of your accomplishments now?

GWEN: No, it just seems expected.

THERAPIST: Maybe if you could feel some positive emotion about your abilities and attributes, that would help your overall emotional balance and decrease your depression. (explanation)

Gwen was asked to come up with a list of positive self-characteristics and to assign an emotion to each one. She generated a long list of self-characteristics including "nice, fair, honest, intelligent, attractive, industrious, motivated, dependable, loving, humble, forgiving, warm, capable, artistic, clean, spiritual." She was not, however, able to come up with any positive emotion words to associate with these self-characteristics.

GWEN: I was never given any recognition for anything positive; it was just expected.
THERAPIST: You have really described a very nice list of positive characteristics; is it possible for you to feel a sense of pride over the positive in you?
GWEN: That's such a foreign idea; no one ever said, "I'm proud of you."
THERAPIST: Would you be willing to try?
GWEN: Yes.

The concept of being self-rewarding and experiencing a sense of pride was one that Gwen took to quite readily. She began to be able to experience positive emotions related to her positive self-characteristics. She felt that developing an ability to do this was very important in helping her maintain a more positive emotional balance.

Dealing with the Loss of Positive Emotions

Besides the loss of her first marriage, Gwen described two other significant losses—the loss of her grandfather and the loss of her capability to rock climb. In both of these instances, we worked on mourning the losses and on replacing the negative emotions with positive.

Since her grandfather's death had occurred at the time she was going through her divorce, she never really mourned his loss. Her grandfather had been a very important person for her growing up, providing a loving counterpoint to her father's negativity. He had continued to be important to her in her adult years, relating to her children in much the same way that he had related to Gwen when she was a child.

As Gwen began to talk about her grandfather, the mourning process was initiated; she was able to express her sadness and sorrow. Eventually, Gwen was able to replace her feelings of sadness over the loss of her grandfather with an image of him that included the many happy memories from her past.

The other thing that happened to Gwen around the time of her divorce was the loss of her capability to rock climb. Rock climbing was an activity that had brought her pleasure since her childhood. She was able to express her feelings over this loss, but had not found any pleasurable activity to replace the riding. Eventually, she began to take some classes at a local university and found this to be enjoyable. She decided to pursue an advanced degree, and this became an activity that stimulated much pleasure in much the same way that her climbing had.

WORK ON DECREASING NEGATIVE ATTACHMENT PATTERNS

Gwen described the attachment pattern that she experienced between her parents as one between a mean, critical other and a neglected, undervalued self with associated emotions of anger and fear. She very much felt that she had repeated this pattern in her relationship with her ex-husband. The goal of this part of the therapy was to help her put this pattern behind her so that she did not repeat it in future relationships. Much of the work on this has already been described in the previous section where we talked about working through her negative feelings concerning her parents and her ex-husband. In other words, the therapy consists of working through the negative self and other representations that are the components of this negative attachment pattern. That is, putting the negative feelings about her parents and husband behind her, and in addition putting the negative feelings about herself in her relationship with them behind her.

The other part of the therapy, which had been attended to from the beginning, is that of experiencing—that is, providing in the therapy an experience of an attachment pattern that is qualitatively different from the negative patterns she has learned in the past. One thing that was different with Gwen was that she already had some positive attachment patterns (grandparents) in her repertoire. Some people need to not only unlearn old patterns but also learn new ones; Gwen was further ahead in this respect.

At the end of therapy, Gwen felt that she was more able to be positive about herself and more able to be proud of her accomplishments. She was less self-critical and now able to experience pleasure in ongoing activities. Emotionally she described herself as calm, and she was no longer experiencing stress-related physical symptoms.

The one issue that remained a concern for Gwen was the relationship between her daughters and her new husband. She knew that family therapy was available through her church, and she planned to look into that.

SUMMARY

Gwen presented with symptoms of depression and symptoms of a psychosomatic nature. The psychodynamic formulation dealt with issues of sense of self, relationship difficulties, adult developmental issues, and conflicted feelings related to her religious belief system.

A relaxation technique was used as a symptomatic treatment. Psychotherapeutic techniques such as empathy, experiencing, explanation, and mourning were used as we worked on decreasing her negative emotional balance and increasing her positive emotional balance.

16

Clinical Presentation: Terry

Terry is a middle-aged white professional woman who came in requesting help with the acute onset of anxiety of several days' duration. Along with a constant sense of nervousness, difficulty concentrating, crying spells, and feelings of vulnerability, on a number of occasions during the last few days, she had experienced herself as if she were outside her body, a dreamlike state in which she felt as if she were floating above herself watching her life go on below. While the acute anxiety went away during these periods, the episodes in and of themselves were very disturbing.

The acute stressor that Terry described had to do with a relationship she had developed several months earlier with a woman who worked in the same office building as Terry. This woman was somewhat older than Terry, but they shared many ideas and interests. They frequently had lunch together and would occasionally see each other in the evening or on a weekend; during these times, they engaged in long conversations concerning topics of common interest. Terry came to feel quite bonded to her friend, whom she described as empathic, giving, and nonjudgmental.

One night Terry had a dream in which part of her was inside her friend. She shared this dream with her friend who, as opposed to Terry, was quite disturbed by this dream. She told Terry that she thought it was best that they not see each other for a while; and it was after this that Terry began to experience the previously described symptoms of anxiety and depersonalization.

Other than what has been described, Terry denied any other major stressors in her life. She had no history of similar symptoms and had never before sought treatment for any psychological problems. In thinking about this current relationship, she did recall one other situation. As an undergraduate in college, she identified quite intensely with one female professor. She never expressed any feelings toward this professor, and when the semester ended, the feelings gradually dissipated. Terry stated, however, that the feelings she has toward her current friend are similar to what she experienced with the professor.

Terry felt that she had been a pretty happy person all of her life, but described what she called "an empty part of me" that was associated with sadness and anger.

There is no history of alcohol or substance abuse, no family psychiatric history, and no history of medical illness.

Socially, Terry lived with her husband and teenage son. She had been married for about twenty years, believed that she and her husband had always had a good relationship, and felt that they were getting closer and closer as time went on. She also described being very attached to her teenage son and spoke with a sense of pride in discussing his various scholastic accomplishments. Professionally, she worked in a career that she had trained for in college and graduate school; she enjoyed her work very much and was well satisfied with her advancement in her field.

Developmentally, Terry grew up with her parents, a brother two years older, and a sister two years younger. She described her mother, an artist, in very mixed terms: on the one hand, she was imaginative, energetic, talented, intuitive, and dynamic; on the other hand, she was eccentric, idiosyncratic, totally unorganized, self-absorbed, and emotionally unavailable. She was engrossed in her work; Terry recalled that trying to talk to her was like shouting at someone with absolutely soundproof ear plugs. When she did listen, her mother tended to be quite opinionated, and quite often the opinions she expressed were critical of Terry.

As the history unfolds, Terry mentions that she has never had close relationships with women; this goes back to earlier relationships, including her mother, her sister, and her maternal grandmother. In fact, she said, "Even now when I talk to my mother I get upset!" She described that she never felt validated in her relationship with her mother, that her mother was never able to make positive statements to her, that she always felt discounted in her relationship with her mother. The affects associated with this relationship included anxiety, sadness, anger, resentment, irritation, and at times rage. "I have avoided relationships with women because the feelings they bring up have such a destabilizing effect on me; the negative feelings that come up in relationships with women prevent closeness, so I keep these relationships on an intellectual level." There have been times when she has not been able to control her feelings in relationships with women. She has expressed anger at women in a manner she feels was out of proportion to the situation, effectively destroying the relationship.

Terry discussed how her mother was frequently critical of her, how whatever she did was not good enough. The affects associated with this included guilt and shame. In adult relationships with women, Terry feared criticism. Terry described a sense of emptiness, a sense that she had missed something in her early female relationships, a desire to have a relationship with another woman.

Her mother was not at all involved in running the household; she never planned meals, cooked, shopped, cleaned, helped the children with homework, or took them to school events. The house was totally unorganized and, when she started grade school, Terry was shocked to see how orderly the rooms were. Despite this, she recalled happy memories of their household, with the work of famous artists hanging on all the walls and classical music playing constantly in the background. "I remember doing cartwheels through the high, vaulted living room to the music of Tchaikovsky!"

Her father worked in the computer industry; "He was the total opposite of my mother." To a large extent, she and he ran the household in terms of cooking, cleaning, shopping, transportation, etc. Terry always felt close to her father; he was there for her—supportive, caring, warm, and understanding.

She also felt that she developed a strong bond with her brother and often enjoyed doing things with him and his friends more than female friends. She and her younger sister were not close; the sister was sickly, and to the extent that anyone got mother's attention, it was she. In interactions among the three of them, Terry was always wrong and the sister was always right.

Terry's maternal grandmother lived nearby but did not seem to be interested in grandchildren, so there was not much of a relationship either positive or negative with her. Terry felt quite close to her father's mother, but she lived across the country, and so there were not frequent interactions.

Terry did very well academically in school, taking enriched classes in grade school and AP classes in high school. She was involved in multiple clubs, organizations, and extracurricular activities. Several teachers from her grade school and high school years were important identification figures for her.

Socially, she always had friends but tended to feel more comfortable with guys than girls. She did not feel she had many "best friend" relationships with females and, in fact, could remember only one from her high school years. Terry dated some in high school, tending to prefer guys a few years older, finding guys her own age too immature. Often her boyfriends were male friends of her brother.

After high school she moved away to college and graduated in four years. College was a very positive experience for her academically. Socially she met a man and developed her first long-term relationship. They stayed together for over two years but eventually broke up shortly before graduation.

After college she attended professional school, receiving training in a field that she still very much enjoys. It was during those years that she met the man she eventually married. While she has been very happy with her family and her professional life, she has not had many close female friends in her adult years.

DIAGNOSIS

We will follow the same format outlined in the previous section (see exhibit 13.1).

Descriptive DSM-IV Diagnosis

Terry presented with symptoms of anxiety and dissociation of several days' duration. Her symptoms, however, had largely dissipated prior to her first appointment. She wished, however, to be in therapy to understand her reaction to this situation, as she believed she had some long-standing unresolved issues from the past. In this case, then, there is no specific treatment aimed at a *DSM-IV* diagnosis.

PSYCHODYNAMIC FORMULATION

How Can We Describe the Inner Psychological World of This Person?

Ego Development

Separation-individuation. Terry manifested a high degree of separation-individuation (figure 16.1). She had completed the separation-individuation process to the point of internalizing mostly positive cohesive self and other representations, though there were some negative elements in both her self representation (lonely, empty spot) and other representation (critical, unsupportive other). Her high degree of separation-individuation correlates with significant ego strength, which she can use to deal with interpsychic issues and also in coping and adapting to the outside world.

Self/other representations and affective balance. Terry's internal self and other presentations were cohesive and whole. She had achieved a level of ambivalence—that is, the ability to see and experience both positive and negative aspects of the self and other within one cohesive image. For example, within her own self-image she could experience a person with positive characteristics (talented, capable, high energy, free spirited) but also some negative characteristics (inner sense of isolation and, at times, melancholy). Her internalized image of mother contained several negatives (self-absorbed, impractical, eccentric, disorganized, unsupportive, insensitive) but, at the same time, many positives (creative, intuitive, talented, wonderful, beautiful). This ability to experience ambivalence, but mostly positive cohesive self and other representations correlates with object constancy, which is very important in one's ability to maintain an inner sense of emotional well-being.

Superego Development

Terry described growing up with a father who was supportive and complimentary, but a mother who was negative, critical, discounting, judgmental, not able to validate her, not able to make positive statements to her. She internalized a superego that had some healthy aspects and some less than healthy aspects. On the punitive side, she felt that she tended to be harder on herself than she needed to be; others had commented on her tendency to be

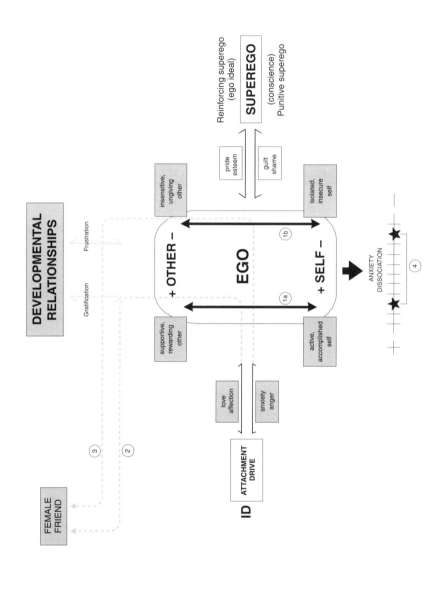

Figure 16.1. Psychotherapy: Terry before Treatment

1. Attachment patterns:
   a. A pattern between a supportive and rewarding other and an active, accomplished self. Expression of attachment drive along this pattern was associated with affects of love and affection.
   b. A pattern between an insensitive, ungiving other and an isolated, insecure self. Expression of attachment drive along this pattern was associated with anger and anxiety.
2. Terry tended to use the first pattern (1a) and repress the second (1b). This was the case in the early phase of her relationship with her female friend.
3. When her female friend suggested that relationship was getting too close, she felt rejected; the other attachment pattern was activated (1b) along with the associated emotions of anger and anxiety.
4. Anxiety and anger overwhelmed the ego and led to symptom formation and shifted the affective balance from its usual positive state to a more negative state.

self-critical. If she did not live up to her expectations, she feared being criticized by others, but noted that in general, the criticism came from within.
Rather, others tended to praise her, but she often had a hard time accepting
that praise, had a hard time being self-rewarding. She also tended to have
rather high expectations of herself and could not be self-rewarding unless
she achieved at a very high level. Though her superego was certainly not
primitive, it did tend to have somewhat exaggerated punitive and
perfectionistic standards. Her ego ideal was very capable of establishing
goals; her conscience seemed consistent with the culture around her.

Id Development

In general, attachment and assertive drives are associated with positive affect
and are expressed, leading to a meaningful career, a fulfilling relationship
with her husband and son, and a variety of recreational interests. Attachment
drives toward women tended to be repressed, leading to a sense of emptiness
with respect to female-female relationships, and creating some degree of
affective imbalance within the ego.

How Does a Person with This Psychological Makeup Relate to Others in the World around Her?

Internalized Object Relationships (Attachment Patterns)

The previous discussion on separation-individuation implies that with respect to internalized object relations, we are dealing with relationships between a whole self and whole other, as opposed to part object relationships.
In this context, Terry described a generally very positive relationship with
her father and older brother. We might describe an internalized object relations (attachment) pattern between Terry and her father as one between a
supportive, rewarding father and an active, accomplished daughter. The
affects associated with this pattern were love and affection. Terry was able to
use this pattern in relating to men in general and her husband more
specifically; she always felt that it was easier for her to relate to men than
women.

   The pattern that she learned in her relationship with her mother might be
characterized as one between a self-absorbed, insensitive, ungiving other and
an unacceptable, isolated, insecure self. The affects associated with this pat-

tern were anger and rage, but then also a sense of guilt for having these nega-tive feeling toward her mother. During her life, Terry had few female friends and stated that she always feared rejection in relating to women. In the rela-tionship described in this case, she had been able to get away from that fear of rejection because the women had been so accepting and supportive. After Terry told her friend of her dream, the friend began to fear that Terry wanted a more intimate relationship than she was willing to give. In fact, Terry de-scribed the fantasy that this relationship might make up for the relationship she had always longed to have with her mother. In this context, the friend abruptly broke off the relationship, effectively rejecting Terry and triggering all the negative effects associated with her mother attachment pattern.

Besides Early Developmental Issues, Are There Issues from Adult Development to Be Considered?

Other than what has been described, Terry did not have any major adult midlife issues. She was happy with her career, her marriage was stable, her parents were both healthy. The only things that she expressed as a concern for the future was that her teenage son was growing up and would be leaving home. She had enjoyed a close relationship with him and was not sure how she would deal with that loss/transition. This event was a few years off and not a major factor at the time of treatment.

Cultural, Religious, and Spiritual Issues

There were no major cultural, religious, or spiritual issues in this case. Terry and her husband belonged to a church and found that involvement to be supportive and rewarding.

In summary, this is a middle aged woman who presents with brief dura-tion symptoms of anxiety and dissociation, which occurred in the context of a relationship with another woman. She had, in general, repressed drives to form relationships with women because the attachment pattern she had learned for relating to women was associated with anxiety, anger, guilt, and shame. She experienced this woman, however, as so accepting, understand-ing, and supportive that she was able to overcome her anxiety and fear of crit-icism and enter into a relationship. When her friend suggested that they cool off their relationship, the ego was no longer able to maintain the repression of anxiety usually associated with relationships with other women, and the ego was flooded with this anxiety. She dealt with this anxiety using the mechanism of defense, dissociation, leading to the symptom of depersonalization. Because she possessed considerable ego strength, she was able to reconstitute quickly but was interested in entering into psychotherapy to understand herself better.

GOALS OF THERAPY

Ego

Work through and resolve the negative aspects of her self and other representations while maintaining and strengthening the positive aspects of her self and other representations.

Superego

Help her develop a more rewarding and a less punitive/perfectionistic superego structure so that her superego can be more of an ally and less of a foe in its interaction with the ego.

Id

Help her learn to associate attachment drives with women with positive affect so that expression of these drives does not destabilize the ego.

Relationships

Work through the negative affects associated with maladaptive attachment patterns and replace those patterns with healthy ones, so that Terry can develop fulfilling relationships with women.

PSYCHOTHERAPY

Terry was seen on a weekly basis for twenty sessions (figure 16.2). She was a very motivated participant in psychotherapy and over the sessions worked on the goals we had agreed upon (i.e., improving the affective balance of her inner world by addressing id, ego, and superego issues and their interactions; and improving her ability to relate to others, especially other women). These issues were not worked on in succession, but she went back and forth between these two areas as we discussed events from the early years of her life as well as those that were ongoing in the present.

The discussion of the therapy will focus on the three general interventions presented previously: explanation, empathy, and experiencing. Some examples of explanation are given next. Here, explanation is used to help Terry understand emotional processes and to maintain the focus of the therapy on the goals that have been set out.

"You have many positive characteristics within yourself, but you also describe some negative aspects which lead to frequent feelings of emptiness and sadness. Perhaps we can work on diminishing or resolving those negative factors so that you can experience a more constant sense of emotional well-being." This is a comment addressing the affective balance of the ego.

"You have described how you tend to be self-critical but find it hard to compliment yourself. If you are always critical and seldom complimenting, it makes it hard to maintain a positive emotional balance within yourself. Perhaps we can reverse this trend—that is, become more self-rewarding and less self-critical so that it will be easier to maintain an inner sense of well-being." This is a comment that addresses her superego function.

"You have told me that relationships with women tend to bring up the same negative feeling you have experienced in your relationship with your mother, resulting in your feeling emotionally destabilized. Maybe we can work on developing a new, more emotionally positive pattern of relating to women and put this old pattern behind you." This is a comment that addresses the issue of attachment patterns.

Next we move on to empathy as a second general intervention. Empathy is one way of addressing the emotional imbalance in the inner world of oneself; several examples follow.

TERRY: My mother never had time for me; when she did interact with me, it was to criticize me. There was always a barrier in our relationship, never any closeness.

THERAPIST: It sounds like you still have a lot of pain inside as a result of that relationship.

TERRY: It's anger (voice getting louder); I can't even talk to my mother on the phone without getting angry.

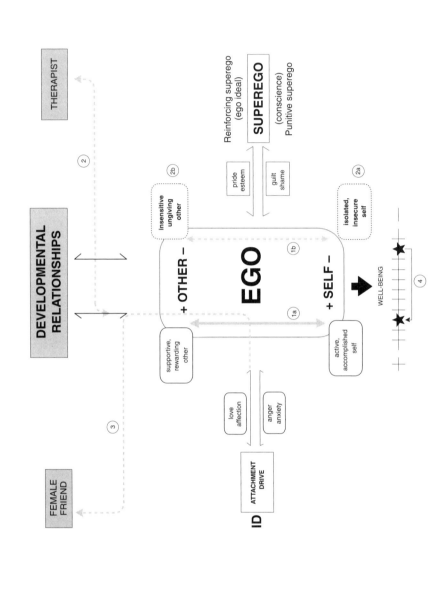

THERAPIST

DEVELOPMENTAL RELATIONSHIPS

FEMALE FRIEND

SUPEREGO
Reinforcing superego (ego ideal)
(conscience)
Punitive superego

pride
esteem

guilt
shame

insensitive ungiving other

2b

isolated, insecure self

2a

+ OTHER –

EGO

+ SELF –

1b

1a

supportive, rewarding other

active, accomplished self

WELL-BEING

4

love affection

anger anxiety

ID   ATTACHMENT DRIVE

2

3

Figure 16.2. Psychotherapy: Terry after Treatment

1. The main movement in the therapy involved the two attachment patterns (1a and 1b). Therapy sought to diminish the negative attachment pattern (1b) along with its associated negative self and other representations and to reinforce the positive attachment pattern (1b) along with its associated positive self and other representations.

2. The therapy relationship provided a supportive environment (a secure base) from which Terry could express and resolve her negative self (2a) and other (2b) representations as well as the relationship between those self and other representations. This allowed her to consolidate a representation of her mother around the positive aspects of her mother and to consolidate a positive representation of her self interacting with that mother.

3. She was able to go on to use her positive attachment pattern to relate to her female friend as well as other women.

4. The above allowed her to shift her affective balance back to a more positive state of well-being.

THERAPIST: Those feelings sound pretty uncomfortable.

TERRY: It's not just anger, it's sadness. There's an empty spot inside of me that often leaves me feeling melancholy.

TERRY: My mother was never able to be sensitive to my emotional needs; in fact, even when I was small, she turned to me to get her emotional needs met.

THERAPIST: That must have been a very difficult position to be in as a child.

TERRY: My mother was never able to give me a sense of security; that's the empty space I talked about.

THERAPIST: Do you mean that it's hard for you to carry around with you an internal image of your mother that gives you a sense of security?

TERRY: Yes, that's it.

TERRY: I ran across a book on mothers and daughters at the bookstore. The book had spaces for you to put in pictures and write statements about happy interactions with your mother from various times in your childhood. There was a part of me that wanted to buy that book, but I realized that I would have to leave almost all of the pages blank.

THERAPIST: That sounds very sad.

TERRY: Yes.

THERAPIST: It must hurt when you realize that you don't have many happy images of interactions with your mother inside you.

TERRY: My thoughts, feelings, and ideas were discounted; all that mattered were my mother's thoughts, feelings, and ideas. I felt unheard; my mother could never make positive statements to me; she could only be negative: "You don't look good in that dress; you should wear your hair different."

THERAPIST: As you talk, there is a real sense of hurt in your voice.

As Terry was able to express more and more feelings about her relationship with her mother, I suggested that we think about this along the lines of the mourning model (one of the specific interactions described earlier). That is, we discussed viewing the negative aspects of the relationship as the loss of something that might have been better, and as something she could work through and resolve. This seemed to make sense to her. Whereas before the most prominent feelings that she experienced toward her mother were anger, she was able to move on to sadness, depression, and grief, to express her feelings of loss in her relationship with her mother. She moved on to a level of acceptance—that is, a level of accepting her mother for who she was—perhaps not the best mother, but her mother nonetheless. Eventually she came to a new level of resolution in which she could value the positive things within her mother and the positive things her mother had given her.

As this process progressed, Terry went from not being able to talk to her mother on the phone about a neutral topic without getting angry, to being able to go visit her mother, spend time with her, engage in activities with her, and enjoy their interaction.

The previous discussion addresses Terry's internalized other image of her mother and movement of that internalization from one that is negatively cathected emotionally to one that is positively cathected, helping to improve her overall emotional balance. Next I will move on to make a few comments about her internalized self representation.

Terry possessed many self characteristics that were cathected with positive affect, but there were others that were negatively cathected, as illustrated in the following sequence:

TERRY: There are parts of me that always make me feel sad.
THERAPIST: What are these?
TERRY: I am a high-energy, creative, artistic person.
THERAPIST: Those sound like positive qualities to me; can you help me understand how they make you feel sad?
TERRY: I guess it is because these are the characteristics that I took in from my mother. My mother was a very different kind of person, and I associate different with weird, unlovable, unacceptable as a person because that's how I felt in my relationship with my mother. If someone comments on my artistic ability, I always feel sad.

As Terry worked through her feelings about her mother, as described earlier, she got to the point where she could value her creative and artistic abilities, to associate them with a sense of pleasure and pride rather than sadness. Thus, in describing Terry's inner world, we have discussed her ability to shift the emotions associated with her internalized self and other representations from negative to positive. The effect of these two shifts was an improvement in her overall sense of emotional well-being. Terry said, "That sense of emptiness is gone, I rarely feel melancholy anymore, most of the time I'm happy."

Before moving on to a discussion of relationships, I will take up one more topic that relates to the emotional balance of her inner world, her superego. Terry described that she felt especially vulnerable to criticism from others and had a hard time accepting praise from others. As mentioned previously, Terry experienced her mother as critical and seldom rewarding. Terry realized that she interacted with herself in the same way: she tended to be self-punitive and had a hard time being self-rewarding.

Obviously, in terms of superego functioning, we would like to see just the opposite (i.e., a superego that can be appropriately self-rewarding and not a superego that is inappropriately self-punitive). An influx of emotions such as pride and esteem from the superego helps to maintain and improve one's emotional balance, whereas the influx of emotions such as guilt and shame diminishes one's emotional balance.

Working through her feelings about her mother, as described earlier, was one factor that helped improve Terry's balance of rewarding to punitive superego. Cognitive techniques could also be used to work on the rewarding to punitive balance. Consider the following sequence:

TERRY: I was assigned a project by a committee I am on at work; I presented the results to the committee last week.

THERAPIST: How did it go?

TERRY: Not very well; I am not happy with my work on that project.

THERAPIST: Oh, how come?

TERRY: It wasn't thorough enough.

THERAPIST: Wasn't thorough enough?

TERRY: No, I should have done better.

THERAPIST: How did the committee feel about the project?

TERRY: Oh, they thought it was great; they went on and on about how wonderful it was.

THERAPIST: It sounds like there is a pretty significant difference between the way you evaluated your work and the way the committee evaluated it. You weren't able to give yourself credit, and yet they were very praiseworthy.

TERRY: Yeah, I've always been very self-critical and always found it hard to accept praise.

THERAPIST: Do you suppose it's possible to consider reversing that trend, becoming less self- critical and more praise accepting?

TERRY: Maybe.

It seemed that the repetition of several such sequences over time was beneficial in helping Terry shift to a more rewarding and less punitive super-ego.

Next I will shift from a discussion of the inner world of emotional balance to a discussion of relationships with others. This shift is somewhat artificial because therapy does not proceed from issues of one's inner self to issues of relationships with others in an orderly sequence; both issues are dealt with together. However, for purposes of discussion, it is easier to sort them out.

It was the stress of the relationship with Terry's female friend that brought her into therapy in the first place, but not unrelated was her concern that she had not had much in the line of female relationships throughout her life. The goal of therapy was to get to the point of being able to establish fulfilling relationships with other women.

One of the concepts that I described earlier in the context of the treatment of relationship issues was that of "experiencing." The concept of experiencing refers to the patient experiencing, in the context of the relationship between the therapist and the patient, an attachment pattern that is different from what the patient has experienced in the past. The hope is that the attachment pattern will be more useful so that the patient can transpose that pattern onto relationships outside the therapy relationship. From the therapist's perspective, this means being constantly mindful of the relationship pattern that is going on in the room at all times. It also means understanding the patterns that the patient has used in the past that have not been successful so that aspects of those patterns are not repeated in the therapy relationship.

Terry experienced her relationship with her mother, but also with her maternal grandmother and sister, as rather negative. As she discussed these relationships, she described an internalized attachment pattern between a self-absorbed, critical other and an insecure, invalidated self with the associated emotions of anger and anxiety.

Conversely, she described a much more positive pattern in her early relationship with her father and brother. She had always found it easier to relate to men and enjoyed meaningful fulfilling relationships with her husband and son. She seemed to be able to use this positive pattern in working with a male therapist, leading to a strong working relationship. Therapy with a female therapist might have evolved along much different lines.

Having identified a relationship pattern that has not worked for Terry, we can understand some aspects of her relationships with women. She described two different types of interactions with women: they were either contentious interactions or nonexistent interactions. In the latter situation, Terry avoided interactions with women to avoid the negative emotions associated with her internalized attachment pattern. If she did interact, the attachment pattern was often activated, usually with negative results. Consider the following interaction that Terry described:

> I ran into a woman that I know at the coffee shop, and we sat down together. There was a part of me that wanted to get to know her better. As we talked, I told her about some of the stresses that were going on in my life. She responded by talking about some of her problems. As she did, I felt the rage welling up inside me. I knew that if I didn't do something soon, I would start shouting at her (as I have in the past in similar situations). To avoid that, I got up abruptly and walked out.

We can consider Terry's reaction in terms of the activation of the previously mentioned attachment pattern between a self-absorbed, critical other and an insecure, invalidated self with the associated emotions of anxiety and anger. The other woman's response to Terry talking about the stresses in her life was to talk of some of her own stresses. Terry experienced this woman as self-absorbed and invalidating, and became anxious and angry, the emotions associated with activation of that attachment pattern.

Terry described several such interactions with women over the years. Obviously this pattern of interacting was not going to lead to long-lasting relationships. Therapy was aimed at helping her put this attachment pattern behind her and at developing a new pattern that could lead to more fulfilling relationships.

The previous discussion talked of Terry's working through her feelings toward her internal representation of her mother. Simultaneously, she was working on the maladaptive attachment pattern that she carried around with her as a result of early mother-daughter interactions. As that pattern dissipated, she was able to develop a more healthy self-other attachment pattern. This pattern allowed her to interact in a much more pleasant manner with her mother. She rekindled the relationship with the older woman, the one with whom Terry had developed the symptoms in the first place. There were no more recurrences of symptoms. In fact, the two of them worked together to complete a project that the other woman had started. In this situation, the older woman was the mentor and Terry the mentee. This interaction stimulated Terry to develop new mentor-mentee relationships, but this time with herself in the mentor role. She would take in students from a local college who were interested in her type of work and would give them an apprenticeship experience (a mentor relationship, a midlife type of activity she had not engaged in previously).

One final thing to mention is Terry's experience working in groups in which all members were to participate together. She would much rather do an individual assignment, and in fact there were times—in college, for example—where she was part of a group that received an assignment, where she would do the whole assignment on her own and distributed it to the other group members. There were other times when parts of the assignment were distributed among the various group members that she would be unsatisfied with their performance and would redo all of their work. As Terry began to relax her perfectionistic standards, she became more comfortable working in a group. She came to realize that she was treating the group in much the same way that her mother interacted with her: putting high expectations on someone, but then criticizing their work. (In this example, Terry had reversed the roles of the attachment pattern, she taking on the mother role and the group taking on her previous self-role.)

As Terry became more comfortable working in groups, new avenues opened up for her. She joined a women's book reading group, which she enjoyed very much, and she also joined a service group through her church, which she also enjoyed. Both of these were activities that stimulated positive affect and helped her maintain her emotional balance.

SUMMARY

This middle-aged woman came to therapy with some acute symptoms of anxiety and dissociation, as well as some chronic symptoms of emptiness and melancholy. She worked hard in therapy and was able to make some significant shifts in her internalized self and other representations as well as her internalized attachment patterns so that her emotional well-being improved and she was much more comfortable interacting with others, especially women.

17

Clinical Presentation: Rosilyn

Rosilyn is a thirty-year-old white woman who came in with a history of depression that she described as lifelong, but which had been worse for the past year. She could not really identify any acute stress that seemed related to the worsening of her depression, though she thought that perhaps turning thirty had something to do with it. Symptoms of depression included sadness, loss of enjoyment, low energy, poor concentration, decreased motivation, low self-esteem, crying spells, initial and intermittent insomnia, poor appetite, and slight weight loss of a few pounds. She felt helpless and hopeless about the future and admitted to suicidal ideation. In fact, shortly before coming in, she had gone to a sporting goods store to purchase a gun. Only a ten-day waiting period required by law prevented her from obtaining the gun. In the interim she told her only friend of her plans. The friend convinced her to give treatment one more try; she agreed; she never went back to pick up the gun.

About a year ago, however, when the depression worsened, she was also quite suicidal. She researched various medications and learned that Tylenol could be fatal. She calculated how much a lethal dose would be and took that amount alone in her apartment. A couple of days later, a friend happened to call, realized that Rosilyn was ill, extracted the history from her, and called the paramedics. By the time Rosilyn arrived at the hospital, she was in severe liver failure, and at one point the doctors thought that she was going to die if a liver transplant could not be obtained. Her liver, however, gradually began to function on its own, and after a prolonged convalescence, she recovered. After discharge from the hospital, she was taken in by a family that belonged to the same church as Rosilyn. She began seeing a therapist on an outpatient basis but stopped shortly thereafter because the family she was living with told her that they did not believe in therapy, medication, or mental illness; her problem was that she was possessed by demons and that the solution was prayer. Rosilyn, who had not had particularly positive experiences with therapy in the past, decided to go along with the family's suggestion. However, when she was not any better a year later, she returned to treatment.

Past Psychiatric History

In addition to depression, Rosilyn had a history of symptoms of post-traumatic stress disorder (PTSD) related to episodes of sexual molestation that occurred in her grade school years. She developed recurrent thoughts and flashbacks of these episodes. The thoughts and flashbacks were often associated with panic anxiety symptoms. During the episodes of sexual molestation, she described depersonalization experiences, a sense that she was out of her body floating above, watching what was going on. These depersonalization symptoms during sex have persisted to the present.

Also in the present during the flashbacks and recurrent memories, she will sometimes become so anxious that she has dissociative episodes, periods where she loses time and cannot account for what happened. These may be brief, lasting a few minutes, or may last several hours and on occasion, up to a day. Sometimes during these episodes only minor things will occur (e.g., she'll misplace her keys in the microwave), but she believed that there have been occasions during which she's gone out, used drugs, and engaged in indiscriminate sex. She does not remember this, but has gotten phone calls and cards from people she does not know, describing the time they had together. She had no awareness of different personalities within her.

Her PTSD symptoms of flashbacks, recurrent memories, and dissociation are often exacerbated by cues in the environment that reminded her of past traumas. One cue might be returning home to visit family. Rosilyn also described the type of arousal symptoms that often accompany PTSD, such as an increased startle response, irritability, hypervigilance, a feeling of being on edge, and decreased sleep. PTSD avoidance symptoms included attempts to avoiding thinking of the molestation, attempts to avoid talking about it, difficulty feeling close to people, and a sense that life will never work out for her.

During seventh or eighth grade, a teacher noted that Rosilyn seemed sad all the time, and she was referred for evaluation. All she remembers is being asked to draw a picture of her family. She drew a happy family and was sent back to her classroom with the conclusion that nothing was wrong.

Sometime during late elementary school or early junior high, she developed a restricting anorectic pattern of eating and essentially stopped gaining weight. Later on in junior high school, she began engaging in some occasional binging and purging behavior. At the start of high school, she weighed seventy-five pounds, but no one noticed a problem; she was performing well in school and involved in band and choir.

In high school her life became more chaotic. She began hanging out with people who drank and used drugs; she began engaging these activities. She began skipping classes, then days, then series of days. Depression became an ever-increasing problem, and she began to cut on herself to relieve symptoms of depression. Because of her concern about her body image, she disliked the scars left by cutting with a knife or razor blade. Her brother was diabetic, and she began using his syringes to withdraw blood for symptom relief.

Her depression continued to deepen, and she became increasingly suicidal. She made multiple suicide attempts via overdose and was hospitalized medically and psychiatrically on numerous occasions; there were eighteen psychiatric hospitalizations from the beginning of her freshman year through her mid-junior year. At that point in time, the decision was made that the treatment she was receiving was not helping; she was sent to a long-term inpatient psychiatric facility for adolescents where she remained for eighteen months. This facility was quite some distance from her family home, and after discharge from the facility, she never returned to live with her family.

In fact, she enrolled in a junior college not too distant from the psychiatric facility from which she had been discharged and continued in an aftercare program with a therapist she had been working with as an inpatient. During these years, there were no recurrences of anorexic behavior, though she did binge and purge about once a month. She had gotten away from self-mutilation and suicide attempts, and depression had decreased in intensity, though she did still draw blood from herself with a syringe when stressed. She continued to have PTSD and dissociative symptoms. During her years of hospitalization and aftercare, she had been on various antidepressant and antianxiety medications; she didn't feel that any of them had been especially helpful for her.

Rosilyn continued in therapy with the previously mentioned therapist for about six years but had not been in any continuous therapy for the last four years because, as noted previously, she had gotten involved with this religious family (with whom she eventually lived), and they did not believe in psychotherapy. During these years, her symptoms of PTSD and dissociation continued, and there was a gradually worsening of her depression to the point where she made the near-fatal suicide attempt on Tylenol, which eventually led to her getting back into treatment.

Family Psychiatric History

There is a history of an older brother who committed suicide and a twin brother with a long-standing history of substance abuse. She believes that her mother suffers from chronic depression, but she has never been diagnosed or treated.

Alcohol and Drug History

Rosilyn abused alcohol, marijuana, and amphetamines during high school prior to the long-term hospitalization but has been drug and alcohol free since.

Medical History

There are no current medical problems. The major past medical problem was the liver toxicity related to the Tylenol overdose. Other than that, she has been physically healthy.

Social History

Rosilyn was working as an administrative assistant for a large company; she was also finishing up her thesis for a master's degree in marketing. At the time that she first came to treatment, she was living in a house on the property of the religious family that she had been affiliated with for the last few years. When she first moved in, she had seen these people as her surrogate family, but a conflict had arisen between Rosilyn and this family over her mental health treatment, and she was in the process of making plans to move to her own apartment. Rosilyn was not dating at the moment, but on and off over the last ten years, she had dated a guy whom she had met back in junior college. They would see each other for a few months, then not see each other for a few months, and so on. They were currently in an off period. Rosilyn enjoyed this man's company; he wanted to pursue the relationship, making it more intimate and committed, including marriage and family. Rosilyn experienced extreme anxiety over the idea of a sexual relationship, and so kept backing out of the relationship.

Rosilyn had one very close female friend whom she had met on a job several years before. The friend was a constant source of support for Rosilyn, and she credits her friend with providing her with the encouragement to finish college and her master's program. In general, Rosilyn was very cautious in relationships. It was hard to trust others, and she feared being let down.

Rosilyn enjoyed music and had played flute and sung in a choir throughout school. She still performed vocally, singing at weddings and other occasions. When feeling well, Rosilyn attends performances of ballet and classical music.

Developmental History

Rosilyn grew up in a large city in a middle-class family that originally consisted of her parents, a twin brother, and four older siblings—a brother and three sisters. The four older sibs were quite close in age, but the youngest of them was ten years older than Rosilyn and her brother. When Rosilyn was four, her older brother committed suicide; this led to a tremendous amount of conflict and blaming back and forth between Rosilyn's parents, and by the time she was seven, they divorced. Rosilyn and her twin brother stayed with her mother, the youngest sister went with her father, and the two older sisters were out on their own by that time. Rosilyn's father remarried and, besides providing some economic support, she has had very little to do with her father since the divorce.

After the suicide and divorce, Rosilyn's mother became very withdrawn. She did continue to work, but after work would come home, lie down on the couch, and stay there until she went to bed. She hired a woman to come in once a week to clean the house, shop for groceries, and do the laundry. Other than that, Rosilyn and her twin brother had to fend for themselves. They survived on dry cereal and peanut butter sandwiches. Rosilyn remembers them having a strong bond and always looking out after each other.

In terms of extended family, there was a maternal aunt who lived nearby. The aunt had a daughter, Rosilyn's cousin, who is several years younger than Rosilyn and to whom Rosilyn was and continues to be quite close.

There was also a maternal uncle who started coming around when Rosilyn was nine, offering to take her to the movies under the guise that she needed a father figure in her life. It was he who molested her; this ended at age eleven when she began refusing to go with him. She never told anyone what happened until years later.

Rosilyn was never close to her older sisters, in part because of the age difference, but also because, during Rosilyn's turbulent teenage years they were never supportive, always critical, telling her to "just grow up."

Rosilyn continued to have a close relationship with her brother up until about age fifteen. His teenage years were as chaotic as Rosilyn's, if not more so. He became heavily involved in drug abuse, dropped out of high school, and for most of the last fifteen years has lived on the street, only occasionally working an odd job here or there. The most common contact that Rosilyn has with her brother occurs when she gets a call from a hospital. Her brother developed insulin dependent diabetes during his teenage years; he usually does not treat himself, preferring to use his insulin syringes for other purposes. Eventually he goes into diabetic ketoacidosis and is taken to a hospital, then Rosilyn gets a call.

Despite the lack of a supportive home environment, Rosilyn's elementary school years went quite well. She was an excellent student, getting mostly A's, had friends, and participated in band, orchestra, and choir. Usually her friends were other girls who also participated in one of these activities. She tried to spend as much time at her friends' homes as she could (as did her brother at his friends' homes). She remembers that the mothers of these friends were significant adult figures in her life. They were the ones who would take her to the after-school performances, as her mother never attended.

Junior high continued to go quite well for Rosilyn in terms of her academic performance and participation in musical activities. The stress of the transition to high school proved to be overwhelming. The idea of integrating sexuality into her identity, given the history of abuse, was extremely difficult. Symptoms of PTSD with attendant anxiety, dissociation, and depression became prominent symptoms. She began using alcohol, drugs, and self-mutilation to try to control her emotional imbalance. Her depression increased, and she made repeated suicide attempts, usually via overdosing, and was hospitalized several times. Her academic performance deteriorated, though she tried to keep up her musical interests. After multiple acute hospitalizations, the decision was made to attempt long-term hospitalization midway through her junior year of high school.

The one and one-half year hospitalization had the effect of stabilizing her self-destructive behavior and substance abuse. She received individual therapy and group therapy and participated in a ward milieu. She felt that these treatments led to some improvement in depression, anxiety, dissociation, and eating disorder symptoms. Medications were tried, but her memory of them was that they caused lots of side effects, and she did not feel they were especially beneficial. While in the hospital she attended classes and obtained her GED.

After discharge from the hospital, she continued in the aftercare program, participating in individual and group therapy. Rosilyn began to take classes at a community college and did well. Eventually she got a part-time job, continued to take classes, finished her AA degree, and moved on to a four-year university where she graduated with honors. She never felt that her symptoms completely went away, but her depression and PTSD symptoms were under much better control. She occasionally binged and purged, but her weight remained stable and within a normal range for her age and height. She continued to have episodes where she lost time and times when she would draw blood when she felt stressed, but these symptoms had decreased in frequency. Other than the one girlfriend and the on-again, off-again boyfriend, her social life was quite limited and her contact with her family was minimal. A few years after discharge from the hospital, she did join a choir and sang at a church.

Through the choir she met a person who introduced her to the family that eventually persuaded her to drop out of treatment. She began to spend a lot of time with this couple and came to consider them her surrogate family. Gradually, however, her depression worsened, and she made the near-fatal suicide attempt described earlier.

DIAGNOSIS

Descriptive DSM-IV Diagnosis

Clearly there are many diagnoses to consider both in the present and over time.

Major Depressive Disorder

Depression was the most acute problem she came in with, and as described previously, she was experiencing suicidal ideation. She had made an agreement with her best friend not to act while she was in treatment; she made the same agreement with me. Rosilyn saw the depression as very chronic, dating at least back to age twelve or thirteen. While it had gotten better at times, she did not feel it ever completely went away, so the modifier "chronic" added to the diagnosis of major depression seems appropriate.

Post-traumatic Stress Disorder

PTSD was related to the sexual abuse that occurred in her latency age years. She described recurrent memories and flashbacks concerning these episodes. Typically the recurrence symptoms were worse at night and were associated with much anxiety and difficulty sleeping. Rosilyn felt that the anxiety related to the memories and flashbacks was one of the major triggers of the dissociative symptoms, to be discussed later. In addition to the recurrence symptoms, Rosilyn also experienced arousal symptoms and avoidance symptoms. Of these groups of symptoms, the one that Rosilyn felt was most problematic for her was difficulty in relationships, difficulty feeling emotionally close to others. She felt a desire within herself to have relationships, but there was a big part of her that felt she could not trust people, that people would let her down. She did have the one five-year relationship with a female friend who had stood by her through all her ups and downs and who had accepted her unconditionally. She also had the on-again, off-again relationship with the boyfriend but clearly felt that the reason that relationship did not progress was because she would not allow it to.

Dissociative Disorder

Rosilyn described two different types of dissociative experiences. The first was depersonalization, which she dated to the period of sexual molestation. During those episodes, she would experience herself as outside of her body hovering above, looking down on what was going on. She has continued to have these experiences into adulthood, though they are not necessarily related to sexual activity; they may occur during a stressful time in her life. She gave the example of how she might be sitting typing at her computer and have the sensation that she was outside herself watching herself type; or sometimes she would look down at her hands and have the sensation that they were not part of her body.

The other dissociative experience she described was that of losing time. These experiences had begun during her teenage years, had continued into adulthood, and could last anywhere from a few minutes to several hours. During the more prolonged episodes, she suspected that she went out and drank and had sex. She had no memory of this, but would wake up in her apartment dressed seductively (not her usual manner of dress), with the feeling of a hangover.

Over the years, the question of multiple personality disorder (dissociative identity disorder) had come up several times. Rosilyn had no history of hearing voices of different identities within herself, and there was no history of other people who knew Rosilyn seeing her in a different identity. It was not entirely clear that Rosilyn did not have multiple personalities, but there was never enough evidence to say that she did. What was clear to Rosilyn was that the frequency and duration of the dissociative experiences had decreased over the years.

Eating Disorder

Rosilyn's anorexic symptoms began during her junior high years. During high school she experienced periods of bulimia alternating with anorexic periods. While she was in the inpatient setting for one and one-half years, she received treatment for her eating disorder, and these symptoms largely resolved. During her twenties, her weight had been stable and within the normal range for her age and height. Other than a rare binge and purge, she was asymptomatic. She never completely lost the tendency to evaluate her self-image based on her weight, but it was much less of an issue than it was in her earlier years. It resurfaced as an issue when she eventually started dating, fearing that no man would want her because of her size and shape (which were very normal). This fear dissipated quickly when she found men very accepting of her and very attracted to her.

Polysubstance Abuse

Abuse of alcohol, marijuana, and amphetamines had been a problem during her high school years prior to the long hospitalization, but this was another issue that was addressed during the hospitalization and had not been a major problem throughout her twenties. Rosilyn felt she had significant control over her substance abuse problem, but as stated earlier, at times during her episodes of dissociation she would drink.

Borderline Personality Disorder (BPD)

BPD was a diagnosis she was frequently given during her teenage years, especially during the period of multiple acute hospitalizations. During the period of therapy after the long-term hospitalization, the descriptor borderline traits was more commonly used. If we review the case material presented along with the current *DSM-IV-TR* (exhibit 17.1) criteria for borderline personality disorder, the ones that are clearly consistent with the current history are (3) identity disturbance, (5) recurrent suicidal behavior, and (9) transient, stress-related severe dissociative symptoms.

Criterion (2), unstable and intense interpersonal relationships, is not met; she has more of an avoidant pattern. Criterion (1), frantic efforts to avoid abandonment, is not met. Though Rosilyn did not like to be alone, since she was usually not in a relationship, abandonment was not an issue. When she was in a relationship with her boyfriend, it was usually she that initiated the breakup. Of the impulsivity behaviors listed in criterion (4), binge eating was the only one that was applicable, but at this point in her life, the binges were

---

Exhibit 17.1 Diagnostic Criteria for 301.83
Borderline Personality Disorder

A pervasive pattern of instability of interpersonal relationships, self-image, and affects, and marked impulsivity beginning by early adulthood and present in a variety of contexts, as indicated by five (or more) of the following:

1. Frantic efforts to avoid real or imagined abandonment. Note: Do not include suicidal or self-mutilating behavior covered in Criterion 5.

2. A pattern of unstable and intense interpersonal relationships characterized by alternating between extremes of idealization and devaluation.

3. Identity disturbance: markedly and persistently unstable self-image or sense of self.

4. Impulsivity in at least two areas that are potentially self-damaging (e.g., spending, sex, substance abuse, reckless driving, binge eating). Note: Do not include suicidal or self-mutilating behavior covered in Criterion 5.

5. Recurrent suicidal behavior, gestures, or threats, or self-mutilating behavior.

6. Affective instability due to a marked reactivity of mood (e.g., intense episodic dysphoria, irritability, or anxiety usually lasting a few hours and only rarely more than a few days).

7. Chronic feelings of emptiness.

8. Inappropriate, intense anger or difficulty controlling anger (e.g., frequent displays of temper, constant anger, recurrent physical fights).

9. Transient, stress-related paranoid ideation or severe dissociative symptoms.

---

only once every few months. Criterion (8), inappropriate, intense anger, was not consistent with the clinical picture. Criterion (7), chronic feelings of emptiness, is an interesting one. Rosilyn did not describe emptiness, but also did not describe a sense of cohesiveness. As noted previously, she felt that she had bits and pieces of a self but that the bits and pieces were not glued together. She seems to be describing a point somewhere between an empty self and a whole, cohesive self.

PSYCHODYNAMIC FORMULATION

The Inner World of the Self

Ego Development

Separation-individuation. The previous discussion of borderline personality disorder segues nicely into the discussion of what is the level of separation-individuation within the ego (figure 17.1). She clearly was not operating from the position of a person with fully integrated mostly positive self and other internalizations. On the other hand, she did not seem to be operating from the completely split all good–all bad borderline position. In the therapy relationship, her pattern of relating was always constant—not the rapidly shifting attachment patterns one sees with a person at the borderline position. Perhaps Rosilyn put it best when she said, "I can see that there are various parts of me, some of them are even good, but they don't all seem to stick together very well." One way to conceptualize Rosilyn's degree of separation-individuation at the point that she came into therapy this time is that she operates from the depressive level of separation-individuation, but at times is overwhelmed by depression and anxiety and thus dissociates.

Internalized other. If we look at the significant others who were present in Rosilyn's developmental years, we find a father who abandoned her, a mother who was present but who had limited ability to meet her emotional or even physical needs, an older brother who was dead via suicide, and three older sisters who were out of the home when Rosilyn was very young. When the sisters were around, Rosilyn experienced them as negative, critical, and judgmental of her and her brother. Finally, we have the uncle who molested her.

On the positive side, Rosilyn described a very close relationship with her twin brother with whom she banded together for survival. Other positive other figures for Rosilyn during her developmental years included various teachers and especially the mothers of some of her friends.

All-in-all though, her internalized other consisted of an other who could not be trusted, who would let her down, who would hurt her. Emotions associated with others included anxiety, anger, and fear.

Internalized self representation. Rosilyn was able to see that she had some positive characteristics, but was not able to invest any of those with positive emotions. On the other hand, she saw many negative things about herself, and the emotions associated with those characteristics were much shame and sadness.

What Is the Level of Affective Balance within the Ego?

If we look at the positive versus negative affective cathexis of self and other representations with the ego, we can see that there is much more negative than positive. This leaves us with an affective balance significantly to the right of center on our scale of affective balance and is consistent with the depressive state with which Rosilyn presented.

Superego and Its Relationship with the Ego

Rewarding superego. This was not well developed in Rosilyn, which perhaps makes sense, as there was no one present in her immediate family to model rewarding functions. Thus Rosilyn had very limited ability to experience a sense of pride, an emotion which, if experienced, could certainly help with her overall affective balance.

Ego ideal. Rosilyn definitely had an ego ideal that was capable of setting goals, especially in the areas of academic and job performance. She also possessed an ego that was very capable of achieving those goals. One problem, however, was her inability to reward herself for goal accomplishment (i.e., to feel a sense of pride). Another problem was that when she got really depressed, she felt that life was worthless; at that point achieving any goal was meaningless.

Conscience. Her conscience seemed consistent with her sociocultural environment.

Punitive superego. Rosilyn described a very active tendency to be self-critical. The major affects stimulated by the punitive superego was shame, which made her feel worthless and obviously had a deleterious effect on her affective balance.

Id and Its Relationship to the Ego

1. Assertive drives to act on the environment are expressed in a productive manner in terms of school, work, and her recreational interests in music. Unfortunately, Rosilyn had limited ability to experience any pleasure in these

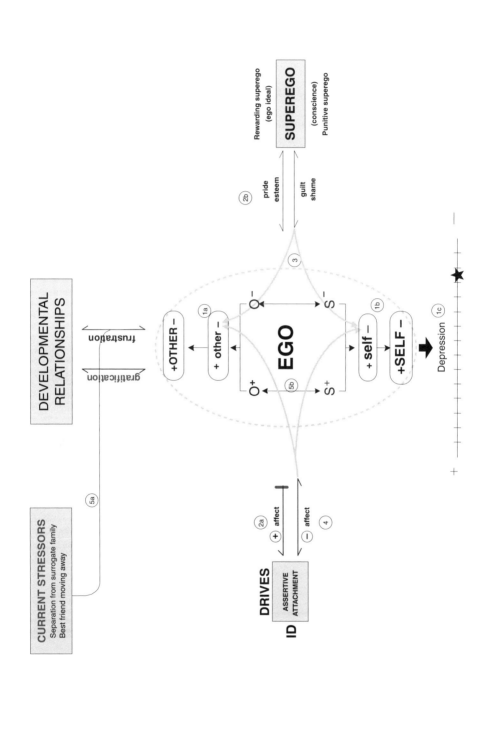

Figure 17.1. Psychotherapy: Rosilyn before Treatment

1. Within the ego, Rosilyn seemed to be at a depressive level of separation-individuation with a mostly negative internalized other representation (1a) and a mostly negative internalized self representation (1b), resulting in an affective balance consistent with depression (1c).

2. Rosilyn was able to express assertive drives resulting in productive activity in work or school, but had little ability to associate that with either positive emotions (2a), such as joy or pleasure, or superego affects, such as pride or esteem (2b), all of which could have helped her affective balance.

3. While rewarding superego functions were underactive, punitive superego functions were overactive, inducing guilt and shame, which further contributed to her negative affective balance.

4. Expressions of attachment drives in relationships with men were associated with significant anxiety and so were generally repressed; if expressed, the associated anxiety had a negative effect on her affective balance.

5. Stresses such as the separation from her surrogate family and best friend (5a) stimulated many feelings of sadness and loss, which also had a negative effect on her affective balance.

ongoing activities. Rather, her activity seemed to be more motivated by a wish to avoid the shame of inactivity. When she became severely depressed, motivation diminished significantly—so activity declined, shame increased, and she became even more depressed.

2. Attachment drives to interact with others are in some situations expressed and in some situations repressed. In terms of expression, she was very capable of interacting with others in a job situation. Her work put her at the interface between her company and the public, she had excellent interpersonal skills, and she was highly valued by her supervisor for the work she did. Unfortunately, she had very limited ability to experience any sense of pleasure or pride in these interactions or any ability to emotionally take in the praise she got from her supervisor.

The other major form of affiliate expression was with her female friend. On one level, this was somewhat of a dependent relationship in that this friend seemed to function as a coach for Rosilyn, constantly encouraging her and giving her advice. On another level, there seemed to be some real intimacy in this relationship. This friend was the one person Rosilyn had grown to trust; Rosilyn felt free to tell her friend all the intricacies of her current and past life, and likewise her friend could share her thoughts and feelings with Rosilyn. This was a relationship that was associated with the influx of pleasure and thus was a stabilizing force on the otherwise negative affective balance of the ego.

With respect to men, the expression of attachment drives fluctuated between expression and repression, leading to the previously mentioned on-again, off-again relationship with her boyfriend. A part of Rosilyn really wanted a relationship, but interpersonally intimate and sexual relationships with men were associated with so much anxiety and anger that she tended to repress these attachment and sexual drives because the triggering of these negative affects would further destabilize the affective balance of the ego.

In summary, then, we have a person with a rather negative affective balance within the ego. It sits between an id and a superego, both of which have the ability to infuse significant negative affect, destabilizing the ego further. Neither the id nor the superego is very good at stimulating positive affect and stabilizing the ego's affective balance.

Relationships

From what we know of Rosilyn's developmental history and from our previ- ous discussion, we can go on to talk about what internalized attachment pat- terns she used to interact with others in the world around her. The predomi- nant pattern that Rosilyn described was between an untrustworthy, abandoning other and an unworthy, needy self. The affects associated with this pattern were anger, anxiety, fear, and shame. This obviously was not a very effective pattern on which to base relationships, so for the most part at- tachment drives were repressed, leading to a lack of relationships.

Rosilyn did have what she called her superficial mode of relating, which she used mostly at work but to some extent in social situations. This was a pattern between an other (customer) in need of some assistance and a self (employee) there to help, associated with a superficial pleasant emotion. Rosilyn was actually very good at utilizing this attachment pattern. Problems came up, however, if someone—for example, a person she met at or through work—wanted to make the relationship more personal. Rosilyn would gen- erally shift to her other attachment pattern, which was associated with re- pression and would not allow a relationship to develop.

With her female friend, Rosilyn did have another pattern, which she lik- ened to her relationship with her twin brother. This was a pattern between a trusted other and a worthwhile self with associated affects of pleasure and se- curity. She had some hope of being able to expand upon this pattern in fu- ture relationships.

Are There Adult Developmental Issues to Be Considered?

If we look at two developmental tasks of early adulthood as (1) establishment of a career or life direction for oneself and (2) formulation of a major intimate relationship, we can see that Rosilyn is doing very well with the first. Despite all the problems of her past, she was about to finish a master's degree, she al- ready has a job in her field of study, and she is poised for advancement once she graduates. The one problem here is Rosilyn's inability to see all this as fulfilling.

But it was really the second developmental task that was of more concern to Rosilyn. She was thirty and had a desire for marriage and family. She acknowledged that she had a long way to go if she was going to realize that goal and was beginning to believe that time was running out.

Cultural, Spiritual, or Religious Issues

Rosilyn grew up as a member of the mainstream culture, so there were no major differences in cultural belief systems between herself and those around her. She did not grow up in a religious family but became associated with a church through friends and her interest in choir. After her long-term hospitalization, she joined a church and eventually became acquainted with the family that she referred to as her surrogate family. While she believed there were many positive aspects to her relationship with this family, the one problematic aspect was their belief that mental illness was a result of demonic possession (a belief that was unique to this family and not part of the belief system of the church as a whole). They eventually convinced Rosilyn of this, and she dropped out of the treatment, which seemingly had been quite beneficial for her.

As she became more and more depressed, Rosilyn had to deal with the decision of whether or not to get back into treatment. She was conflicted over this decision because it meant going against the belief system of the family who had been so helpful to her. She did opt to leave the family and restart treatment, but experienced a sense of loss of this family. Interestingly, there was some resolution to this many months later when she ran into the female member of this family and found out that she herself had gone through a depressive period and had gotten some treatment, and as a result the family had reassessed their views toward mental illness.

In summary, this is a thirty-year-old woman with a history of many problems of several years' duration, including depression, post-traumatic stress disorder, dissociative symptoms, anorexia/bulimia, substance abuse, and difficulty in interpersonal relationships. Of these, the most acute problem was depression, which was associated with significant suicidal ideation. The PTSD symptoms and dissociative symptoms were still active problems for Rosilyn. The anorexia, bulimia, and substance abuse problems were markedly improved.

Rosilyn had been in treatment for many years, and while she had some ambivalence about treatment, she did believe that it had been helpful for her.

She had been out of treatment for the last few years and had been quite depressed for at least the last year, so despite the wishes of her "surrogate family," she decided to come seek treatment again.

The variety and duration of psychological symptoms and syndromes that Rosilyn experienced is truly remarkable. Perhaps what is equally impressive is the fact that she has coped with all of these problems for so long and, in at least some areas of her life, has thrived and grown. I believe this speaks to an incredible inner strength, a strength that, unfortunately, Rosilyn had not yet acknowledged.

GOALS OF THERAPY

Obviously, the number one goal was to treat her acute depression and reduce—and hopefully eliminate—her risk of suicide.

Psychotherapy goals aimed at underlying psychodynamic issues include the following.

Ego

Help Rosilyn decrease the negative affective valence associated with internalized self and other representations, and help her begin to associate positive affect with the existing positive aspects of her self so as to (1) improve the overall affective balance of the ego and (2) further the separation-individuation process and develop a more cohesive sense of self.

Superego

Work on decreasing the critical punitive aspects of the superego and improve the rewarding reinforcing aspects of the superego so as to have a means via which to maintain and improve the affective balance of the ego.

Id

Help Rosilyn develop ways to express affiliative and assertive drives associated with positive affect, again with the goal of being more able to maintain and improve the affective balance of the ego.

Relationships

Help Rosilyn work through old attachment patterns that were associated with negative affect and were inhibiting the development of interpersonal relationships; help her develop new attachment patterns associated with positive affect so that she can develop fulfilling relationships.

TREATMENT

Treatment of Depression

Antidepressant medications were discussed (figure 17.2). Rosilyn had always been very negative about medication and had never felt that medications had been helpful; nonetheless, she agreed to a trial of medication. Suicidality was discussed; though she admitted to active suicidal ideation, she told me that she had promised her friend that she would not act on those impulses. She was willing to make the same agreement with me.

Fortunately, this time, the antidepressant medication seemed to have a therapeutic effect. Within two to four weeks, her symptoms had decreased and she was no longer suicidal. One time, about halfway through the treatment, she decided she wanted to go off the medication, but depressive symptoms returned. She restarted the medication, symptoms decreased again, and she resolved to stay on the medication long-term. Throughout the treatment, Rosilyn felt that the medication accounted for at least 40 to 50 percent of her improvement.

PSYCHOTHERAPY

Rosilyn was seen for twenty-five sessions over a period of about one year. The therapy will be presented longitudinally with an attempt to illustrate the general interventions of empathy, explanation, and experiencing as well as more specific interventions aimed at the id, ego, and superego and their interactions (the inner world of the self), and also relationships with others.

When we first discussed psychotherapy, Rosilyn stated that she wanted to be less depressed, to feel better about herself, and to function better interpersonally. She had been in therapy for many years but had not been in treatment for the last four years. She stated that most of her therapy had involved talking about the negative things that had happened in her past, and while she acknowledged that the therapy had been helpful for her, she was loath to talk about all those things again.

ROSILYN: I can't fathom talking about all those negative things from my past.

THERAPIST: Those things must be very painful (empathy).

ROSILYN: Yeah (with a tear in her eye), and if I talk about them, I will just get more depressed and then I will dissociate more.

THERAPIST: Maybe we can focus on building up the positive in you.

ROSILYN: What do you mean?

THERAPIST: You've told me that you've been depressed and anxious all of your life. That suggests to me that you have an imbalance of negative emotions over positive emotions within you. Perhaps we can increase the positive to help correct the imbalance (explanation).

ROSILYN: Oh.

THERAPIST: Are there any things about you that you feel good about?

ROSILYN: Yes, I have some islands of function, work, school, music, but I don't have any global sense of me!

THERAPIST: That must be pretty uncomfortable (empathy).

ROSILYN: Yes!!!

THERAPIST: Would you like to try to work on developing a more global sense of you that you can feel positive about?

ROSILYN: (Surprised) I never thought that was possible; are there actually people who feel good about themselves?

We agreed to meet for psychotherapy. The outline of the following discussion will follow this format:

1. Working on increasing positive within the self
2. Working on decreasing negative within the self
3. Working on improving relationships

While talking about the therapy in this format does have the advantage of being able to discuss each of these areas in detail and does generally follow the longitudinal course of the therapy, please keep in mind that in this ther-

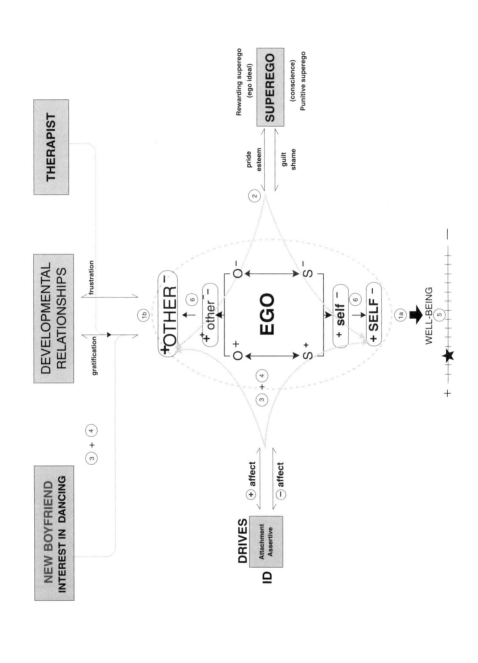

Figure 17.2. Psychotherapy: Rosilyn after Therapy

1. Within the ego, we looked at the positive and negative affective cathexis of her internalized self (1a) and other (1b) representations, with the goal of first increasing positive affective cathexis and then decreasing negative affective cathexis.

2. In the relationship between the superego and the ego, Rosilyn was able to become less punitive and more rewarding, experiencing affects such as pride, which helped improve her affective balance.

3. In the relationship between the id and the ego, Rosilyn became more able to experience positive affect (joy, happiness) in assertive drive expression in her work and in her new recreational activity, dancing. This also helped improve her overall affective balance.

4. As Rosilyn's affective balance improved and as she worked through the negative affects associated with old attachment patterns, she was able to enter into new relationships with men that did not overwhelm her with anxiety. Relationships became an activity that stimulated positive affect, again helping her overall affective balance.

5. As a result of the above, Rosilyn was able to shift her degree of affective balance from its previous depression state to one of well-being.

6. Concomitantly, she also seemed to be able to take a step from her previous depressive level of separation-individuation to a more positive cohesive level.

apy, and in most if not all therapies, there was much back and forth among these issues over time.

Working on Improving the Positive within the Ego

THERAPIST: Are there any things that you associate with a feeling of pleasure?

ROSILYN: Yes, reading, singing, and playing the flute.

THERAPIST: And are you able to feel a sense of pride in those abilities?

ROSILYN: Pride. I don't think I'm familiar with that emotion.

THERAPIST: Are you able to be self-rewarding, to tell yourself you did a good job?

ROSILYN: No, I've never been able to do that. No one in my family ever did that. When I was in school and played in the orchestra and sang in the choir, my family never came to the performances. My friends' parents came and were pleased and proud of their kids, but not my family.

THERAPIST: That seems very sad (empathy).

ROSILYN: (Cries) It's just the way it was.

At this point, I asked Rosilyn to do a homework exercise: to make a list of her positive self-attributes and to assign an emotion to each one. She brought in the following list (see table 17.1).

In looking at Rosilyn's list, I believe it is good that she is able to come up with some positive characteristics, and her positive list is as long as her negative list. (Some people can come up with no or few positives but have a long list of negatives.) On the other hand, in discussing this with Rosilyn, she said that the positive emotions she wrote down next to her positive characteristics were just emotions she thought she was supposed to feel, not ones that she actually felt, whereas the negative emotions that she wrote down were characteristic of the way she felt most of the time.

Again, using explanation, we discussed the goal of being able to experience positive emotions with her positive characteristics and to put the negative emotions behind her. Rosilyn said, "That's why I can't feel whole, there are too many negative pieces."

In building up the positive, staying attuned to experiencing in the therapy can be useful; that is, can the therapist help the patient experience the positive emotions he or she has not previously been able to experience? For example:

Table 17.1 Rosilyn

Positive Self		Negative Self	
Characteristics	*Emotions*	*Characteristics*	*Emotions*
Thoughtful	Proud, good, nice	Secretive	Unworthy
Considerate	Humble, good	Isolated	Lonely
Friendly	Happy	Selfish	Ashamed
Intelligent	Worthy	Crazy	Different, bad, ashamed
Playful	Joyful	Greedy	Ashamed
Giving	Happy	Needy	Ashamed

ROSILYN: At work I helped someone with a problem they could not figure out.

THERAPIST: That was very nice of you.

ROSILYN: (Smiles) That's what she said, and three other people at work complimented me for figuring it out.

THERAPIST: Were you able to feel a sense of pleasure and pride?

ROSILYN: I'm starting to.

Example:

ROSILYN: I finished my thesis prospectus.

THERAPIST: That's great!

ROSILYN: Yes, I'm able to feel that now, too.

As therapy progressed, Rosilyn seemed more capable of experiencing positive emotion, beginning to shift the emotional balance with the ego toward the positive. She reported being less depressed and having fewer and fewer episodes of losing time. She made statements such as the following:

"I've never seen life as all that meaningful, but now I realize that other people do, and I think I can now."

"I'm focusing on the normal parts of me; I'm able to see myself as more normal."

Around this time in therapy, the following interchange occurred:

ROSILYN: I've given up my practices (referring to her bloodletting).

THERAPIST: Can you tell me about that?

ROSILYN: I threw away all the blood drawing paraphernalia. It's what I used to do to help me feel good; but now I see it as pathological. I'm more able to feel good on my own!

In addition to working on trying to improve the emotional balance within the ego, we worked on improving the emotional interaction between the superego and the ego, and the id and the ego.

Superego and Ego

Example:

ROSILYN: I sang a solo at church last Sunday.

THERAPIST: How did it go?

ROSILYN: I felt a sense of shame, I made lots of mistakes.

THERAPIST: Did you get any reaction from members of the congregation?

ROSILYN: Oh yes, when I was finished they all clapped, which is something people don't usually do in the middle of a church service; and afterwards many people came up to me and complimented me.

THERAPIST: And how did you feel about that?

ROSILYN: Well, all I could focus on was the mistakes I made.

THERAPIST: Did anyone else notice the mistakes?

ROSILYN: I don't think so.

THERAPIST: It sounds like the vast majority of your performance was excellent; is it possible to focus on that and feel a sense of pride in what you accomplished?

ROSILYN: That seems so foreign.

Example:

ROSILYN: I was talking to a guy at work and happened to mention that I played the flute; he was amazed. He said, "I can't believe that you are so talented; you perform so well at work and you are musically accomplished as well."

THERAPIST: And . . .

ROSILYN: I guess I am starting to be able to feel proud of the positive parts of me.

Example:

ROSILYN: (Excited) I finished my thesis, and it was accepted by the committee!!

THERAPIST: That's wonderful!

ROSILYN: I know what you are going to ask; can I feel a sense of pride in myself and the answer is "Yes!!!"

Id and the Ego

In addition to helping to strengthen and maintain the emotional balance of the ego via interactions with the superego, we also worked on the relationship between the id and the ego (i.e., what can a person do to stimulate an influx of positive affect such as pleasure from the id to the ego?).

At the time she first came in for therapy, Rosilyn was very depressed and had nothing going on in her life that she enjoyed, yet she did have a history of enjoying some activities previously; we talked about restarting some of the activities that had given her pleasure in the past. Rosilyn did the following over time:

1. She went back to church, an activity that she had previously enjoyed but had stopped engaging in after she left her "surrogate family."

2. As mentioned earlier, she began singing at church and came to enjoy that.

3. She also began to perform at other venues besides the church services. She sang at a wedding, enjoyed that, and noted how happy and normal both families seemed. She thought, "Maybe that's possible."

4. As she became less depressed, she began to enjoy work more and, at school, rekindled her interest in learning.

5. Rosilyn also took up a new activity: she signed up for dance lessons, began dancing with a group, and won first place in a dance competition. Dancing gave her much pleasure as well as a sense of pride.

Around this time Rosilyn came in with a dream:

ROSILYN: I've been having the same dream for the last several nights.

THERAPIST: Would you share it with me?

ROSILYN: In the dream I am going somewhere with several friends; we are ambushed and many of my friends are killed.

THERAPIST: That sounds very frightening.

ROSILYN: It was at first.

THERAPIST: But not now?

ROSILYN: Well, I know it seems strange, but I think some of these friends represent the negative parts of me, and the dream is saying I'm ready to leave them behind.

Working on Decreasing the Negative within the Ego

One of the stresses that occurred during the therapy was that Rosilyn's female friend moved away when that friend's husband was transferred to another city. Rosilyn expressed much sadness over this loss but was able to see it as different from other losses. Other losses had left her with only negative feelings. This loss was not totally negative because the relationship continued via phone, e-mail, and weekend visits. This separation also seemed to propel Rosilyn on to a new degree of individuation. Whereas she had been very dependent on her friend and had always referred to her as her safety net, she now felt more capable of being self-reliant.

Nonetheless, this loss triggered many feelings of past losses. Whereas at the beginning of therapy she did not want to talk about her past, she now began to talk about past losses. We used the mourning model along with explanation of how the mourning model applies to past losses to work on the following losses. In addition, empathy was used to aid in the expression of feelings.

Her Surrogate Family

Not long after her friend moved, she learned that her "surrogate family" had recently moved to another state. She had not had any contact with them for many months, but this news triggered a sense of loss as well as many feelings of anger, which she was able to express—anger at the fact that they told her she was possessed by demons, anger over the fact that they had convinced her to drop out of therapy. At the same time, she was able to express a feeling of gratitude for the support they had given her during a difficult time in her life.

Her Older Brother Who Committed Suicide

Rosilyn expressed a profound sense of loss for this brother who died when she was very young. She really had no memory of him and only knew him through pictures and family stories. She experienced a sense of loss of a relationship that might have been.

Her Mother

The suicide of her brother triggered the breakup of the family, the loss of her father, and a chronic depression in her mother. Her major memory of her mother was of this woman lying on the couch, not interacting with anyone. She expressed sadness and anger over a relationship that might have been, a sense of having been let down in this relationship, a fear that has continued concerning relationships.

As she talked of her relationship with her mother, she also talked about her relationship with her three older sisters, all of whom had always been critical of her. Rosilyn had hoped that by moving away and gaining some physical distance from her family, she would not have so many negative feelings. This had not worked, but by expressing these feelings, she seemed to be able to come to a level of resolution and gain some psychological distance from the negative aspects of her family.

As Rosilyn expressed her feelings about negative feelings about interactions with her family, she began to have some memories of positive experiences. Though there were not a lot of these, they seemed very important to Rosilyn. In addition, she came to value the fact that though her developmental years had been stormy, she had coped and could continue to cope with adversity.

Her Twin Brother

Rosilyn described a close bond with her twin brother as a child that has continued into adulthood. Her brother, however, has had significant problems with substance abuse, frequently living on the streets, his whereabouts unknown to Rosilyn and the rest of the family.

When Rosilyn started therapy, her brother was doing well, off drugs, working, and in a stable living situation. After several months, however, he disappeared again, and Rosilyn could not contact him. She was very distressed by this and expressed much anger at her family because they were, at best, critical of him and, at worst, disinterested. She said, "My family has always been negative towards him; they have never taken care of him." The way her family interacted with her brother was very much the same way in which they interacted with her. Expressing her feelings about the relationship between her family and her brother became another way of working through her feelings about her own relationship with her family.

Relationships in the Present

As Rosilyn was able to increase positive internal emotion and decrease negative internal emotion, she became less depressed and began to talk more about her desire for a relationship. For some time, various people at work had offered to introduce her to someone, but she had always declined, stating she was too busy with work and school. She realized, of course, that the first step in starting a relationship was meeting someone, and she felt more ready for that.

Previously, she had felt that it was not possible to trust people; they would let you down. The attachment pattern she described learning via developmental relationships was that of a critical or unconcerned other and a worthless, undeserving self. The affects associated with this pattern were anxiety and shame. Besides anxiety over interpersonal closeness, Rosilyn, as a result of the molestation, also experienced anxiety about having a sexual relationship. One of the goals of all of the previous work described under the heading of "Working on Decreasing the Negative within the Ego" was to improve the emotional balance of the ego. Simultaneously, this work deals with the negative affects associated with maladaptive attachment patterns, freeing one up to learn new attachment patterns. The hope is that one can use experiencing in the therapeutic relationship to help a person experience a qualitatively different attachment pattern from what he or she has known in the past, which the patient can then transfer outside the therapy and use to form healthy interpersonal relationships.

Several months into the therapy, Rosilyn came in one day and said, "I had a date with a normal guy." When asked what she meant, she described that since she had always seen herself as defective, she thought she could only have a relationship with a defective guy. This guy didn't seem to have any emotional problems, and the date went well. They dated for a number of weeks, and then Rosilyn terminated the relationship. This time, though, she did not end the relationship because of interpersonal or sexual anxiety. She said, "He was vacuous, he never had anything to say, he couldn't open up and talk in a relationship. I want a relationship where I can share back and forth with my partner. I've always seen myself as the negative one in a relationship, but this time I could see myself as the one with better social skills, better interpersonal skills, more willingness to be open."

After several weeks, she started dating someone else. She found him to be more interpersonally open. He could open up to her; she cautiously told him some of the details of her past life and found him to be accepting. She and her boyfriend began having a sexual relationship, which she described as a very positive experience. She said, "I have been able to enjoy the sexual relationship, something I never thought I would be able to do."

About this time, Rosilyn graduated with her master's degree. Her family, including her mother, three sisters, brother, and niece, came to the ceremony. This made her very happy; she felt that she had finally received some acknowledgment from them.

After Rosilyn received her master's degree, her company offered her a job promotion that included a doubling of her salary and a transfer to their home office, which, coincidentally, was in the same city that her best friend had moved to several months before.

And so the treatment came to an end; we made arrangements for follow-up in the city in which she would soon be living. I heard from Rosilyn once after the move; she was happy with her new job, settled in a new apartment, and glad to once again be near her friend. Her relationship with her boyfriend had not survived the move, but she felt confident that she would find someone with whom to have a fulfilling relationship. We said our goodbyes and I wished her a happy future. As I reflected on the therapy later, I marveled at all the problems that Rosilyn had experienced, all that strength she had shown to cope with these problems, and hoped that the next part of her life would go better than the first part. Yet, given her history of severe depression and significant suicidality, I remained cautiously optimistic.

SUMMARY

Rosilyn presented with many symptomatic diagnoses, the most acute of which was major depression. An antidepressant was helpful in treating her depressive symptoms.

Psychodynamically, Rosilyn manifested problems related to sense of self and relationship ability, as well as issues associated with adult development and spiritual beliefs. From a psychodynamic point of view, we discussed the negative affective balance of her ego, as well as the tendency of both the id and the superego to make that worse. Therapy was aimed at improving the affective balance of the ego as well as developing ways for both the id and superego to sustain and improve that affective balance. Therapy techniques including empathy, experiencing, explanation, and mourning were used to effect these affective changes.

Summary & Conclusions

This book began with a quest to understand psychodynamics and psychotherapy, to understand something about the problems within a person's inner representational world, and to develop ways to treat those problems. In part I, various concepts of psychodynamics were discussed with the goal of developing a picture of the inner representational world of a person. First I talked of internal mental structures such as the id, ego, and superego and illustrated them interacting along a horizontal axis. I gave examples of how these interactions might become conflicted, leading to psychopathology. Next I discussed the process of separation-individuation of self and other representations and illustrated this process along a vertical axis; understanding a person's internalized sense of self and sense of other is one important aspect of understanding a person's inner world. I went on to talk of attachment theory and introduced concepts such as attachment drives and attachment patterns (internal working models), which are important components of one's inner world; these concepts are also very helpful in understanding how a person relates to others in the outer world. Finally, I discussed affect theory including the ideas that (1) the affective balance of the ego is determined by the affective quality of one's self and other representations, and (2) the ego's affective balance may shift from its baseline depending on the affective inputs from the ego and superego.

Part II discussed development across the phases of the life span. In each phase of development, I considered two major developmental tasks: (1) the development of a healthy sense of self (i.e., a healthy inner world) and (2) the development of healthy relationships (i.e., an ability to relate to one's outer world). I then went on to discuss pathology of both sense of self and relationship ability and illustrated these problems with clinical examples.

Part III took up the topic of treatment and focused on psychotherapy. I discussed various techniques such as empathy, explanation, mourning, and the experiencing relationship between the patient and the therapist. Several clinical examples of psychotherapy were presented. Emphasis was placed on looking at the affects of various components of the inner world, including the affects associated with self and other representations and the affects associated with attachment patterns. Therapy was focused on helping a person resolve negative affects and develop positive ones.

The goal of this book has been to try to paint a picture of our inner world and then to use that understanding to help persons who are having problems with their inner world. By understanding where the problems are in a person's inner representational world, the hope is that we can design treatments to help a person achieve a positive inner emotional balance and an ability to relate to others in a positive manner.

In conclusion, let me point out that our relationship with our self is our longest, most persistent relationship. Achieving some emotional balance in that inner relationship is important if we are to maintain a sense of well-being in our inner world and develop healthy relationships with those in our outer world.

References

Ainsworth, M. D. S. (1989). Attachments beyond infancy. *American Psychologist, 44,* 709–716.

Ainsworth, M. D. S., Blehar, M., Waters, E., & Wall, S. (1978). *Patterns of attachment: A psychological study of the strange situation.* Hillsdale, NJ: Erlbaum.

American Psychiatric Association. (2000). *Diagnostic and statistical manual of mental disorders* (4th ed.). Washington, DC: American Psychiatric Association.

Archerbach, T., & Edelbrock, C. (1986). *Manual for the teacher's report form and teacher version of the child behavior profile.* Burlington: University of Vermont, Department of Psychiatry.

Basch, M. F. (1980). *Doing psychotherapy.* New York: Basic Books.

Basch, M. F. (1988). *Understanding psychotherapy.* New York: Basic Books.

Basch, M. F. (1995). *Doing brief psychotherapy.* New York: Basic Books.

Beck, A. T. (1981). *Cognitive therapy of depression.* New York: Guilford Press.

Beck, J. S. (1995). *Cognitive therapy: Basics and beyond.* New York: Guilford Press.

Bowlby, J. (1969–1980). *Attachment and loss* (Vols. 1–3). New York: Basic Books.

Bowlby, J. (1988). *A secure base.* New York: Basic Books.

Breur, J., & Freud, S. (1955). On the psychical mechanisms of hysterical phenomena: Preliminary communication. In *The standard edition of the complete psychological works of Sigmund Freud* (Vol. 2). London: Hogarth Press. (Original work published 1893)

Brown, G. W., & Harris, T. O. (1993). Aetiology of anxiety and depressive disorders in an inner city population: 1. Early adversity. *Psychological Medicine, 23,* 143–156.

Cassidy, J. (1994). Emotion regulation: Influences of attachment relationships. In N. A. Fox (Ed.), The development of emotional regulation: Biological and behavioral considerations. *Monographs of the Society for Research in Child Development, 59* (2–3, Serial No. 240).

Cassidy, J. (1995). Attachment and generalized anxiety disorder. In D. Cicchetti & S. Toth (Eds.), *Rochester symposium on developmental psychopathology: Vol. 6. Emotion, cognition and representation* (pp. 343–370). Rochester, NY: University of Rochester Press.

Cole-Detke, H., & Kabak, R. (1996). Attachment processes in eating disorder and depression. *Journal of Consulting and Clinical Psychology, 64* (2), 282–290.

Darwin, C. (1969). *The expression of emotions in man and animals.* Chicago: University of Chicago Press. (Original work published 1872)

De Rivera, J. (1977). *A structural theory of the emotions.* New York: International University Press.

Docherty, J. P. (1985). Therapeutic alliance and treatment outcome. In Hales, R. E., & Francis, A. J. (Eds.), *Psychiatry update: American Psychiatric Association annual review* (Vol. 4, pp. 525–633). Washington, DC: American Psychiatric Association Press.

Dozier, M., Stovall, K. C., & Albus, K. E. (1999). Attachment and psychopathology in adulthood. Chapter 22 in J. Cassidy & P. R. Shaver (Eds.), *Handbook of attachment.* New York: Guilford Press.

Ekman, P. (1992a). Facial expressions of emotion: New findings, new questions. *Psychological Science, 3* (1), 34–37.

Ekman, P. (1992b). Are there basic emotions? *Psychological Review, 99* (3), 550–553.

Ekman, P. (1992c). An argument for basic emotions. *Cognition and Emotion, 6* (314), 169–200.

Ekman, P., & Davidson, R. J. (1994). *The nature of emotion.* New York: Oxford University Press.

Ekman, P., & Friesen, W. V. (1975). *Unmasking the face: A guide to recognition emotions from facial cues.* Englewood Cliffs, NJ: Prentice-Hall.

Fairbairn, R. (1952). A synopsis of the development of the author's views regarding the structure of the personality. In *Psychoanalytic studies of the personality* (pp. 162–182). London: Tavistock.

Feeney, J. (1999). Adult romantic attachment and couple relationships. Chapter 17 in J. Cassidy & P. R. Shaver (Eds.), *Handbook of attachment.* New York: Guilford Press.

Fenichel, O. (1945). *The psychoanalytic theory of neurosis.* New York: W. W. Norton.

Fonagy, P. (1999). Psychoanalytic theory from the viewpoint of attachment theory and research. Chapter 26 in J. Cassidy & P. R. Shaver (Eds.), *Handbook of attachment.* New York: Guilford Press.

Freud, A. (1946). *The ego and the mechanisms of defense.* New York: International Universities Press. (Original work published 1936)

Freud, S. (1955). The interpretation of dreams. In *The standard edition of the complete psychological works of Sigmund Freud* (Vol. 4). London: Hogarth Press. (Original work published 1900)

Freud, S. (1955). Fragment of a case of hysteria. In *The standard edition of the complete psychological works of Sigmund Freud* (Vol. 4). London: Hogarth Press. (Original work published 1905)

Freud, S. (1955). Instincts and their vicissitudes. In *The standard edition of the complete psychological works of Sigmund Freud* (Vol. 14). London: Hogarth Press. (Original work published 1915)

Freud, S. (1955). The ego and the id. In *The standard edition of the complete psychological works of Sigmund Freud* (Vol. 19). London: Hogarth Press. (Original work published 1923)

Freud, S., & Breur, J. (1955). Studies on hysteria. In *The standard edition of the complete psychological works of Sigmund Freud* (Vol. 2). London: Hogarth Press. (Original work published 1893–1895)

Gabbard, G. O. (1994). *Psychodynamic psychiatry in clinical practice.* Washington, DC: American Psychiatric Press.

George, C., & Soloman, J. (1999). Attachment and caregiving: The caregiving behavioral system. Chapter 28 in J. Cassidy & P. R. Shaver (Eds.), *Handbook of attachment.* New York: Guilford Press.

Goldsmith, H. H., & Alansky, S. A. (1987). Maternal and infant predictors of attachment: A meta-analytic review. *Journal of Consulting and Clinical Psychology, 55,* 805–816.

Guntrip, H. (1961). *Personality structure and human interaction.* New York: International Universities Press.

Harlow, H. F., & Harlow, M. K. (1969). Effects of various mother-infant relationships on rhesus monkey behaviors. In B. M. Foss (Ed.), *Determinants of infant behavior* (Vol. 4, p. 15). London: Methuen.

Harlow, H. F., & Harlow M. K. (1971). Psychopathology in monkeys. In H. A. Kimmel (Ed.), *Experimental psychopathology: recent research and theory* (p. 204). New York: Academic Press.

Harlow, H. F., & Novak, M. A. (1973). Psychopathological perspectives. *Perspectives in Biology and Medicine, 16,* 461.

Harris T. O., Brown, G. W., & Bifalco, A. Y. (1990). Depression and situational helplessness/mastery in a sample selected to study childhood parental loss. *Journal of Affective Disorders, 20,* 27–41.

Hartman, H. (1964). *Essays on ego psychology.* New York. International Universities Press.

Hartman, H. (1986). *Ego psychology and the problem of adaptation.* New York: International Universities Press. (Original work published 1939)

Hartman, H., Kris, E., & Lowenstein, R. M. (1949). Notes on the theory of aggression. In *The psychoanalytic study of the child* (Vols. 3–4, pp. 9–36). New York: International Universities Press.

Hartman, H., Kris, E. & Lowenstein, R. M. (1964). *Papers on psychoanalytic psychology* (*Psychological issues, Monograph 14*). New York: International Universities Press.

Hartman, H., Newman, L. M., Schur, M., & Solnit, A. J. (Eds.). (1966). *Psychoanalysis: A general psychology.* New York: International Universities Press.

Hazan, C., & Zeifman, D. (1999). Pair bonds as attachments: Evaluating the evidence. Chapter 16 in J. Cassidy & P. R. Shaver (Eds.), *Handbook of attachment.* New York: Guilford Press.

Kernberg, O. (1975). *Borderline conditions and pathological narcissism.* Northvale, NJ: Jason Aronson.

Kernberg, O. (1976). *Object relationship theory and clinical psychoanalysis.* Northvale, NJ: Jason Aronson.

Kernberg, O. (1980). *Internal world and external reality.* Northvale, NJ: Jason Aronson.

Kernberg O. F., Selzer, M. A., Koenigsberg, H. W., Carr, A. C., & Appelbaum, A. H., (1989). *Psychodynamic therapy of borderline patients.* New York: Basic Books.

Kirschenbaum, H., & Henderson, V. L. (Eds.). (1989). *The Carl Rogers reader.* Boston: Houghton Mifflin.

Klein, M. (1975). *The writings of Melanie Klein* (Vols. 1–4). London: Hogarth.

Kohut, H. (1971). *The analysis of the self.* New York: International Universities Press.

Kohut, H. (1977). *The restoration of the self.* New York: International Universities Press.

Lambert, M. J., Shapiro, D. A., & Bergin, A. E. (1986). The effectiveness of psychotherapy. In S. L. Garfield & A. E. Bergin (Eds.), *Handbook of psychotherapy and behavioral change* (3rd ed., pp. 157–211). New York: John Wiley & Sons.

Langs, R. (1989). *The technique of psychoanalytic psychotherapy* (Vols. 1–2). Northvale, NJ: Jason Aronson.

Langs, R. (1990). *Psychotherapy: A basic text.* Northvale, NJ: Jason Aronson.

Liotti, G. (1996). Disorganized/disoriented attachment in the etiology of the dissociative disorders. *Dissociation, 4,* 196–204.

Lorenz, K. (1957). *Instinctive behavior.* New York: International Universities Press.

Luborsky, L., Singer, B., & Luborsky, L. (1975). Comparative studies of psychotherapies: Is it true that "everyone has won all must have prizes?" *Archives of General Psychiatry 32,* 995–1008.

Mackinnon, R. A., & Michels, R. (1971). *The psychiatric interview in clinical practice.* Philadelphia: W. B. Saunders.

Mahler, M., Pine, F., & Bergman, A. (1975). *The psychological birth of the human infant.* New York: Basic Books.

Main, M., & Solomon, J. (1990). Procedures for identifying infants as disorganized/disoriented during the Ainsworth strange situation. In M. T. Greenberg, D. Cicchetti, & E. M. Cummings (Eds.), *Attachment in the preschool years* (pp. 121–160). Chicago: University of Chicago Press.

Malan, D. H. (1979). *Individual psychotherapy and the science of psychodynamics.* London: Butterworths.

Masterson, J. (1976). *Psychotherapy of the borderline adult.* New York: Brunner/Mazel.

Mesulam, M. M. (2000). *Principles of behavioral and cognitive neurology.* New York: Oxford University Press.

Minuchin, S., Rosman, B. L., & Baker, L. (1980). *Psychosomatic families: Anorexia nervosa in context.* Cambridge, MA: Harvard University Press.

Nathanson, D. L. (Ed.) (1987). *The many faces of shame.* New York: Guilford Press.

Patrick, M., Hobson, R. P., Castle, D., Howard, R., & Maughan, B. (1994). Personality disorder and the mental representation of early social experience. *Development and Pychopathology, 6,* 375–388.

Raskin, A., Boothe, H. H., Reatig, N. A., Schulterbrandt, J. G., & Odel, D. (1971). Factor analysis of normal and depressed patients' memories of parental behavior. *Psychological Reports, 29,* 871–879.

Reedy, M. N., Birren, J. E., & Schaie, K. W. (1981). Age and sex differences in satisfying love relationships across the adult life span. *Human Development, 24,* 52–66.

Robertson, J., & Bowlby, J. (1952). Responses of young children to separation from their mothers. *Courrier of the International Children's Center, Paris, 2,* 131–142.

Rogers, C. R. (1961). *On becoming a person.* Boston: Houghton Mifflin.

Sable, P. (2000). *Attachment and adult psychotherapy.* Northvale, NJ: Jason Aronson.

Sern, D. N. (1985). *The interpersonal world of the infant: A view from psychoanalysis and developmental psychology.* New York: Basic Books.

Sifneos, P. E. (1979). *Short-term dynamic psychotherapy.* New York: Plenum Medical.

Smith, M. L., Glass, G. V., & Miller, T. I. (1980). *The benefits of psychotherapy.* Baltimore, MD: Johns Hopkins University Press.

Soloff, H. P., & Millwood, J. W. (1983). Developmental histories of borderline patients. *Comprehensive Psychiatry, 24,* 574–588.

Spitz, R. (1965). *The first year of life.* New York: International Universities Press.

Sullivan, H. S. (1953). *The interpersonal theory of psychiatry.* New York: W. W. Norton.

Summers, F. (1994). *Object relations theory and psychopathology.* Hillsdale, NJ: Analytic Press.

Tasman, A., Kay, J., & Lieberman, J. A. (Eds.). (2003). *Psychiatry Therapeutics.* West Sussex, England: John Wiley & Sons.

Tomkins, S. S. (1962–1963). Affect/imagery/consciousness (Vols. 1–2). New York: Springer.

Warren, S. L., Hutson, L., Egeland, B., & Stroute, L. A. (1997). Child and adolescent anxiety disorders and early attachment. *Journal of the American Academy of Child and Adolescent Psychiatry, 36,* 637–644.

Weiner, I. B. (1975). *Principles of psychotherapy.* New York: John Wiley & Sons.

Winnicott, D. W. (1965). The theory of the parent-infant relationship. In *The maturational processes and the facilitating environment* (pp. 37–55). New York: International Universities Press.

Index

*Page numbers in **boldface** type refer to figures, tables, or exhibits.*